'An extraordinarily rich, complex, and moving account. A skillfully plotted narrative.'
— Professor Stuart McIntyre, University of Melbourne

'A quite wonderful book.'
— Professor Richard Tanter, University of Melbourne

'Moving ... of great historical interest ... finely written ...'
— Valerie Krips, co-editor *Arena Magazine*

'Awesome ... good writing ... a wonderful book.'
— Nigel Buesst, filmmaker

'It tells a very real story of the lives of ordinary people in extraordinary circumstances.'
— Sandy Jeffs, author of *Flying with Paper Wings*

'It is a fabulous read ... The compromises Natalie and Paul had to make to stay alive. The choices they made ... So brilliantly captured and conveyed.'
— Alan Behm, Director Canberra Writers Festival, author of *No Minister*

'Great writing leads you to change your perception of the characters and that's what Eugene Schlusser's book allows. His characters have to make hard moral choices. It is compulsive reading.'
— Humphrey McQueen, Socialist Historian, author of *A New Brittania* et al.

'A compassionate and dispassionate interrogation of the author's shrouded past. Honors the resilience of displaced persons.'
— Professor Alan Rosen, Community Psychiatrist, Professorial Fellow, University of Wollongong

'Surviving not only one, not two, but three Tyrannies!'
— Phillip Adams, ABC Radio RN

ESCAPE FROM THE SUN

Surviving the Tyrannies of Lenin, Hitler and Stalin

ESCAPE FROM THE SUN

Surviving the Tyrannies of Lenin, Hitler and Stalin

EUGENE SCHLUSSER

Australian Scholarly

© Eugene Schlusser 2017, 2021

First published 2017, reprinted 2021 by
Australian Scholarly Publishing Pty Ltd
7 Lt Lothian St Nth, North Melbourne, Vic 3051

Tel: 03 9329 6963 / Fax: 03 9329 5452
enquiry@scholarly.info / www.scholarly.info

ISBN 978-1-925588-27-9

ALL RIGHTS RESERVED

Cover design Wayne Saunders

The past is never dead. It's not even past.
William Faulkner

Contents

Preface xi
Brief Chronology xvii
Key Family Members xix
Maps xxi

Part 1: Lenin
The Riddle 3
A Challenging Childhood 14
A Troubling Heritage 24
Incarceration 31
Paul Meets His Love 39
Archaeology of a Family 45
Spooked 53
Lost Property 56
If Only 64
Tsunami Approaching 69

Part 2: Stalin
Saving Lies 73
Love Finds a Way 83
Preparing for Freedom 89
Full Swing in Berlin 107
The Rise and Fall of Evil 111

Part 3: Hitler
Another Fascist Sun Rises 127
Naughty Zinaida 135
Paul Schlüsser PhD? 139
Diminishing Options 142
The Arsonists 146
Focus on the Innocent 148
Closer to the Sun 151
Preparing the Fire 155
More Lost Fortunes 159
An Idyll in the Sun 182
Eclipsed 186

Part 4: Stalin Reduxed
Chaos Threatens 199
Fear Rising 209
Educating for Democracy 220
Surviving on *Ersatz* 225
The Circling Sun 230
Marshalling the Economy 233
Win Some, Lose Some 236
Life Goes On 238
Paul's Final Escape 245
Mystery Solved 255

Appendices 267
Select Bibliography 279
Index 281
About the Author 297

Preface

Much is written and many stories are told of incarceration, torture and death at the hands of tyrants. What is told less often is the story of those who survived, retaining their integrity despite being caught in the middle of crushing forces. The 'Sun' in the title is a reference to the tyrants who shine, attract a wide following but then turn on them and incinerate them in their millions – burnt by the 'Sun'. Paul and Natalie, through good and bad times, through a combination of luck, opportunity and intelligence, succeed in keeping their distance from three successive 'Suns' and thereby escape their lethal power.

I borrowed the metaphor from the Russian filmmaker Nikita Mikhalkov's film *Burnt by the Sun*, where the 'Sun' is Stalin. In the 1930s 'Show Trials' he destroyed all his inner circle, and up to three million others such as the World War I hero Mikhail Tukhachevsky and Leon Trotsky. Lenin is responsible for the death of up to twelve million Russians in the Civil War that followed the Revolution. Hitler rose to power promising adherence to democracy then killed millions, including members of his closest circle.

The story of my cross-cultural origins and upbringing provokes many questions and frequently scepticism. What is a Russian family doing with a German name? Are you Russian, then, German, or what? A German name but your family are members of the Orthodox church; how did that happen? The questioners often stop listening before a full explanation can be given. I am grateful to those who persisted and came to appreciate the importance of my need to understand. They spurred me on, encouraged me to tell this story, the experience of living under the rule of tyrants. The most provocative and challenging questions were the ones which implied that there may be a dark side to the family's history, so dark that examining it more closely would lead to revelations of an embarrassing, shaming, if not criminal nature – a variant on the ironic question popular a few years ago: 'What did you do in the war, daddy?' One implication was that there might be episodes in the family's life which could reveal guilt and participation in the extermination camps. It unsettled me every time, though I understood the reasons for the questions. On two occasions at least, I followed a line of research that ended in my identifying two persons with the name Schlüsser who were implicated in the horrors of massacres and death camps. Having examined as many aspects of their story as I could, I concluded that they are either not related to me or so distantly related that the connection cannot be traced.

As will become evident in the story, my regard for my mother increased even as I learned new details of her and father's life. They had a great love for each other, tested almost daily once they had a family to protect and nurture in the face of Soviet tyranny and Nazi repression. No one said a bad word about mother, and her capacity to deal with changing fortunes elicits awe and admiration from a wide range of listeners.

Father was a keen photographer. It was, after all, merely an extension of the use of light – his profession as an electrical engineer, a specialist in lighting and illumination. The extensive albums, one for each year from 1927 to 1944, record their activities, holidays and the growing family. Remarkably though, like most family albums, the pictures chronicle a happy life. Almost totally absent are images of the social conflicts, financial hardships, stresses and strains in the family, community and society. There is no photo of my uncle Vladimir in his *Wehrmacht* uniform or of brother William in his Hitler Youth outfit or Svetlana in her League of German Girls outfit. There are no photos of the consequences of war in the village of Allendorf, the presence of American Occupation troops or the ruins of the devastated city of Frankfurt. The photos alone give the impression of a harmonious life. Perhaps that is the role of family albums, to celebrate the triumphs of life but not the tragedies. A number of photos included here were taken by my father, Paul. He developed and printed many of them in the family bathroom, adapted to an improvised dark room. Duplicates were often sent to relatives in Russia, Switzerland and France. In return, they sent photos to show the life they were leading, or at least what they wanted to show. While benign and seemingly innocuous, the pictures reveal much about the time and place, relationships, mores and moods.

I have written the story as largely my own story. I discovered early on that I could not presume to describe the experiences of my two older sisters and brother. They have their own experiences, their own priorities, their own emphases. We each are entitled to present our past in our own way. It forms part of our identity and becomes valuable personal property.

What about objectivity and definitive truths? They can be aimed for but I do not believe that they can be achieved: everything is filtered through a personal prism. In fact, that is the value of this account and others like it: they reveal a personal point of view. I put special value on Konrad Heiden's work (*The Führer*), as he had experienced the beginnings of fascism in Nazi Germany; and William Shirer (*Twentieth Century Journey* and *A Native's Return*), whose writing is informed by his own life in Berlin during crucial periods of the Nazi regime. They write of details and attitudes unique to their experience.

As a filmmaker, I often travelled with my video camera at the ready. This allowed me to record many encounters during my search. I draw on these in the writing of this book. Some people are offended when a camera appears unannounced, and for this reason I missed recording some important revelations. My brother, when with me, tried to ease those times by referring to me as coming equipped with a 'third eye' – and indeed that's what it was. Being able to examine the material at leisure, after the pressure of the occasion has eased, proved invaluable. I revised my opinion on many occasions in the light of viewing the video material, even years later.

My first language was German, my second Russian and my third English. I have lived among Germans, Russians and native English-speaking people.

Not surprisingly, I am acutely conscious of the meaning and structure of words, of spoken languages and their dialects, of speaking a foreign language and how all of these affect meaning and communication. Understanding is difficult and misunderstandings are easy. Many times, my Russian cousin has alerted me to a subtlety in a Russian word or sentence which has changed the meaning significantly. In return, there are occasions when the perversity of the English language makes my cousin misunderstand the intent of a statement, which I can correct for her. Caution and respect for language and its subtleties are even more important when taking information from native speakers of a language other than one's own or documents in other languages. Some time ago, I was asked to comment on a television script where a Viennese character during World War II was to dis-inform a Prussian German general with false radio reports. I felt that this could be near to impossible, no matter how well the Viennese German dialect was disguised. When reading some pages of Chekhov's *The Cherry Orchard* to my mother, she observed how characters' surnames could identify which part of Russia they came from – a subtlety I had been unaware of and which could have implications for casting and staging. Languages are constantly changing as social, cultural and historical context shape them. With this in mind, I have tried to be aware of the facts and subtleties in every report and document that I examined.

As a filmmaker and story-teller, I have presented the facts as I came to know them. But I have also claimed the prerogative of a story-teller to fill in some of the gaps with imaginative reconstructions. These are mostly informed by my own experience when I physically retraced the paths that Paul and Natalie had taken. Areas of their lives remain inaccessible, which in the future may hold more revelations. I have learned that the most improbable can become probable.

With time, changing attitudes and a greater tolerance of diversity in society, I feel that a burden is being lifted from my shoulders. My small regret is that I didn't write this story earlier.

What follows is my version of my family's life in two parallel universes: the one which I had believed to be true most of my life, and the other that I now know to be true following my research in archives, among friends and relatives, and in the books of respected authors, academic and non-academic. It has been a challenging process, often moving me more than I had expected. There have been times when, had I followed the advice of others, I would have kept the lid on the boxes of letters, photos and documents. I would have been much poorer had I done so. I have tried never to hide from the truth and, in the end, it has been full of revelations bringing me much personal resolution. I hope to have told the story so that the reader can share some of my profound pleasure and satisfaction in discovering the truth, and pride in the way my mother and father conducted their lives.

This book is published in the centenary year of the Russian Revolution – or rather, the Bolshevik Revolution – of 1917. For many, there is little to celebrate. For me, it is the occasion to celebrate all those knowing that the system created through force could not last. Paul was prepared to return to Russia all his life, expecting to do so virtually every year. In readiness, he never ventured far from Russia's borders. A Russian rhyme that mother taught me was: Белый, Синий, Красный, Русский флаг прекрасный (white, blue, red, Russia's flag is magnificent); this refers to the colour of Russia's flag since 1696, not the hammer and sickle of the Communist regime. Natalie and Paul believed in the older, enduring Russia and taught me to do the same.

***

What's in a name? My family name, varied to suit changing fortunes, is an important part of this story. I have used the name Schlüsser throughout, except for the period after World War II when the umlaut was dropped to seem less German and help the family to emigrate from Europe. Strictly speaking, the name in Russian is Шлиссер (Schlisser). This happens because, in Cyrillic script, the cursive, written 'u' forms an 'i'. This 'shift', as the name itself, has dangerous and even tragic consequences. Even so, perhaps suggesting how Westernised they were, our Russian grandmother's calling card is printed as 'Madame Sophia Schlüsser'.

With all our aunts, uncles and cousins, I thought that it would be tedious to differentiate between degrees of separation in the text, whether first, second or third. The relationships are made clear in the Key Family Members listing.

Eugene Schlusser
March 2017

I wish to acknowledge the many people who assisted me in researching and writing this book; to confirm the fate of lost family members I am indebted to the Red Cross Organisation in Melbourne and its international network, the Tolstoy Foundation in New York, the Russian Federal Security Bureau in St Petersburg and Novgorod (Russia), the Sachsenhausen Concentration Camp museum. I was given invaluable information by family members Svetlana Kamenzeva, Natalie Kamenzeva, Vasily Schlusser, Tatjana Daddi, Svetlana Risco, Lev Samoilov, Beatrice den Ouden, Oleg Schlusser, Kira and Marina Makarova; family friends Kaethe and Heinrich Damm, Dr Rudolf. Heiss, Dr. Christa Maar. I greatly appreciated the support given by Anna Schlusser, Tony Llewellyn Jones, Cynthia Troup, among others.

I note especially the Karl May School museum in St Petersburg, its Director V. Blagovo, the head of the Karl May School Friends Society, M.T. Valiev and his wife Natalia, who established numerous ties with the Schlusser clan in Russia, Germany, Italy and Estonia. Their work in the archives and the subsequent publications were invaluable. Lev Samoilov's faultless memory, his knowledge and his enthusiasm added immeasurably to the quality of my book. He gave me insights into Russia's Soviet past and introduced me to interesting Muscovites. Tatyana Slepnova, local historian shared her extensive information of life at the Schlusser dacha in Sablino, south of St Petersburg. Yuri Artsutanov kept me safe in my travels to locate a grave in Nivki, western Russia. In the editing I was greatly assisted by Diane Carlyle and Susan Hancock. For general encouragement and support I am deeply indebted to Dr. Margaret Leggatt A.M.

Finally, for showing faith in my book and publishing it I remain grateful to Nick Walker and his staff.

Brief Chronology: Europe 1900-1953

1905	Attempted revolution in Russia. Nicholas II forced to accept limited constitutional democracy
1914	August: outbreak of World War I
1917	February: Revolution; Nicholas II abdicates
1918	March: end of 'The Great War' for Russia
1918–20	Civil War between the 'progressive forces' (Bolsheviks) and 'reactionary forces' (Whites)
1921	The naval garrison at the Kronstadt base (near Leningrad) revolts forcing Lenin to introduce the New Economic Policy (NEP), legalising limited private enterprise
1924	Death of Lenin leads to power struggle among his successors
1928	Stalin abandons the NEP replacing it with the first Five Year Plan, aiming to fulfil ambitious economic targets
1929	Stalin expels his rival Trotsky from the USSR on trumped up charges of disloyalty
1932–33	Stalin's drive to control agriculture in Ukraine leads to famine and millions die

1934	Leningrad Communist Party boss, Kirov, and perceived rival to Stalin assassinated
1936–38	Rigged trials ('Show Trials') purge Stalin's rivals
1939	September: German and Russian foreign ministers, von Ribbentrop and Molotov sign notorious non-aggression pact with secret protocol to divide Poland between them; World War II declared
1941	June: Hitler invades Russia; 872-day siege of Leningrad begins
1943	February: Battle of Stalingrad, heralding defeat of Nazis
1944	January: siege of Leningrad lifted
1945	Roosevelt, Churchill, Stalin at Yalta conference. Their agreements favour Stalin, including forced repatriation of Soviet POWs and others in Western Europe. Many will die. Against expectations repression in Russia intensifies
1948–49	Russia opposes formation of Federal Republic of Germany and blocks transit routes through Russian Zone to supply West Berliners with food and other essentials. Allies respond with massive airlift and break the economic siege
1949	Russia challenges Western military superiority by exploding its first nuclear bomb
1950	June: outbreak of war in Korea averts war in Germany
1953	March: death of Stalin leads to release of many prisoners in Russia and satellite states, like East Germany

Key Family Members

Paul Schlüsser (Pavel Feodorovich, Pavlusha), 1900–50

Justus Friedrich Schlüsser, 1760–1840 (Paul's great-great-grandfather)

Fyodor (Friedrich) Schlüsser, 1860–1912 (Paul's father)

Sophia Schlüsser (née Dahler), 1861–1905 (Paul's mother)

Theresa Schlüsser (née Opfermann, Theresa Vasilievna) (Paul's stepmother)

Nadezhda (Nadya) Schlüsser, 1886–1963 (Paul's sister)

Natalie Schlüsser (née Kamenzeva, Natalya Vasilievna), 1900–85

Evgenia Trofimovna Kamenzeva (née Rakitski), 1878–1954 (Natalie's mother; Paul's mother-in-law)

Vasily Ephimovich Kamenzev, 1870–1931 (Natalie's father; Paul's father-in-law)

Michael Kamenzev (Misha), 1903–56 (Natalie's brother)

Olga Shapoval, 1900–84 (Michael's wife; Natalie & Paul's sister-in-law)

Svetlana Kamenzeva, 1935–present (Natalie's niece)

Natalie (Natasha) Kamenzeva, 1938–present (Natalie's niece; Michael's daughter)

Nicolai Schlüsser, 1893–1960
(Paul's brother)

Vladimir Schlüsser (Volodya),
1897–1943
(Paul's brother)

Zinaida Schlüsser (née Kungurzeva),
1900–54?
(Vladimir's wife; Paul's sister-in-law)

Dagmara Schlüsser, 1903–77
(Paul's second cousin)

Alexander Makarov, 1888–1973
(Paul's second cousin)

Marina Makarova, 1928–2004
(Alexander's daughter)

Frederick Sevier (Fedya), 1903–75
(Paul's cousin)

William Schlusser (Vasily), 1933–present
(author's brother)

Eugene Schlusser (Eugen, Evgeni, Zhenya, Kuka), 1939–present

Beatrice Schlüsser, 1924–2011
(Nicolai's daughter; Paul's niece)

Oleg Schlüsser (stage name – Sabline),
1925–2011
(Nicolai's son; Paul's nephew)

Antonia Schlüsser, 1864–1936
(Paul's great-aunt)

Artur Schlüsser, 1898–1938
(Paul's second cousin)

Kira Makarova, 1926–2013(?)
(Alexander's daughter)

Konstantin Bruni (Kostya), 1901–70
(Paul's second cousin)

Svetlana Schlusser, 1929–2003
(author's sister)

Tatjana Schlusser (Tanya), 1936–present
(author's sister)

Spread of the extended Schlusser Family, and localities referred to in the text

Post-Nazi Germany, 1945–49, showing borders of the four zones of Allied occupation and localities mentioned in the text

PART 1
LENIN

The Riddle – A Challenging Childhood – A Troubling Heritage – Incarceration – Paul Meets His Love – Archaeology of a Family – Spooked – Lost Property – If Only – Tsunami Approaching

The Riddle

It was one of those beautiful mornings on Sydney's northern beaches. Cool and clear and looking out to sea, you felt you could see forever. In a small two-bedroom house, halfway up the hill, my beloved mother was sitting at the window chain-smoking, reflecting. Her well-proportioned face had shrunk with age and her false teeth were now slightly too big, giving her a sterner demeanour than she would otherwise have. You could still see what an attractive woman she had been. A black and white photograph on a shelf behind her, taken when she was in her early fifties, confirmed her handsome face, and revealed something of her strong character. People didn't hesitate to comment on her qualities as revealed in the photograph and added that her smile, almost laughter, suggested an optimistic disposition. I had boasted to my friends that she was still in medical practice but now, finally, she had retired to the then modest seaside suburb of North Curl Curl. She had at last found a tranquillity in life which the cataclysmic events of the twentieth century had conspired to put out of her reach for so long. While she had given up her practice, she had continued working as a locum. Her modest weatherboard house, which fulfilled her dream of living by the sea, was paid for and reasonably comfortable. She liked to refer to it, with a smile through clenched teeth, as her 'Buckingham Palace'. But the only aspects to suggest a palace were the lawn at the front and back, the 'million dollar view' of the sea and her collection of orchids. Sheer luxury. Aged eighty-four, she now had time to recollect. Like all families, hers had had its ups and many downs. Despite everything, she was now resigned to her circumstances. She had to be content, she knew. She lived alone. My eldest sister, after several successful careers, divorced, childless, was a mature age student at Macquarie University; my brother, a highly sought-after, well-paid instrument engineer (designing and constructing instrumentation for aluminium refineries and off-shore oil and gas platforms), was working in Venezuela, leaving his family behind in Sydney. The cultural tension between mother and her German daughter-in-law, exemplified in Natalie's outdated approach to child-rearing, had become a rift so she had no contact with her grandchildren. My other sister, a library technician living in Perth on the other side of the continent, was already widowed, had two adult sons and, while with a positive disposition – mother called Tatjana her 'ray of sunshine' – was given to episodes of anxiety and depression. And here was I, an averagely talented and moderately successful filmmaker, on a visit from my home in Melbourne. I also suffered episodes of anxiety and depression, and had done so over some years.

'So, a funny world, isn't it!' A sigh followed, though it was more like a groan, and then she took another puff on her cigarette.

'People are crazy', followed by a long silence. I never took my mother's words as mere throwaway lines. I respected her intelligence and experience too much for that. What did she mean, 'a funny world' and 'people are crazy'? The tone of voice suggested deep irony and I recognised the bitterness in her voice, emphasised by a shift of her weight on the vinyl sofa. As for people being crazy, it was a flippant way of staving off the hurt she had felt at the hands of others, and fate. While she thought a lot about the past and avidly read histories and biographies set in her lifetime, she could rarely be persuaded to speak of the past. Who did what, when and why, why, why? Something about me must have signalled to her that I felt frustrated, again. She had stonewalled my requests over the years to unburden herself of her past. Whenever I attempted to open a conversation about her life, she would answer as she did now:

'You don't understand anything'.

At the time, that was in many ways an accurate statement. It was not until almost a decade after her death when I painstakingly opened one secret after another that I found the answer to how it came about that she was now sitting with me, widowed for many years and so far from her Russian homeland. I couldn't understand as she hadn't confided in me what had brought about our present circumstances: why father's grave had been moved, why she had not had an autopsy performed on him, what had happened to my uncle and aunt who had disappeared in the 1940s, what had happened to mother's family in Russia, and a score of other questions.

'The times was different.'

Her English grammar faltered at times, but then she had begun to learn it seriously only at fifty. Her mother tongue was Russian, while she had learned French at home and German and French at school. But she learned English only after the war, when she found herself in the American Occupied Zone in Germany, and once she came to Australia. In her student days, English had not been essential; French and German were more useful.

She threw the next statement away as if it were self-evident.

'Papa took the decisions and as his wife I didn't question them. I told him we should emigrate, leave Germany, even before the war', she added, somewhat contradicting the first part of her statement. She fell silent. If only she could have told me what was going through her mind. But even though it was decades since the end of World War II, she remained afraid to talk. I waited expectantly, hoping my silence would encourage her to elaborate. Not so. Instead we were interrupted by an extraordinary phone call. The phone was on a small coffee table next to her. My older brother William and I had made that table for her thirty years earlier, and the magazine rack next to it. The phone now rang. It so startled mother that she jumped at her end of the couch. She grabbed it resentfully and half shouted into it.

'Hello!'

This was her gruff personality. Today it was partly a response to the intrusion, partly induced by our conversation.

'Vladimir Vladimirovich!', she exclaimed, almost incredulous but still retaining that tone of resentment in her voice. Mother's circle of Russian friends was small and I immediately placed the name: a retired engineer living in Vasteras in Sweden. I had met him once in 1956 when he had made his house available for my sister Svetlana to recover from her kidney operation. He had been a student with father at the Institute of Technology in Karlsruhe, Germany.

'No, no, no, no, no, do not ... no details. You know who they are.' She listened, lit another cigarette and leant forward, elbows on her knees. She threw an occasional look out over the ocean, as if she might see Vladimir at the other end if she looked hard enough.

'Are you a fool or something? Ring me immediately you hear anything.'

'What's happened?' I asked, falling into the Russian she had been using on the phone.

'Nothing that concerns you.' And for emphasis, she added: 'None of your business'.

When I persisted, she retorted: 'Why are you always such a sticky beak?' The use of the Australian colloquialism suggested that she was becoming less agitated.

That small-framed woman, a mere 1.52 metres tall, was the strongest that I ever encountered. Everything fate had thrown at her had tested her and she had prevailed, the experience shining out of her grey eyes, aquiline nose and slightly pouting lips. She had stopped curling her thinning hair and it now had a blue rinse and permanent curls.

Inside her were at least two personas and this frustrated me: on the one hand, there was an almost regal demeanour exuding ability, compassion, control and competence. That was the persona she used with her family and her Russian friends. However, once in the company of people outside her circle, particularly native-born Australians, she became diffident, which struck me as sycophantic and out of character. When I was conscious of her dissembling like this, I remained silent or distanced myself, or worse, fell in with her attitude. Harsh my judgement may seem: it was a thinly disguised hypocrisy, which made me most uncomfortable. On those occasions, it threatened my belief in her.

Still, I was in awe of mother's intellectual sophistication. She was widely read and there were few topics on which she couldn't express an informed opinion. She had specialised in bacteriology and once worked at Berlin's renowned Robert Koch Medical Institute. I was impressed, but not as much as I would become as I learned more about her life and career. When uninformed on some topic, she eagerly learned from others. I lacked that ability. My memory was poor and I found it difficult to concentrate for long. My parents had anticipated a mediocre career for me when they sent me to a non-academic secondary school, a decision I had resented. Now and for a long time, it was my ardent wish that she claim her gift for compassion and her capacity to adapt. Perhaps therein lay the problem: she adapted but never asserted herself, and I wished fervently for her to do so. If she could be seen to claim her place, then so could my sisters and I, and it might have been possible for my brother to succeed without the need for the inordinate anger that he frequently showed. It may seem hard to lay this at the feet of our mother and it is not an accusation, merely a part of my attempt to understand my own nature and accept it.

I was forty-five years old, had a wife and two sons, but to mother I remained her youngest and somewhat unpredictable, even perhaps unreliable, son. At 1.70 metres, while not tall I had a healthy gymnast's physique and moved easily. As a pre-schooler I had often been coaxed to perform a little improvised dance for guests in our apartment, and I enjoyed the attention that I provoked.

She had consistently refused to speak to me in any detail of her experiences, especially how she felt about them then and now. I was yearning for answers and explanations, what had happened, what motivated the actions, what different choices may have been available and what emotional effect it had on each of us in our family. When I was about thirty years old, my need for answers grew daily stronger as I struggled with my recurring inexplicable episodes of suicidal thoughts and debilitating depression, trying to contain the disabling effect of thoughts of self-harm, random panic attacks and a wide range of phobias. I believed mother might have a key to their cause. Mother and father had survived the Russian Revolution, lived in Nazi Germany from its beginning to its end, and survived World War II and its aftermath. 'We were lucky to stay alive', mother wrote to her niece, late in life. A litany of memoirs and reminiscences and scientific research showed that such traumatic events could cause serious mental and emotional injuries, even if they didn't have visible physical consequences.

My mother bore me while living in Frankfurt on the Main, Germany, on 19 January 1939, six months before the outbreak of insanity that was World War II. I can recall events from about August 1943 onwards, with flashes of experiences before that. As these events receded in time, I became ever more aware of the uniqueness of our family's situation and a need to know how it had come about: Russians in Germany with a German surname. But not only was I denied any satisfactory explanation, I was also misinformed and deliberately misled about the origins and causes of the family's singular circumstances. I had no accurate facts and no satisfactory explanation to myself or for others, whether I asked the questions or whether the questions were asked of me, frequently, by friends and acquaintances, teachers, doctors, all kind of officials and others I had to deal with. Everyone seemed to have the right to question my legitimacy. I created explanations over the years but never fully believed them. I knew they were a mixture of self-justifications, half-truths and exoticism, to make myself appear 'interesting' and to some extent fulfil my interrogators' expectations. The phone call from Sweden became a key spur in my search for my unknown past. Various pieces of information gradually became comprehensible and some matched up with others to form a larger picture, but despite concerted efforts then and later, it took many years – long after mother's death – before I was able to form a reasonably complete picture. And I know for certain now that that's precisely how mother and father had intended it. They knew that the information and the truth were so dangerous that to speak of them would have seriously threatened our lives. Our parents had lied to us in order to protect us.

My father was by nature a good and gentle man. Circumstances had made him an anxious man. The end of World War II might have led to a lessening of his anxiety but instead, whenever he was at home, there was tension in the family. This frequently erupted into a row between mother and father. In our two-bedroom apartment in Frankfurt, there was no escaping it. The sign of an impending quarrel was clear. One or the other slammed the kitchen door shut and a heated exchange ensued. The argument was always conducted in Russian – an indication that it was about matters which were to be withheld from us. I understood little of the Russian they spoke and I certainly knew nothing of the issues. My sister Tatjana, three years older than I, recalled our mother once confiding in her that they withheld information from us lest we be interrogated. Interrogate us? Who would have wanted to do so? What was so important or threatening that justified keeping us in ignorance even into adult life? I could not know then that, far from being a thing of the past, the threat to our lives had become even greater in the immediate postwar years.

After some time of raised voices from the kitchen, one of them – usually father – stormed out, slamming the glass door behind them. An ominous silence hung in the air while we remained intent on reading or playing, trying to appear unperturbed. Shortly afterwards father would leave, closing the apartment door more gently and then the front door at the bottom of the steps. Calm would return. In a little while, mother called her oft-repeated refrain from the kitchen, in German: *Hände waschen, Stühle machen, setzen, essen!* (Wash your hands, set the chairs, sit down to eat.) To defuse any remaining tension, she would explain that father had returned to work. He was then teaching Russian to members of the US Occupation Forces and had come home for lunch. She never referred to the dispute. That pattern of secrecy was the norm in our family. It was understandable during the Nazi period, but Hitler was now dead. 'Your father made the decisions', she would repeat when questioned in later years. Only when the consequences of those decisions had been almost fully played out did she allow herself to doubt the wisdom of his decisions. Hindsight also made her revise her own feelings about these decisions with the unfolding of events in Eastern and Western Europe.

I expect father was full of remorse as he rode his bicycle along our street, *Fallerslebenstrasse*. From there he turned left into *Raimundstrasse* and rode until he came to a three-metre-high, barbed-wire fence and continued along it. I imagine he felt that this wasn't the way he wanted his family life to be. Anger had no place in any relationship. He seemed unable to control it and blamed himself. His anxiety and fear turned into aggression at the slightest provocation. He knew his exhaustion was part of the cause, but he wasn't able to shake that with sleep. He rode another 500 metres along the fence, on either side of which was a further barrier of coiled barbed wire. He dismounted when he reached a sentry point. A military policeman wearing a steel helmet and gun holster on his hip inspected father's identity card. An open Jeep stood by where a soldier smoking a cigarette was listening to US Forces radio. He was on standby to speed along the perimeter should there be any cause for alarm. Father walked his bicycle past the guard before mounting it again to ride to the Army Education Centre. The barbed-wire fence marked the no-go zone between the German population and the US Occupation Forces. Within it lay the confiscated part of the city. The fence formed a barrier secure enough to deter any attempts to climb it or ram it. The US Forces had feared that remnants of Nazi loyalists would conduct guerrilla-style attacks. Such rumours had been encouraged in the last months of the war, but no insurgencies eventuated. It seems that the German people were exhausted after thirteen years of the Nazi regime – six of them in war – and cowed by the heavy bombing of civilians during the final stages of the war. Any talk of German nationalism, so prevalent while Hitler was alive, for most Germans largely disappeared and didn't resurface for a decade.

I believed that this was sufficient explanation for the lack of German resistance after the war, but I had to reassess this after learning about the Morgenthau Plan. I could scarcely credit it that the Secretary of State to President Roosevelt had persuaded the Western Allies to implement a programme to keep the German population docile by restricting their food supply, literally starving the population into submission. Daily food allowance was limited to 1,200 calories per adult per day, when 1,800 calories are considered the necessary minimum. It was rigorously enforced, with a total ban on the importation of foodstuffs. That explained why the period between the end of the war and 1947 was a desperate one for us. Until then, I had believed the desperation to have been the inevitable result of shortages caused by the war. It was a time when mother padlocked the bread cupboard so as to prevent us from stealing bread. It was a lawless period when neighbour stole from neighbour and marauding thieves took advantage of the chaos. For years, I thought that it had been postwar turmoil that caused the catastrophic shortages, never crediting that they were also the result of a deliberate plan to starve us. The Morgenthau Plan even prescribed that German manufacturing and the mining industry were to be dismantled, and Germany reduced to an agrarian economy. I had believed the Soviets to have been particularly brutal when they implemented the plan in their Soviet Zone of Occupation. But in fact it had been agreed on by common treaty between the Allies. My own ignorance, I learned once again, had led to wrong or misleading conclusions.

My mother was also right when she accused me of being naive. Why should I have been astonished about the opportunism and lack of principles? I knew that the Western Allies and the Russians had given asylum to rocket scientists, chemists and other specialists notwithstanding that they had been Nazi Party members or enthusiastic supporters of the Nazi regime. And asylum was given even to individuals outside the technical fields. I still find it difficult to credit that the Nazi spymaster Reinhardt Gehlen, for instance, moved almost seamlessly from organising Nazi spy networks in the USSR to working for the American Central Intelligence Agency (CIA), and from there to establishing the new West German spy network in the 1950s.

As I researched and assembled this book, I grew less naive and more open to possibilities which I had until then rejected as fanciful. But when I researched the life of my Russian aunt Zinaida, widowed and alone in postwar Germany, and discovered that she had been involved in this murky world of intrigue, spying and betrayal, alarm bells rang in my head. Could she be the key to what had befallen my family? She had become enmeshed in clandestine activities involving Nazi Germans, Americans and Soviet Russians. And I believe that it involved my father.

Ever since I was old enough to reflect on it, I was mystified why father, a highly qualified engineer, abandoned his profession soon after the end of the war. It seemed such a mistaken decision. Nor was I mollified by my sister Svetlana's explanation that father had told her his German employers, Schanzenbach & Co., had dismissed him after the war. The reason they had allegedly given was that he was a Russian, and this despite the fact that he was officially stateless and had given loyal service to the firm since 1937. When, after mother's death, the family papers came into my hands, I was able to verify certain details but the truth long remained elusive. What, for instance, was I to make of father's 'dismissal' correspondence from Schanzenbach & Co.? The first letter of this series, a few paragraphs long and typed on company letterhead, even now makes uncomfortable reading. Herr Paul Schlüsser, it states cryptically, was a loyal employee of the firm since joining in 1937. At one point, it continues, the firm was warned by the Gestapo – the Nazi German Secret Police – that an order had been issued for Herr Schlüsser's arrest. The Gestapo questioned his allegiance to Nazi Germany and Hitler. But the firm defended him, the letter claimed, asserting that father was a valuable and indispensable member of their staff. The firm undertook to keep him under surveillance and to guarantee that Herr Schlüsser would not engage in any subversive activities. The letter's intent was clear but it totally contradicted what Svetlana had been told. It was an unequivocal statement of support. So who had reported him to the Gestapo and on what grounds? Reading the letter took my mind back to our apartment in Frankfurt and the many times that the family living upstairs in the third-floor apartment, the Waggeg family, were spoken of critically and in hushed tones. Herr Waggeg, his two sons and a daughter had been members of the Nazi Party. Shortly after the war, one of the sons hanged himself in our attic for reasons unknown to me. We had been forbidden to speak to the family, even though their daughter had been Svetlana's close friend. Did one of them report father?

Confirming father's precarious position was another document issued by the police, prohibiting father from leaving Frankfurt and ordering him to report twice weekly to the nearby Dornbusch police station. What did they fear that he might do? Or was it designed to intimidate him? Could I trust this information? I knew that other family documents had been 'adapted' to suit circumstances and purpose. Was the Schanzenbach letter one of them? I don't believe so. Father's alleged dismissal contradicted everything I knew and defied a rational explanation. Manpower was critically short. Germany had suffered heavy casualties beginning with its defeat at Stalingrad in early 1943. With shortages across all professions, it would surely have been self-defeating to dismiss father after the war. But if he wasn't dismissed, then why did he resign? This question became central to my quest. A second letter from the company states that father resigned on 28 February 1948, almost a full three years after the end of the war. The Morgenthau Plan had been abandoned and the worst of postwar hunger and deprivation had eased significantly. In only a short while, the German economy would begin to recover dramatically. I could scarcely believe it when I read that he had left of his own free will. Why then the pretence that he had been dismissed? Was the character reference a face-saving letter that father had extracted from the firm when they let him go? It seemed unlikely. Perhaps the firm wished to present itself as a caring, supportive employer during the Nazi period and thus escape retribution from the Occupation Forces?

I became even less sure of the truth when I recalled one of my last conversations with mother. On another sunny day in Sydney, she told me for the first time – there was anger in her voice – that father had been 'schizophrenic' with fear. I believe she used the word 'schizophrenic' as Russians do to describe extreme states of mind, not a mental illness. But, despite my urging, she refused to elaborate. I could not ignore this assertion. It was some years before I had the time and means to examine her extraordinary claim. I felt that it would be a betrayal of my parents' integrity if I did not try to find an explanation for such a sweeping statement. One question led to another and, like Alice in Wonderland, I followed down each passage of the family's fortunes and misfortunes, looking deeper into the past, delving into the lives of other family members, looking for any compelling incident or event in father's life which might help to explain this fear.

A Challenging Childhood

An important event took place for me on 28 March 1900, in St Petersburg, Russia. On that day a local midwife who had already delivered six children to Sophia Dahler-Schlüsser delivered her a seventh child, a boy, my father, to be christened Paul at the St Andrew's Orthodox Cathedral on Vasilievski Island. She was thirty-nine years old and it would be her last child. Not uncommon at the time, Sophia's first child, Alexander, had died aged three in 1891. Paul's next eldest brother, Fyodor, died two months after Paul's own birth, aged ten. Another death, most tragic of all, was soon to follow. The moist air of St Petersburg was notorious for its affect on human health. The many canals ebbed and flowed with the tides and frequently flooded cellars, basements and low-lying houses. Whether winter or summer, the air was often humid. Peter the Great had selected a marshy place for building Russia's 'Window on the West', as he called it. Many people escaped the city to their country houses during the worst of the humid summer months and sometimes during the damp winter period as well. Paul's family was no exception. Yet tragically his mother succumbed to tuberculosis. Despite efforts to arrest the disease by taking her to a drier climate in Finland, and even for a time to the Crimea on the Black Sea, Sophia died in September 1905. Paul had turned five that March. If I was looking for a single traumatic event in father's life to explain some of his character, this could have been it. The illness must have set in at least a year prior to her death and, as it was highly contagious, she would have been quarantined from the children. Thus Paul hardly knew his mother, may have seen her infrequently, and was left with few memories of her. Her body was taken to St Andrew's Cathedral, where she received the last rites. I have yet to discover her grave. I might have despaired if I had had to go through yet another death so soon after, but Paul and his widowed father were at St Andrew's Cathedral only a few months later to attend the last rites on the death of Paul's brother Andrei. The cause of his death is not known to me. He was eleven years old and had only recently started school. I weep for my father as I reflect on the traumas he endured in the first years of his life and on how fraught his life would become in his final years. I believe that the Schlüsser persona, if there is such a thing, is sensitive and empathetic and Paul's father must have felt these losses deeply. Yet he had little time for grieving, with four surviving children to raise. But he couldn't do it alone. The children had had a nanny and home teacher, Theresa Vasilievna Opfermann. She was born in St Petersburg, the daughter of a businessman with a similar Baltic German background to the Schlüsser family. Photos taken in later years show her to be of small stature and rotund. She knew the children, spoke German and French, and was qualified as a home teacher. Sophia had hired her and it was sensible to maintain some continuity in the children's lives. Paul's father, Frederick, married Theresa for convenience, whereas the marriage to Sophia had been a true love match. They had two more children, Olga in 1907 and Raymond in 1910, perhaps as compensation for the loss of Andrei, Fyodor and Alexander. I have few personal details of my step-grandmother. There are no documents referring to her, although Paul's cousin Frederick Sevier gave me some details of their family life. I came to know him in 1975 in London. He recalled having meals with the Schlüsser family at their home at 3 *Bolshoi Prospekt* (Grand Avenue) in St Petersburg. (I discovered the address in correspondence among the family papers.) The meals were formal events. At mealtimes, the children each stood behind their chair, had their hands and fingernails checked for cleanliness, before their father would arrive to sit at the head of the table. From there, the paterfamilias would give the signal for the children to sit and all were importuned to be on their best behaviour. Any show of bad manners was immediately reprimanded: using the wrong cutlery, for example, was an offence, and no food could remain on the plate and no one was allowed to leave the table unless permission had been sought and given by the paterfamilias himself. Should any child require to go to the toilet during a meal, they were strongly admonished – such ablutions should have been attended to before the meal.

The apartment had at least eight rooms and each child had their own bedroom. Paul would invite his cousin to his room, where Fred marvelled at the tools, equipment and models on display, and the crisscross of wires serving as aerials for Paul's crystal set. Paul, it was clear to Fred, was passionate about electricity, electric motors and wireless transmission. (Tesla and Marconi were still developing the technology at the time.) He made many of the parts he needed and received money to buy components as required. His father was probably too busy to concern himself with such matters, but his stepmother as a qualified home teacher may have encouraged him. In 1956, in Paris, I met another of my father's cousins and childhood friends, Konstantin Bruni. He recalled that Paul at that time was experimenting with Geissler tubes: glass tubes filled with a variety of gases emitting different coloured lights, depending on the gas used. An early sign of what was to become Paul's life work.

Regimentation was seen as both a practical imperative and desirable training for children. Yet I have a sense that my grandfather was a vulnerable soul, which seems confirmed by events soon to follow. The hardships and deaths in the family and growing uncertainty in his business combined to create almost unbearable stress as the world lurched toward World War I. By June 1912, he found the burden overwhelming. The shocks that he had weathered had weakened him and he suffered a heart attack and died. He was just fifty-two years old. The funeral service was held in St Andrew's Cathedral but I have not been able to find his grave. I fancy that since I have found neither Sophia's or Frederick's grave, they are buried together somewhere. Some touching notes, exchanged during their courting days, suggest their deep love for each other.

With his difficult early years, Paul might have become bitter and resentful, yet it speaks for the love, care and guidance that he had in and out of the family that, despite everything, he grew up to be a decent, compassionate and deeply caring man. Despite my occasional equivocal feelings toward him, I admired him and was anxious to learn how he had come to hold the beliefs and values that he did. His culture and upbringing had a variety of sources and he acquired values of mutual respect, individual freedom, choosing negotiation and persuasion over force and compulsion, and a passion for his spiritual beliefs and actions.

His extended family came from a variety of backgrounds, interests and professions. The Bruni family, father's uncle and cousins, lived only 300 metres away, on the premises of the splendid neo-classical ensemble, the Academy of Arts, facing the Neva River. It still exists and I have walked the large exhibition halls, with their enormous murals painted by Konstantin's great-uncle, the renowned painter, muralist and teacher, Fyodor Bruni. Through the high lace curtains, the Neva River can be seen flowing past the Academy of Arts quay, with steps saluted by two 3,000-year-old large granite sphinxes leading to the water's edge. Paul was a frequent visitor at the Brunis. In these magnificent surroundings, he discussed art and architecture with his uncle. He later even contemplated becoming an architect. St Petersburg with its incomparable buildings could have been a rich source of inspiration for a student of architecture.

On festive days, grandfather assembled his family and took them across the river to St Isaac's Orthodox Cathedral. Paul's parents had both converted to Russian Orthodoxy as a response to Tsar Nicholas II's policy of Russification. It is redolent with history, where the Russian tsars had been crowned since its completion in 1858. The scale of the cathedral is breathtaking. On my first visit in 1993, it was a Cathedral Museum; no religious services had been held there since Stalin banned them in 1931. The frescoes by Fyodor Bruni, and his contemporary Bryullov, of Old Testament subjects on the ceiling, and the giant pillars depicting Old Testament figures including Abraham, Noah and Isaac, gave warnings of the consequences of disobedience to God's laws. The mosaics on the *ikonostasis* masterfully created by Fyodor Bruni depict episodes from the New Testament. Today Russian and foreign tourists can again stand in awe before these images dedicated to the spirit of humankind. Here father learned to respect religious teaching, tradition and the arts, as well as Russian history and culture. He ordered his life by these values, observing the rituals and festive days of the church, no matter where he was or what effort it required.

My search took a leap when, after many failed attempts, I learned the significance of another document. In itself it is clear what it is: father's Matriculation Certificate. I could accept that he had kept it as a souvenir, but I felt that there might be other reasons. I examined it at intervals, hoping every time that it would reveal why it might be important, why it had been kept.

I noted that it was issued on 18 March 1918, only a few months after the November 1917 Revolution. The word 'Revolution' suggested chaos to me, so I was surprised that the bureaucracy was functioning well enough to issue such a certificate. Mother had cited Paul's exceptional school results, aiming to motivate me, rewarded as his were with a silver medal. I was puzzled by the school's unusual name, not at all Russian: Karl May *Gymnasium* (academic state secondary school). One of the first full-length books that I had read as a youth, *Across the Desert*, was written by the German-Hungarian author Karl May. Could the school have been named after him? Not likely, I thought, after I had scanned his biography.

I subscribed to a website which periodically issued a bulletin listing new publications in Russian. I scrolled through each bulletin, alert for titles relating to my family's period in Russia. It was a long shot; many titles referred to scientific and scholarly books. But then I had, not for the last time, a stroke of great luck. On one memorable occasion, I spotted a book in Russian, whose translated title is: *A School on Vasilievski Island: A History of the Karl May Gymnasium*. My scalp prickled – a sign that I was onto something. My next step was obvious though it had only recently become possible. The Internet was expanding daily and, when I Googled 'Karl May', I was rewarded to find an extensive entry on a school by that name – my father's school. The school had been of a special kind. I avidly read about its history, the principles on which the teaching was based and, remarkably, a list of its graduates. And here was why my scalp had become itchy: my father's name was in the list!

There are many 'firsts' in a search such as mine but this one was special: my father's name on a Russian website. Other than on some correspondence, I had never seen my father's name in writing. Sometimes it felt as if he only existed in my imagination; he had no reality for me in Russia – it could all have been made up. Not that I thought so but I did feel defensive at times when asked by others about his background. Was I perhaps in part or whole making it up? Here it was in print. But why? As I eagerly joined the dots of what I knew and surmised, this find revealed much then and in time to come. It was like 'show me the school he went to and I'll show you the man'. At least that is how it felt to me.

I ordered the book from the US distributor and in due course it arrived. It was a substantial history of the school, written by a Mr Blagovo, and it contained a list of graduates including the name of my father, with his dates of enrolment and graduation. There it was again, the family name made real by being in print.

The school was founded in 1856 by a Karl Ivanovich May – not the author of the same name, clearly. He was a professional educator who had graduated with distinction from St Peter's Principal German College, and, in 1845, from the philological faculty of the Imperial St Petersburg University. The school he founded was progressive, incorporating the teaching methods of Pestalozzi, Diesterweg and Fröbel. I was keen to learn more about these pedagogues and to gain insight into father's education. Johann Heinrich Pestalozzi held that each child was unique and learned in their own way: child-centred education. He believed that an education should precede a vocation and developed the idea of a *Kindergarten* for early childhood education, and gave the concept its name. Friedrich Fröbel was influenced by Pestalozzi, as was Adolph Diesterweg. (Fröbel became a teacher at the *Musterschule* in Frankfurt, a 'model school' secondary college to which my brother William would later go. I attended a school in Frankfurt called Diesterweg.) 'First love then teach' was another of Pestalozzi's guiding principles, eagerly adopted by the Karl May School. Pestalozzi wrote in very enlightened and progressive terms:

> Give the students true knowledge; the mind, moral qualities, aesthetic sense, will and health of the student should all concern the teacher to an equal degree. Value enlightenment, discipline alone is not education. A young being can succeed in everything if he is trusted. The family, the school and the church are the three forces that educate humankind.

Father had clearly been influenced by these precepts and had brought us up on a combination of the values promoted at his school, and in his family life. I was gaining an insight into the essence of my father's beliefs and values, which might help to explain his later actions, and perhaps part of my own nature.

At the time, children of well-to-do parents were home-schooled for the first few years and so it was with Paul and his siblings. On turning ten, Paul was admitted to the Karl May *Gymnasium* at the beginning of the new school year, in September 1910. His oldest brother, Nicolai, had completed his schooling there the year before, and his other brother, Vladimir, was in third class. As I read through the list of names, I discovered that other members of the immediate and extended family had also attended the school. Frederick, Paul's father – my grandfather – had been a student from 1870 to 1877. Other cousins and uncles went through the school. In fact, the Schlüsser family provided the largest number of students from any single family. Cousin Konstantin Bruni had also been at the school, confirming what Konstantin told me years later that he and Paul had been friends since their school days.

Paul was academically gifted and a good sportsman as well. I have two medals, which he won, both inscribed 27.VII.1912: for winning a doubles tennis title and the singles title. Is it a reflection of his own strength of character, or his stepmother's, that he won these tournaments within weeks of his father's death?

I discovered that the reason for the school's history being written and the creation of the website was the large number of distinguished alumni. The list includes such renowned names as Benois, Roehrich, Bulgakov, Rimsky-Korsakov – people from families who made outstanding contributions to Russian society and culture. For instance, Lev Uspensky graduated with Paul, served in the Civil War and in World War II, and became a philologist and a popular science fiction writer. He was honoured by being elected a member of both the Academy of Science and the Academy of Arts. He was one of many graduates distinguished by their achievements and the honours that followed. Paul, too, had been part of the unique educational experience and here it was recorded in great detail. Sad to reflect that father, cut off from his culture, became part of the unnecessary waste that was a result of the 1917 Revolution. I believe that he might have made a significant contribution to his society and culture had he been given the chance.

In a routine as old as photography, members of the graduating class of 1918 took a short walk to 23 *Kadetskaya Linya* where a Mr Manteufel had his photographic studio. There, all nineteen students and one neatly bearded teacher posed for a class photo. Perhaps because of the long exposure needed, the expressions on the students' faces are unsmiling but it also adds to the slightly ominous quality of the photo taken at such a momentous time in history. The photo became my calling card to the Karl May School Museum.

Convinced that I could learn more about my father on my next visit to St Petersburg, I went to the last known address of the Karl May *Gymnasium*. According to the website, there was a museum located there celebrating the school's history and achievements. I had no difficulty finding it and I introduced myself to the Director, Mr N.V. Blagovo, author of the school history, which had brought me here, and I was warmly welcomed. He was delighted that I had brought the class photo. He quizzed me for several hours, asking me not only of the Schlüssers but also of other relatives and acquaintances: the Makarovs, the Grimms and the Brunis. He was eager to show me a photo of the fourth class in the school year of 1913–14 and asked expectantly whether I recognised anyone. There, in the front row next to the teacher, sat my father. The teacher I recognised to be the same one as in the graduation photo. Evidently, the same teacher took the class through its higher years, which spoke further of the values at the school.

I was perplexed by two other names in the list of graduates: Artur Arturovich Schlüsser and Dagmara Arturovna Schlüsser. I had first noted these names in a will that had come into my possession and whose content was then still a mystery to me. I would agonise about their names for a long time, eventually to learn of their fate and the crucial role that one of them had played in Paul's life.

Paul's final school report was exceptional, as mother had impressed on me – though typically, she never revealed that she had graduated with a gold medal herself. 'In recognition of his outstanding scholarly achievement, he is hereby awarded the silver medal' reads a handwritten entry. It was issued according to 'Sections 130–132 of the Act to establish *Gymnasia* and *Pro-gymnasia*', on 30 July 1871 – a Tsarist not a Bolshevik law. The report is a foolscap-sized certificate with an embossed front page, issued by the Ministry for People's Enlightenment. The grades are entered in ink with comments, and all eight teachers and the Secretary of the School Education Council signed it. Soviets were established to determine content, work practices and administration at all levels. Broadly speaking, they fulfilled the combined functions of trade unions and city councils, giving voice to the needs and aspirations of their members. The Soviets – from the Russian word *sovyet* (to advise or counsel) – elected representatives who voted at congresses and supported endorsed members in the elections for the Duma, the Legislative Assembly. With different leadership instead of the disastrous one of Lenin (or Tsar Nicholas II, for that matter), they might have formed the building blocks of a future social democracy.

The first subject listed in Paul's Certificate is 'God's Laws'. There is a dash where a grade should have been entered. Presumably, atheism being the state 'religion' by then, the subject was no longer taught or, perhaps, the school authorities thought it wise not to record a grade. The head of the church and of the state, one and the same person, Nicholas II, had abdicated – soon to be executed – and God's Law had been transmuted into the law of the state. Just weeks after the Revolution, on 20 January 1918, the Bolsheviks outlawed the teaching of religion to minors and confiscated all church property, claiming it for the state while also denying the clergy income. Paul's devout family must have reacted with fear and horror. Where would the destruction and violence end? Who would be next? The Patriarch of the Orthodox Church spoke out against what he identified as 'these monsters of the human race' and was put under house arrest. But rather than destroy religious belief, the persecution merely drove it underground. Paul never lost his faith in the Orthodox Church. (The historian Orlando Figes, in his book *The Whisperers*, documents how religious belief was kept alive during the Soviet years, passed from grandparents to grandchildren, with only the immediate generation accepting atheism as a creed.) Paul's second subject gets the top mark, 5, for 'Russian Language'. The subject included 'Church Slavonik and Literature'. Church Slavonic is an older form of the Russian language, in which the Bible and other church documents are written. Were the students taught 'God's Law' under this heading? Possibly. 'Elementary Philosophy' is next, earning father another 5, and he received top grades in Mathematics, Physics, Mathematical Geography, History, Geography, Jurisprudence, German and French. He scored a 4 in Latin, which was presumably why he was awarded a silver medal rather than a gold one. His had clearly been a very thorough education – something I might never have known about had I not remained curious about the unusual, if not improbable, name for a school in Russia.

A Troubling Heritage

The Russian people endured massive upheavals in the early part of the twentieth century: the 1905 Revolution, World War I, and the Revolutions of February and November 1917. How did father live through these events and how did they affect him? I believe that we learn much from the models we choose. The examples of family and friends, even strangers and literary heroes, can influence learning greatly: the use of language, personal mannerisms, attitudes and values modelled by a trusted peer, friend, parents and teachers – expressed in the phrase 'If you can't see it, you can't be it' – can be profoundly effective. However, modelling can also be negative. If a deeply ingrained habit, learned from a respected source such as a parent or sibling, is contradicted or opposed it can lead to serious mental stress. Keeping possible 'models' in mind, I formed my impressions of father's early life and how he dealt with personal and family crises. I was alarmed to learn that while I had frequently experienced father's anger, relatives suggested that it was even more extreme in his brother Nicolai and Nicolai's son Oleg. They each seemed to have learned this often damaging way of dealing with frustrations and contradictions. I, too, have this trait. I have caused great hurt and hurt myself when I have responded with anger to both important and trivial incidents and situations. Some try to explain it as being due to genes, but I believe that modelling plays the more important role.

Paul's inquisitive mind, fostered at home and at school, involved him in ongoing debates with his school friends about the rapidly changing political and social developments. They debated them in the schoolroom, led by the teacher – although he had learned to be circumspect to avoid the attention of the Tsar's secret police, the *Okhrana*. Their information came from bulletins and newspapers; each political faction published their own pamphlets promoting their manifesto, publicising meetings and urging action. It was a potent mix of reliable and unreliable facts and opinions. But the school itself was perhaps the best source of information. Fellow students, even some of Paul's relatives, came from homes where fathers were actors in the unfolding drama. At that time, the sources of power, authority and influence were the Imperial Court of Tsar Nicholas II (heavily influenced by the Tsarina and the infamous 'mad monk', Rasputin), the parliament, the university, the church, the military, artists and – to a lesser extent – the business community. Paul's fellow students came from families associated with all these power bases and information brought into the school acquired a special authenticity. This information and the varying attitudes, assessed and mediated by the mostly liberal teacher, would become the orthodox view of class members. Had not Karl May stipulated in the school's programme the belief that the school, together with family and church, was the most important influence in a child's education? (My brother recalls that in a comparable situation during the Nazi period, when he was attending school in Germany, the class teacher became the authority on the correct attitude to take with regard to social and political questions.) With much of the population, the students of Karl May School welcomed the events of the February 1917 Revolution led by liberals against an out-of-touch tsarist regime. They had read about the inept conduct of the war against Kaiser Wilhelm's Germany, especially after Nicholas II declared himself commander-in-chief in September 1915, which eventually led to five and a half million Russian casualties. On the streets, maimed and wounded soldiers stood begging, a constant reminder of the consequences of the war. Paul's brothers, Nicolai and Vladimir, had been drafted into the Tsar's Army and when on furlough would report on the deteriorating conditions and morale at the front. Nicolai's daughter Beatrice – safe in her comfortable home in Münster, Germany, where I visited her – told me that in later years her father could even laugh at how his own military career in the Tsar's Army came to a sudden and ignominious end. After taking part in several military actions, he and his company found themselves sitting in their trenches casually relaxing, smoking cigarettes. Disorganisation in the Tsar's Army was such that they had no accurate information about the state of the battle. Their smoking came to a sudden end as a German cavalry unit overran them. They had no chance of escape and were instantly taken prisoner. Nicolai remained a prisoner of war until the amnesty was negotiated at Brest-Litovsk in March 1918.

In Petrograd – St Petersburg had been renamed in 1914 to make it sound less Germanic – the transport system was in chaos and shortages of food, fuel and clothing were daily getting worse. Whenever a shop received fresh supplies, Paul was sent to queue, sometimes for hours, hoping to get to the front before supplies ran out. By late winter, the store of potatoes, pickled vegetables and fish – so carefully planned for in the previous summer and autumn, and kept in the cellar – was running low. A wave of illnesses – including influenza, mumps and measles – hit them. Travel restrictions were imposed as trains were requisitioned to transport military supplies and soldiers to the battlefront. It became more difficult to reach the family *dacha* to retrieve food supplies stored there, and where enterprising smallholders still had some produce to sell. Yet, compared to many others, Paul's family was coping well. The thousands of factory workers who had streamed to work in Petrograd over the previous years had no such food reserves. Those few who could return to their village to collect food forfeited pay. Lucky ones had relatives who could bring food to the city. With increasing shortages, disquiet and unrest intensified.

In the wings, waiting to exploit the people's misery, was Lenin promising a basic but simplistic solution: bread, peace and land. The situation grew more confused. The discontent came to a head with strikes in Petrograd on 8 March 1917. Two days later, troops joined the workers on strike. In a dramatic move, the Duma appointed a Provisional Government under Prince Lvov (Leader of the Union of District and City Councils), who immediately negotiated the abdication of the deeply unpopular Tsar in favour of his younger brother, Grand Duke Michael. The populace, but not the church, applauded and a workable solution seemed to have been found. But in a surprise move, Grand Duke Michael declined the Imperial throne. To fill the vacuum, a Provisional Government took power under Prince Georgy Lvov, who had already gained a positive reputation working for land reform.

The change in the ruler of the Russian Empire was momentous. It and events surrounding it took place within a short distance of Paul's home and school. Georgy Lvov was not a Romanov. The 300-year Romanov autocracy came to a sudden and almost bloodless end. As head of the church, the Tsar had received on a daily basis the prayers of Orthodox Russians for the health and guidance of both himself and his family, but that authority vanished overnight. *Batyushka*, their 'little father' as they referred to him, was no more. These events took place in the centre of Petrograd in the Winter Palace, the Duma, the industrial district of Petrograd District, and the business centre and port on Vasilievski Island, where the Schlüsser home and business were located.

The rapid economic and social decline and the consequent uncertainty made it difficult for the Schlüsser firm to continue operating. As a trading company, they were sizeable employers with clerks, coachmen, lorry drivers and storemen. While the workers had some loyalty to the firm, they feared for their future. Following the example of others, they agitated for better conditions, better pay and a voice in the management of the company – demands for change by workers who had high expectations of the Provisional Government. They looked for a quick end to the war and thus to shortages.

The population desperately wanted peace. Paul's brothers Nicolai and Vladimir were two of the fifteen million men and women who, in the event of war's end, would be able to return from the front and from prisoner of war camps to become productive again. Vladimir may have hoped to take up his studies in the science faculty to which he had gained admittance in August 1915. Nicolai, by the time he was repatriated in March 1918, found the Schlüsser firm closed, though only temporarily, he hoped. Before being drafted into the Tsar's Army, he had expected to become the major partner because, although his father had died in 1912, the Schlüsser family still owned 50 per cent of the company. He had been training in accountancy. In the interim, the firm had been headed by three of its accountants: a Mr Huvalet (there is some doubt about the name, which may have been Chevalier), a Mr John and a third whose name remains unknown.

The idealistic liberals in government after the February Revolution had enacted a remarkable number of reforms, which appealed to educated and progressive Russians. They introduced freedom of conscience and freedom of the press, worship, and assembly. They outlawed all religious, class and ethnic discrimination; separated church and state; overhauled the military code; proclaimed a political amnesty; abolished capital punishment and exile; instituted trial by jury for all offences; created an independent judiciary. They introduced the eight-hour day, arbitration, and rural self-government. The prime ministership had passed from Prince Lvov to a lawyer, only barely competent in other areas; the newly elected Prime Minister Kerensky made a fatal mistake when he misread the people's mood and continued the war against Germany. His July offensive against the Germans became a military disaster and, with it, he and the liberals lost the support of the people. But it played to the Bolshevik leader Lenin's advantage. With the freedoms that the Provisional Government had created, he could return and set about almost legally to subvert all the achievements of that Provisional Government, believing that an imminent worldwide Workers' Revolution – as predicted in Karl Marx's 'Communist Manifesto', his operational bible – justified his actions. His slogans for bread, peace and land resonated with city and country people. These promises, and Kerensky's ineptitude, seduced the population and Russia's hope for social democracy was doomed. Kerensky was outside the capital leading a disheartened Russian Army when Lenin staged a *coup d'état*. The unthinkable became fact, and would rob the lives and liberty of so many. It would deprive Paul of his culture, his language, his spirit.

Paul's stepmother had strong convictions. Hardly had her stepsons returned from the war when Theresa Schlüsser, convinced that the Bolsheviks would not stay in power long, encouraged Nicolai, then twenty-six years old, and Vladimir, aged twenty, to join the anti-Bolshevik White Army to fight for control of

Russia against the Bolsheviks' newly formed Red Army led by the brilliant Leon Trotsky. There is no record, but very likely they served with General Yudenich's White Army, which attempted to regain Petrograd in October 1919. However, Trotsky armed every working man and woman, brought troops from Moscow and was able to force Yudenich to withdraw and finally disband. (I do not know whether Paul, then aged nineteen, was armed to fight against his brothers.) But anti-Bolsheviks had to be punished and Nicolai recounted to his daughter Beatrice his own terrifying experience when he was arrested: he was sentenced to death by drowning, since scarcity of ammunition meant that bullets could not be spared for executions. Instead, he was taken in a boat to the middle of the Neva River, tied inside a hessian bag to be thrown into the water. He believed that his end had come when two men threw him over the side. Yet when he was moments from drowning, for some unknown reason they pulled him out of the water – an experience not unlike that of Dostoevsky, who was led before a firing squad, blindfolded and then reprieved at the last moment. Dostoevsky was scarred for life; Nicolai was profoundly traumatised. And it had deep and lasting effects on his sense of self and his ability to deal with the world. It was a mixed blessing for him when he met Olga Malinovskaya. She had also been a student at the Karl May *Gymnasium*. They fell in love, married, and their first child, Beatrice, was born in March 1924. They left Russia for Paris, where Olga's affairs soon marred their relationship. According to his family, Nicolai often reacted extremely violently.

After the Bolsheviks took control of his apartment block, Paul was summoned by the house committee, which now administered the building. On 23 May 1918, Paul was issued with a house pass. His photo on the document reflects the tension that the then eighteen-year-old was under. Worse was to come, but for the moment the committee gave Paul permission to occupy one room of the Schlüsser family's apartment, on Central Avenue, Vasilievski Island. Presumably they judged that this young bourgeois could be ideologically re-educated. There was no shortage of accommodation. Apartments had been left empty as a result of the deaths in the Great War, the Revolution, and the many people who had fled the country. The population of

Petrograd declined from two and a half million in 1917 to 600,000 in 1920. Some of Paul's close contemporaries, and even family, were among the tens of thousands of his social class who were sent into exile or executed. The threat of death was never far away and came very close when his great-uncle, Alexander Alexandrovich Makarov, was shot. A graduate of the Karl May *Gymnasium*, and St Petersburg University, he was a prominent jurist before becoming Minister of the Interior following the assassination of the reformist Prime Minister Stolypin in 1911. In late 1916 he was appointed Minister of Justice, a post he held until the February 1917 Revolution. The record of service to his country and his advanced age of sixty-three could not save him from arrest when the Bolsheviks came to power. They executed him in 1919.

Incarceration

Paul was due to begin his engineering course in September 1918. I puzzled over this. Wasn't he an enemy of the people? The reason why this son of a bourgeois was given permission to study at the Electrotechnical Institute, as mother told me, was beautifully pragmatic: because he was able to pay for his tuition in foreign currency. Proletarians, members of the working class, received free tertiary education. Where did the money to pay for Paul's course come from? According to mother, in the confusion of those early months after the 1917 Revolution, an arrangement was made to send him money via England, couriered by a friendly seaman whose ship made regular voyages to Petrograd. As foreign currency was much needed, few questions were asked. But it did leave Paul potentially open to charges of currency speculation. And where had the money come from and whose money was it? These facts, with many others, are lost.

But he was not about to escape retribution for being a class enemy. He was arrested. What could be worse than to have your personal freedom taken away from you? The Russian writer Alexander Solzhenitsyn recorded his own experience:

> Arrest! Need it be said that it is the breaking point in your life, a bolt of lightning, which has scored a direct hit on you? That it is an unassailable spiritual earthquake not every person can cope with, as a result of which people often slip into insanity?

An earthquake? Insanity? Hadn't mother described father's fear as 'schizophrenic'? Paul was arrested following Lenin's call in August 1918 for his followers to implement a Red Terror: 'Lock up all the doubtful ones in a concentration camp outside the city' and 'carry out merciless mass terror'. No specific charge was necessary: he was simply identified as an 'enemy of the people'. No evidence was needed for such a charge. Being born into a bourgeois family was a sufficient crime. One day Paul no longer appeared in his communal building and no one knew where he had gone. Nor did they ask. Lenin's 'mass terror' was having its desired effect of cowing the populace. He was given a sentence and sent to the prison in the Schlisselburg fortress, sixty kilometres east of Petrograd. Soon afterwards he was sent to join a work gang on the Volga River, where he laboured in appalling conditions to secure the riverbank. How long he spent there is not known but he was released, presumably when it was deemed that he had been sufficiently well 're-educated' and purged of his bourgeois ways and beliefs. But perhaps it was because the authorities could no longer feed him. In January 1919 the Bolsheviks, in an effort to feed city dwellers, imposed a massive tax on the peasant farmers of Russia which was payable in the food they produced. By the next harvest, the peasants refused to pay the tax and a famine threatened. Without food, urban society in Petrograd almost totally broke down. The legacy of the war, the millions of returning soldiers, the chaos everywhere, left the majority of people struggling desperately to survive. Many became 'bag men' – men who took their valuables to the country, to barter for food (as we would do after World War II). Along the way they gathered dropped fruit, windfall. Picking hanging fruit had been made a crime and orchards were heavily guarded. They collected edible plants growing on verges and in forests: nasturtiums, flax, stinging nettle, and wild berries, fruits and mushrooms. Occasionally a bag man could find a peasant who was willing to barter some of his hidden grain. Lenin called these peasants 'speculators' and tried to eradicate this 'black market', sending armed men in groups of twenty to thirty to roam the countryside and raid grain stores. The peasants fought back in the only way they could: by passive resistance. Knowing that any surplus food would be confiscated, they grew only enough to feed their families. They sold any small surplus on the black market or exchanged it for the services of a doctor or veterinarian. Such practice further damaged the economy. Hunger became so widespread that factories were forced to send marauding groups of workers to bring food to the workers' canteen. This was often done violently. With the de-mobbing of soldiers, there was no shortage of trained sharpshooters with rifles and pistols ready to use to obtain food. The famine grew worse and the people more desperate. Paul, released from 'correctional labour camp', now faced death by starvation.

'They ate cats and dogs, any domestic animal or pet!' mother told me bitterly as she described the suffering.

'They had nothing, nothing to eat and father almost died.' There was real outrage in her voice that the situation in Russia had been allowed to deteriorate to such a level. 'Nobody cared. They were terrible times.' I could sense the hopelessness she had felt then and the resentment now that no one had been made to take responsibility. She feared that those acts of cruelty and barbarity of people against people were being forgotten, which is why she was telling me this. She also feared that my political views were becoming unacceptably 'socialist', to be challenged with these stories of abuse.

Half the population of the city fled to the country, where they set up camp to grow food on any available land. The abandoned apartments in the city became sources for fuel and food. In the bitter winter of 1920–21, Paul kept himself alive by dismantling doors and window frames to burn for heating and cooking.

'Papa told me', mother recalled, 'he became so desperate he tore the wallpaper off the walls to get at the glue. He scraped it off the back of the wallpaper and put it into a pot of boiling water to give it some semblance of a soup. There couldn't have been much nutrition in it.' Her tone of voice left me in no doubt of the vividness of her memories. He fell ill. In his emaciated condition, he succumbed to the disease rampant during famine: typhus. By creating conditions of famine, Lenin's policy (copied by Stalin in the Ukraine ten years later) to 'terrorise the masses' was working. When Paul fell ill, he was alone in his room on Vasilievski Island. His food had run out and he hadn't even the strength to leave his room. Worse, no one knew of his plight so he might well have died there.

A near miracle saved him. I have a document, a will, which had come to me with the family papers. It was handwritten, in Russian, making it hard to decipher. Laboriously, I was able to establish that Paul and his brother Nicolai had been left some land. The land referred to a fifteen-hectare property at a place called Sablino. It was to be inherited by Nicolai and Paul Schlüsser, with some special provisions for a certain Artur Schlüsser and Dagmara Schlüsser (whose names I discovered in the list of Karl May *Gymnasium* graduates). It took me years to piece together the details and to locate the property. This is how I believe that Paul was saved. It seems Paul's second cousin Antonia and her sister Ludowika had been living at their farmstead in Sablino. (At that time, I did not know where this was.) It had been nationalised by the Bolsheviks, but as they had set up an orphanage on the property and were thus doing 'social good', the law allowed them to remain there. Paul had in the past been a regular visitor, but they now became concerned when he did not make contact for some time. They took the train from Sablino Station to Petrograd's Nicolaievski Station (today, Moscow Station), and from there took a *droshky* to *Bolshoi Prospekt*. They reached his apartment and found him convulsing in his room, near death. He was delirious and had the telltale rashes on his body, indicating that the fever was at its height. He was one of a reported thirty million victims of typhus in Russia at this time. Three million died. Antonia and Ludowika took Paul back to Sablino and nursed him. With the coming winter they took him to the warmer, drier climate in Balaclava in Crimea, on the shores of the Black Sea, where they rented a *dacha*. As it turned out, they escaped not only the famine but another epidemic as well. The Spanish flu was raging through Russia and much of Europe, killing millions. With the warm weather and gentle exercise – some tennis, and sailing on the Black Sea – he slowly recuperated. Photographs show him totally bald, a consequence of the disease, and while he has a healthy tan, he looks emaciated with a piercing – almost haunted – look in his eyes. His appearance belied that he was only just nearing his twenty-first birthday.

The Bolsheviks, on seizing power, had promised peace. In March 1918, the Brest-Litovsk Treaty established terms that guaranteed Germany would not invade Russia, if Russia capitulated and ceded Poland and parts of Ukraine to them. Despite the harsh terms, the treaty gained support for the Bolsheviks as it gave respite to the war-weary Russians. But the peace treaty did not totally eliminate the threat to Lenin's regime in Petrograd. In March 1918, Lenin moved the government several hundred kilometres from the German border, southeast to Moscow. The move represented a psychological shift as well. Moscow has always been more Asiatic in its outlook and culture, reflected by its architecture. At such a distance from Western Europe, it practically forms the centre of another continent, sometimes referred to as Eurasia. In the 1830s, the French travel writer Marquis de Custine praised Moscow for its uniqueness, while he thought that St Petersburg was a pretentious, pale imitation of Western culture. The five-domed Russian churches in Moscow reflected influences of the architecture of the Byzantine cultures of Asia. When Nicholas II built a church in St Petersburg in 1905 – commemorating the assassination of his grandfather, Alexander II – the new Church of the Saviour on Spilled Blood was in the familiar onion-domed Moscow style, one of only a few built in St Petersburg. It gets a very mixed response from St Petersburg's residents. The Russian Orthodox Church has a decidedly Byzantine aesthetic. For me, the cupolas – like the onion-domed church spires of Central Europe – echo the Islamic minarets. The five cupolas represent Christ and the four apostles, authors of the New Testament. Inside the church, the *ikonostasis* that separates the earthly from the heavenly world is taken from the Greek tradition, as are the depictions in hierarchical order of Orthodox saints. Despite de Custine's writings, the perception persists that Moscow is less cultured and less law-abiding, closer to what are thought to be the mores of Asian origin. Loyalty is more to the clan than to the nation. This atmosphere may have influenced the development of Lenin's Bolshevik Party, its tendency to secrecy, violence and lawlessness, and its resistance to the moderating influences from Petrograd throughout the period of Communist rule. The differences in culture between the two cities can still be seen today. The St Petersburg origins of Vladimir Putin and Dimitri Medvedev gave them an added status in the eyes of many Russians, even while Putin acted like a Muscovite tsar.

The cost in lives of the Revolution climbed. 'Man can be corrected', Lenin told the eminent Russian physiologist, Ivan Pavlov. 'Man can be made what we want him to be.' In his quest to change man to conform to his conception of what man should be, by 1921 ten million people had fallen victim to the revolution, civil war and famine. Death had touched virtually every family. The failure to manage the economy had led to a catastrophic fall in industrial and agricultural production, bringing the government near to collapse. Disastrously, in December 1920, industrial production was only 10 per cent of what it had been in 1913.

Paul would have been encouraged when the desperate conditions that Lenin had created provoked revolts in various parts of the country. The most menacing to the revolution was that of the sailors on Kronstadt, the country's largest naval base on the Gulf of Finland, off Petrograd. The sailors had supported the Bolsheviks in 1917 but, in March 1921, more than 20,000 seamen rebelled and demanded an end to the dominance of the Bolsheviks and their economic policies. The Red Army led by World War I hero Tukhachevsky (later to fall victim to Stalin's great purge), with Trotsky as commissar, ruthlessly quelled the rebellion. But the uprising shocked Lenin and forced him to modify his economic programme by introducing the New Economic Policy. The change was announced in the Communist Party newspaper *Pravda* (Truth), and the mouthpiece of the governing body, the Supreme Soviet, *Izvestia* (News). While the Schlüsser family business was closed, this change may have given Paul hope that it signalled the beginning of the restoration of private enterprise and private property. While other members of his family had gone into exile, they urged Paul to remain in Russia to wait for just such an event.

The New Economic Policy (NEP) permitted sole operators to conduct a business provided that only family members were involved; employing labour remained illegal and was considered 'exploitation'. The NEP eased the burden on peasant farmers, who could now pay their taxes in cash rather than in produce and crops, which also became an incentive for peasants to increase crop yields and to sell the surplus. The liberalisation had immediate consequences, ensuring the population could survive the difficult period ahead. The freer cash economy encouraged cottage industries: food, clothing, hardware, furniture all reappeared on roadside stalls – goods which had not been seen since 1917.

Dark clouds formed when Lenin died at his *dacha*, south of Moscow, on 21 January 1924. His death had been expected since his first stroke, two years earlier, had paralysed him. A reported 900,000 people came to see Lenin's body as it lay in the Hall of Columns in Moscow's Trade Union building. Paul was almost twenty-four years old, had lost virtually everything and was lucky to remain alive. All members of his immediate family had fled, his own health was seriously affected, the family's business with its proud hundred-year history had been destroyed, and all family property had been confiscated. Did this son of a bourgeois merchant trader of foreign origin, albeit several generations ago, have a future in Russia? Might it have been better to flee the country, to make his life abroad? Paul hoped that the New Economic Policy introduced in 1922 would continue and expand under Lenin's successor, Stalin; he further hoped, however faintly, for the restitution of the family property. It was a vain hope. The eminent American historian Richard Pipes categorised the men who led the Communist cause as:

> The Russian Revolution appears as the unfolding of a tragedy in which events follow with inexorable force from the mentality and character of the protagonists ... human individuals pursuing their own interests and aspirations, incapable or unwilling to make the allowances for the interests and aspirations of others.

Maxim Gorky, the Russian writer, foresaw the events to come in November 1917:

> The working man must know that there are no miracles, and that he will have to confront hunger, complete disorganization of industry, prolonged and bloody anarchy followed by reaction no less sanguinary and dark. That is where the proletariat is being led … One must understand that Lenin is not an all-powerful magician, but a deliberate juggler, who has no feeling for the lives or the honour of the proletariat.

This is the context in which Paul had to make his decisions. Similar attributes would soon be ascribed to Stalin. With authority in the hands of such capricious, deluded, self-seeking men, Paul learned not to trust officials or even most relatives or friends. He relied only on a few who were closest to him and whom he had learned to trust, having shared common crises. The Bolsheviks enacted laws to destroy trust between individuals, not least among relatives. The aim was to make every person loyal to the state rather than to the family. While claiming to create 'New Man' – a superior, rational being – in reality, they were setting out to destroy many of the basic, decent impulses in people. Paul understood this and opposed these forces all his life, often putting himself in danger. But after these bitter experiences, aged twenty-four, where would he get the strength to fight with?

Paul Meets His Love

Natalie brought a new life force into Paul's life. They met while they were both students. Natalie, like Paul, was an exceptional student, studying for her medical degree. As chance would have it, her younger brother Michael had been accepted into the same Engineering Institute as Paul and they became friends. They shared academic interests and both loved sport: tennis, sailing, winter sports. Michael had been a physical education instructor in the Red Army during the Civil War. On one occasion when Michael was calling on his sister, he suggested that his friend Paul come with him. Natalie and Paul were introduced and immediately took to each other. Natalie was an attractive, witty, intelligent woman of twenty-five. She was the eldest child of three, much loved by her father, a doctor, and her mother, a dentist, who as professionals were considered members of the 'intelligentsia'. Together with their youngest brother Sergei, they were a close family. Her small stature belied her strength of character. Her grooming was immaculate, something she had learned from her mother. Her nails were manicured, her hair curled into a roll from front to back, accentuating her oval face. She wore fashionable full blouses and ankle-length skirts, clothes that were a combination of hand-me-downs, and homemade skirts and dresses.

Her class of women had had many freedoms in tsarist Russia. Even so, the policy of greater gender equality introduced under Lenin was in her favour and she took advantage of it. She spoke an attractive Russian, fluent French and some German. Her maternal grandmother, Louise, who lived with the family, had come to Russia as a child from Bulle in the French-speaking part of Switzerland. Her grandmother's sister Anna had also come to Russia and in time helped to rear the children. Natalie exchanged letters with her Aunt Anna, in French, until she died in Geneva in 1958. Natalie had an easy and outgoing personality; she laughed spontaneously, her sharp intelligence quickly perceived any irony in conversation. She was generous to others, knew her own needs and how to set priorities. Not everybody could be helped nor could everything be undertaken. One had to prioritise. Paul at the same age had already been scarred by life with his hair loss, deep-set eyes and a downward turn to his mouth. But even so, he remained a handsome man. Natalie's lighter nature proved a counterweight to his heaviness, the cause of many future disagreements. She had inherited her father's lightness and, as the eldest, had been given great encouragement in everything she attempted. He, on the other hand, had inherited the seriousness of his male line and, as the youngest, had perhaps been given responsibilities beyond his capacity.

Paul became a welcome visitor in Natalie's home. Her mother, whom he addressed by her patronymic Evgenia Trofimovna, respected his intellect and his seriousness, which would give stability to her daughter. Paul's background as a bourgeois and of foreign extraction mattered little to her. Such relationships were not uncommon and his wider cultural background appealed to her. Evgenia Trofimovna looked to Europe for Russia's future.

I have many gaps in my knowledge of mother's years in Russia; I know even less about my aunt Zinaida, whose life would end in tragedy but not before she played a crucial role in our family's life. Natalie and aunt Zinaida were born within a month of each other. Natalie Vasilievna Kamenzeva was born on 29 August 1900, in Tver, known during the Soviet period as Kalinin, 150 kilometres northwest of Moscow. Zinaida Demianovna Kungurzeva was born a month later, on 21 September 1900, a thousand kilometres to the east, in Irkutsk, Siberia. Both joined the caring professions: mother as a medical doctor, Zinaida as a nurse. Their lives would become fatefully intertwined in their place of exile, my birthplace: Frankfurt, Germany. Zinaida, according to information I obtained in part from a Russian Military Tribunal, trained as a nurse and then joined General Kolchak's White Army in Siberia. General Kolchak had declared himself master of the Irkutsk and Central Siberian regions in the Civil War of 1918–21 and set out to rout the Red Army. However, Trotsky's forces defeated Kolchak's army and, in February 1920, he was hanged in Irkutsk. Zinaida escaped and joined General Denikin's army in southern Russia but with his defeat and that of his successor, General Wrangel, the Civil War was lost and Trotsky's Red Army prevailed. The remnant of the White Army was evacuated from Sevastopol in the Crimea, first to Istanbul (then called Constantinople) and from there to France where Zinaida would meet and marry Paul's brother, my uncle Vladimir.

What qualities brought Paul and Natalie together in a lifelong union? Natalie's mother Evgenia had a great sense of self. She was born in Warsaw, Poland – then part of the Russian Empire – where her father was an officer in the Russian Army. Her maiden name Rakitsky identifies her Polish origin on her father's side. Natalie's father, Vasily Ephimovich Kamenzev, came from a Smolensk family. The Kamenzevs had come from Belarus (then Byelorussia) perhaps two generations earlier. (The Byelorussian connection becomes important after World War II.) My cousin Svetlana gave me a one-page family history written by our Kamenzev grandfather, which shows that the family name was changed from Kamenits to Kamenzev, perhaps to Russify it, my cousin believes. In the Soviet era, my cousin recounts, the name was used to persecute the family when an unknown informer claimed that it was a variation of Kamenev, the name of a contemporary of Stalin who fell foul of him and was one of the first to die in the purges of the 1930s. Another unknown informer claimed that the name was Jewish and a variation on the Russian word *kamen* (stone). Natalie's parents, Evgenia and Vasily, married in Smolensk in 1898. Evgenia had qualified as a dentist and Vasily, six years her senior, had been practising as a medical doctor. When Natalie was born in August 1900, her father was stationed in Tver, employed as the company doctor for the Russian railways. Tver is on the St Petersburg–Moscow train line (the same line as Sablino), where it is an important junction with extensive railroad workshops. The line is one of the oldest in Russia, built in 1837.

When Natalie was five years old, by then with two younger brothers, Michael and Sergei, her father was transferred to Orekhovo, eighty-five kilometres east of Moscow. This was the third largest industrial area in Russia after St Petersburg and Moscow, with extensive textile manufacturing. Mother rarely expressed pride in anything but she was proud to talk to me about her father's part in the 1905 Revolution. The workers from his plant marched on Moscow after 22 January 1905, when tsarist troops in St Petersburg shot an unarmed crowd wanting to bring their grievances to the attention of the Tsar. A thousand people were killed and wounded, and the day became notorious as Bloody Sunday. Riots and demonstrations broke out in many parts of Russia. In Moscow, heavy-handed Cossack troops from the Don region were sent in to disperse the crowds and a number of Vasily Kamenzev's workers were injured. He treated their wounds but for this he was branded a revolutionary and was gaoled in Moscow. Fortunately, in the chaos at the time and with few guards to stop him, he was able to walk out of the prison and return to Orekhovo. The shootings alarmed all levels of society and, recognising the justice of the workers' grievances, moderates like Vasily and many of the intelligentsia supported their protests. Mother repeatedly referred to her father's loyalties to and sympathies with the workers.

When the Great War broke out, my grandfather Vasily and his family, including my mother, had moved from Orekhovo back to Smolensk. That summer of 1914 they were living in a *dacha*, resettling for the three hottest months of the year to their summerhouse where they tended vegetables and fruit trees, pickled vegetables and dry-stored fruit. Vasily remained to work in Smolensk and joined his family for weekends. Habitually, they returned to their city home at the commencement of the school year in late August. This year, their summer stay was cut short. The family was relaxing at the *dacha* by the banks of the Dnieper River when Vasily arrived unexpectedly. He brought news that the Archduke of Austria had been assassinated and that Austria had declared war on Serbia. Russia, feeling its security threatened, had declared its support for Serbia and ordered general mobilisation. Confusion followed but the family could not immediately return to Smolensk, as the trains were transporting troops, equipment and supplies to the frontier.

Further confusion followed. Austria–Hungary had declared war on Serbia on 28 July. On 29 July, Russia mobilised its forces on the frontiers of Austria and its ally, Germany. As a result, Germany declared war on Russia on 1 August, and on Russia's ally, France, on 3 August. That month was a one of infamy, as Solzhenitsyn chronicled in his book *August 1914*. At the battle in East Prussia, later known as the battle of Tannenberg, there were 170,000 casualties and thousands more were taken prisoner by the Germans, including Natalie's favourite uncle, Nicolai Kamenzev (and Paul's brother Nicolai, the same first name a coincidence). She learned that he had been taken prisoner and sent him food parcels, but none reached him, she found out.

'They treated our people terribly, they were cruel, cruel!'

She was looking at a photo of herself and her uncle at their *dacha*. The Germans treated Russian prisoners of war (POWs) deplorably and when, after four years, her uncle returned, he was so damaged physically and mentally that he could not speak.

'They starved our POWs', Natalie recalled in anguish. The Germans had been the first to use poison gas as a weapon. Nicolai was injured in a gas attack, and the damage to his body was irreversible. Her beloved uncle was incapacitated for the rest of his life. Perhaps her dislike, if not hatred, of Germans had its beginnings in these experiences.

As mother told me in my video interview with her, at war's end she, as a seventeen-year-old who had just completed her schooling, was employed to work at the Smolensk railway station recording details of returning soldiers. By this time, virtually all railway traffic had come to a halt. The returning soldiers came walking along the tracks, many of them without boots, their feet bandaged in rough cloth. Natalie helped to identify each soldier, where they had come from and where they were going. The majority were illiterate peasants from villages across Russia. If they weren't wounded physically, the ordeal of war had scarred them mentally, often beyond hope of recovery. Natalie was authorised to issue them with a certificate, to provide each with a bowl of soup, a small amount of money and then send them on their way. They would have had to spend their money quickly, as the Bolsheviks soon abolished the currency. (One way to destroy capitalism, Bukharin and Preobrazhensky in their book *The ABC of Communism* believed, was to do away with money.) The scene as mother described it was chaotic and desperate, but she remained empathetic and resilient.

Natalie's family was part of the 'working intelligentsia', as distinct from the 'leisured intelligentsia'. She believed that it was the lack of engagement and commitment by the leisured intelligentsia, with their education, income and resources, that allowed Bolshevism to triumph. (Today's oligarchs and their circles might be considered their successors.) The Kamenzevs, while sympathising with the workers, also became losers in the revolution. Natalie's grandparents had acquired some properties in Smolensk, which they leased and which Evgenia inherited, earning rent from them. With the 1917 Revolution, the properties were confiscated and the rent went to 'goodness knows who', as mother expressed it; undeserving individuals had taken advantage of the chaos to deprive Evgenia of her income. The houses were soon turned into communal apartments, while money was declared to work against the interests of the revolution. Once money was abolished and there was nothing to be bought, all shops closed. Replacing money was a system whereby the workers received rations at their place of work, but this applied only to those who came to work. Quantities were kept at barely adequate levels to prevent black market profiteering. Despite these efforts, social and economic conditions deteriorated further. One thing, however, worked in Natalie's favour. In tsarist Russia, women had not been admitted to universities; the Bolsheviks changed this. By 1920 Natalie had moved to Petrograd, to study at the Institute of Medicine. She had found accommodation in an empty apartment and, as fate would have it, this was not far from where Paul lived on Vasilievski Island.

Archaeology of a Family

Having learned a little of father's life and of the events of those years, I was keen to discover where the firm had been located and where father's family had lived. I wanted a concrete image of their lives. In the year 2000, I decided to chance it in the St Petersburg Public Library. I say 'chance' as I did not know what I was looking for. The little I did know at that time was that my family had lived in St Petersburg for many years and conducted a business there. I was particularly interested in pinpointing where the Schlüsser Trading Company had had their offices. My cousin Oleg, at the time living in Cincinnati in the USA, though never having been to St Petersburg himself, suggested that the offices had been on *Nevsky Prospekt*, the Fifth Avenue of St Petersburg. But I had nothing to confirm this. Walking down the *Nevsky*, I thought it unlikely that a trading company would have been located here. It is full of upmarket retail stores, bookstores, antique shops and suchlike. My cousin Svetlana was letting me stay in her two-room apartment in the Petrograd district and she located the library for me. I caught the tube to Gostinyi Dvor, a shopping complex on the *Nevsky Prospekt*, and found it to be near the statue of Catherine the Great. As on previous visits, I felt at ease in the city of my father but would they let me into the library, and what if any useful information might I find? I cloaked my backpack but insisted I be allowed to take my video bag with me into the reading room. I didn't trust anyone, though that was probably unfair on the library staff. Reluctantly they let this quarrelsome foreigner have his way. After explaining to the woman at the information desk that I was seeking details of my family prior to 1918, I was directed to a library assistant on the third floor. There a middle-aged lady patiently heard me out and suggested that I look through the directories of the time. Not knowing how I would cope, I limited my request to three directories: the year of my grandfather's death (1912), the year of revolution (1917), and the year the Schlüsser firm was closed down (1918). No directory was published for the following few years. The first might give me information about the firm and the last two could reveal something about the changes between the year of revolution and the year when all property was nationalised. The library assistant explained it would take about thirty minutes to retrieve the volumes. I felt somewhat apologetic at my presumption that I would find a decrepit system rather than such a well-organised one. Almost to the minute, she brought me the books and I began to examine them. They proved to be directories of private citizens and businesses with and without telephone numbers. The Petrograd directory – known as the *Red Book* – for 1918 contained entries for the Schlüsser Trading Company and members of the family. I surmised that it must have been compiled before November 1917, as the firm had been closed down and some family members had fled by 1918. My heart rate increased dramatically when I read that the firm had been located at 37 *Kadetskaya Linya*, on Vasilievski Island, and not on the *Nevsky Prospekt* as cousin Oleg had suggested. The location seemed confirmed when I established that all Schlüssers listed in the directory lived on Vasilievski Island. With such a singular name, I presumed that they were all relatives, close or distant. The entry described the firm as 'Importers-Exporters' and gave several phone numbers. I noted down other addresses too, especially that of my step-grandmother Theresa Vasilievna Schlüsser, assuming it had been the address of my grandfather until 1912. It turned out that they had lived on the corner of *Bolshoi Prospekt* and Third Line, a five-minute walk from the firm's offices and warehouse. Other family members were listed as living on the Eleventh Line, on *Sredny Prospekt* (Central Avenue) and on the Tuchkov Embankment. (I later learned that the great Russian poet Anna Akhmatova had lived in that same building.)

Speaking with mother in Sydney on another sunny day, she sat opposite a portrait in oil of Justus Friedrich Schlüsser (1760–1840), the founder of the firm in St Petersburg, whose business thrived and made him very wealthy. When we came to talk about the 'lost Schlüsser fortune' she looked up at the portrait and addressed him, with heavy irony:

'So you ask me what did I do with all that money?'

I have the oil painting hanging on my wall as I write. It is a portrait of father's great-great-grandfather, painted in about 1810, and shows a benign man in late middle age, with ruddy cheeks and a receding hairline. His collar and coat suggest affluence, in a Dickensian way. He was a remarkable man who, in his own right and through his nine children, spread his influence to England, Italy, even Bengal and Mauritius.

An important source of information was a family diary. It came to me from brother William, who had, fortuitously, collected family papers and photos from his aunt Nadezhda, who had died in Paris. Besides recording births, deaths and marriages, it detailed trips to and from the *dacha* and trips abroad by various family members. It also recorded some incidental information, such as certain business deals, flood levels of the Neva River, extreme weather conditions, major events in the royal family. While Justus started his business in St Petersburg, it wasn't confined to Russia, and the Schlüsser family were frequent travellers – as was common among the educated – within Russia and abroad. There were relatives and business connections on the Baltic coast; they travelled to their *dacha* in Finland, and south to the Crimea – some two thousand kilometres away – to holiday on the Black Sea. With relatives in Germany and England, there was a steady flow of people for business and social reasons. Business was international, involving various shipping companies and foreign banks over the years. As early as 1812, the Schlüsser firm insured cargo sent from St Petersburg to London with Lloyds of London. The goods they exported came from merchants from across Russia: minerals, timber, rosin, pigs' bristles and furs. Not typical, but indicative of the agents with whom the Schlüsser firm dealt, was Heinrich Schliemann, who accumulated a small fortune in Russia before undertaking his epic archaeological dig at Troy to establish Homer's writings to be history and not merely myth.

With so much movement across borders, why does Russia's reputation as being isolationist persist, and is it justified? The tsarist autocracy could only survive if its population believed the tsarist government to be in control of the vast land, which it did by instilling fear that outsiders could threaten the country's stability at any time. Stalin continued this policy when he turned the Soviet Union into a fortress and ruled it by equally autocratic means. Today's Russian leaders seek to perpetuate these means of political control. In these circumstances, change is difficult to bring about no matter how good the intentions. Under Nicholas II, the Chairman of the Council of Ministers, Sergei Witte (a heroic political figure to mother), in trying to persuade the Tsar to introduce reform, warned of what might happen, in October 1905, as quoted by Pipes:

> The advance of human progress is unstoppable. The idea of human freedom will triumph, if not by way of reform, then by way of revolution. But in the latter event it will come to life on the ashes of a thousand years of destroyed history. The Russian *bunt* (rebellion) mindless and pitiless, will sweep away everything, turn everything to dust. What kind of Russia will emerge from this unexampled trial transcends human imagination: the horrors of the Russian *bunt* may surpass everything known to history. It is possible that foreign intervention will tear the country apart. Attempts to put into practice the ideals of theoretical socialism – they will fail but they will be made, no doubt about it – will destroy the family, the expressions of religious faith, property, all the foundations of law.

Witte might have been predicting father's future. Sadly, because his warning went unheeded, he resigned. Witte's economic policies had encouraged enterprises such as the Schlüsser Trading Company with various trade agreements and tariff measures. Peter the Great had authorised a Stock Exchange in St Petersburg, to which over the years several Schlüsser family members belonged. A grand building had been erected on the spit of Vasilievski Island, where symbolically and in practice maritime activity and finance merged.

With its high Greco-Roman colonnade on three sides, it remains one of the most imposing buildings in the city, a temple to the orderly financing of private enterprise. Today the Stock Exchange is housed in a more modest building.

Catherine the Great was the reigning autocrat (1762–96) when my great-great-great-grandfather, Justus Schlüsser, arrived in St Petersburg in 1784. Of German birth, Catherine further Europeanised Russia as Peter the Great had strived to do before her. She encouraged migration from Germany and, as an Anglophile, attracted many from England and Scotland, among them architects and scientists. It was the Age of Enlightenment and Catherine believed in its tenet of progress through reason, while she was also notorious for indulging her senses. Her very capable chief advisor, Potemkin, was one of many lovers. She invited the French philosopher Diderot to St Petersburg and purchased the whole of the French writer, historian and philosopher Voltaire's library. During her reign, the territory of Russia expanded greatly, with wars in the south, and the east, where Russians even established a settlement in Alaska.

Justus Schlüsser, family lore has it, walked from Berlin to St Petersburg having received a visa in the Danish port of Elsinor. After a time in Reval (now Tallinn), he formed a partnership in St Petersburg with a fellow countryman, Wolff, and their business prospered assisted by an increase in trade once Tsar Paul I had achieved a rapprochement with the French in 1800. Wolff resigned from the partnership and Justus set up business alone. His company suffered a financial blow when, during the Napoleonic Wars, a ship laden with cargo chartered by the Schlüsser Company was impounded by the French authorities in the Baltic port of Reval, and its cargo confiscated – a scenario which would be repeated almost exactly in World War I. The company managed to survive and took their insurers to court in 1820, aiming to recoup the 1812 losses. The court case was lost, but it suggests that the resources of the company were very considerable and reached across several national borders. The insurers were Lloyds of London. When Justus died in 1840 at the age of '79 years, 8 months and 10 days', as it says in the eulogy, he was farewelled with a poem that praises him as a most felicitous person with great business skills, yet not lacking care or compassion. He was buried in the Lutheran section of the St Petersburg Cemetery, where his grave survives, albeit stripped of its Christian symbols and decoration by revolutionary zealots in 1917. From Justus to Paul's grandfather, Fyodor, the family attended the Lutheran church on *Bolshoi Prospekt*. With Tsar Alexander II and Tsar Alexander III's drive to Russify during the 1880s, the family converted to the Orthodox faith, attending services at the St Andrew's Cathedral further along *Bolshoi Prospekt*. In Berlin, the family had belonged to the Reformed Church, roughly equivalent to the Presbyterian church, and I feel that Presbyterianism came down the generations.

Justus entrusted his business to his eldest son Wilhelm, under whose management the firm expanded greatly. The next two brothers, Carl and Heinrich, also added greatly to the success of the firm. A fourth son, Alexander, was ambitious to develop the business abroad, particularly in London. He eventually settled there and became an executive partner with John Henry Schroder in the merchant bank, Schroder & Co. The family now had a secure base in England for expanding their European trade. They became wealthy. The relationship with the Schroder firm was further sealed when Alexander's niece Eveline Schlüsser married Henry Schroder, who was later knighted for his services to commerce. They had no children. Justus's youngest son, Friedrich, saw his chances in England and from there in Bengal and Mauritius.

When I was shown the portrait of Justus for the first time, the story that mother had to tell about him immediately fascinated me, as it does everyone who looks at it. As you examine Justus's portrait, you notice a small puncture in the canvas in the middle of Justus's forehead. It is quickly apparent that its position is no accident and on closer inspection, and judging by the diameter of the hole, a .22-millimetre pistol made it. After painstakingly following information that I had about the Schlüsser firm, I was able to establish a narrative about the portrait's whereabouts during the Revolution. In the week of 7 November 1917, the portrait was hanging in the offices of Schlüsser

& Co. on *Kadetskaya Linya*, on Vasilievski Island. Vasilievski Island was the location and home of many foreign firms and thus an important target for the Bolsheviks. The American journalist John Reed's account, *Ten Days that Shook the World*, describes how elements of the Red Guard went on a rampage one day of that week. I could visualise how some of them broke into the offices of Schlüsser & Co., ransacked them and pilfered everything of value. In a parting gesture aimed against their bourgeois class enemy, they took a shot at the portrait – hence the hole in his forehead, 'death to the class enemy'. Justus Schlüsser had been conducting business in St Petersburg since his arrival in 1784. He had come there to make his fortune and he did. He ran an import-export business in Reval and St Petersburg, was decorated for his contribution to the business community of St Petersburg and made an 'Honorary Hereditary Citizen' for his work (a title which if reinstated would, I believe, be able to be claimed by the current generation of the family). He had been a valued member of the 1st Merchant Guild in both St Petersburg and Reval. All that was symbolically obliterated with one bullet through Justus's forehead.

Where had all that wealth disappeared? I learned what had happened to some of it from an unexpected source. I had two close relatives on father's side: Nicolai's children, cousin Oleg in the USA and cousin Beatrice in Germany. When I approached Oleg, he surprised me by sending copies of correspondence of the firm of Schlüsser & Co. I was not expecting that he would have any documents relating to the firm. The family believed that the Schlüsser Trading Company had owned a fleet of cargo ships, which had been illegally confiscated – during the Revolution, it was thought. It was frequently mentioned, with the implication that the cargo and ships might be found and that the Schlüsser wealth could somehow be regained. Oleg's copy of the correspondence at last provided some facts. According to that document, at the outbreak of World War I in August 1914 (in an echo of the events in 1812), a large consignment of rosin and refined lead was on board a ship, possibly owned or chartered by the Schlüsser firm, *en route* to London. It had docked on the Elbe River in the German port of Hamburg. The following day, Russia declared war on Germany and, in retaliation, all Russian assets in German ports were confiscated. The future of the firm was threatened. The cargo had been insured but would they be able to claim it in time of war?

Despite the loss, the firm continued to operate. The wealth which Paul's stepmother, Theresa Vasilievna, and the accountant-directors were able to take out of the country in or soon after November 1917 confirm that. But with that November Revolution, the capitalist firm of Schlüsser & Co., like all private enterprises, was confiscated, and put under control of the local municipality, where it soon languished for lack of expertise to carry on the business. The banks were nationalised, as were factories and mines. Lenin introduced regulations for foreign trade and repudiated his government's obligation to repay its debtors at home and abroad. He abrogated the civic rights of the wealthier citizens, which included the wider Schlüsser family, and established his own secret police, the Cheka, to enforce the decrees. In a sign of things to come, it is a little-mentioned fact that between ten and fifteen thousand people were executed in the first two months after Lenin announced his 'On Red Terror', in September 1918. With it, he claimed that he had established dictatorship of the working class. More accurately, he had established a personal dictatorship and kept himself in power applying ruthless and arbitrary violence.

Spooked

'From how these things are talked about, I formed the strong impression that your father was working for one of the American agencies.' The speaker was father's cousin Frederick Sevier, always known to me as uncle Fedya. In 1974, I took my wife and two sons, aged two and four, to England. I had twelve months' leave from my position as a television producer with the Australian Broadcasting Commission. Mother had kept in contact with Paul's English cousins, the Sevier family. Robert Sevier had worked for a British insurance company in St Petersburg and very likely had business dealings with the Schlüsser firm. Paul's aunt Elizabeth married into the Sevier family. Mother wrote to Fedya's sister Alice Helmer, née Sevier, who lived in Romaldskirk, Durham, that I was coming to London. Alice, her two sisters and brothers Fedya and Robert had played crucial parts in our family's life. We found an apartment in Hampstead and it turned out that Fedya lived not far away, in Hampstead Gardens. Alice wrote to Fedya with details of our address and soon I received a letter inviting me to call on him. It would be the first time that I had seen him since 1948.

I knew he had left Russia soon after the Revolution in 1917. In the way that ours was a German heritage, his was English and so it was natural for him to resettle in England. Some time later he joined Britain's secret service, MI6 – the external espionage agency (its most famous fictional member is, of course James Bond) – where with his knowledge of the Russian language and Russia itself he served honourably for the rest of his working life. When I learned this from mother, the thought first occurred to me that father might have been working for American intelligence services. This was my opportunity to confirm the suspicion. Also, dissatisfied with reasons I had been given over the years, I hoped that Fedya Sevier could finally help explain why our family had migrated – or should that be 'fled'? – to Australia. Thirdly, now would also be the time to confirm what I'd been told of Fedya's attempt to get us to England after World War II. When father feared the Soviet takeover of the rest of Germany, Fedya had been able to obtain six visas for our family to enter Britain. Germany was divided into four sectors and uncle Fedya was then stationed in the British Occupation Zone, in Cologne.

'It was so foolish of me! So foolish!' he lamented. In a lapse of judgement, he had sent the visas to Frankfurt by post; they never arrived. They were either destroyed or, more likely, six unknown people reached Britain using our visas, probably after altering the names. Fedya had come to explain. My own memory of that occasion was seeing a black, chauffeur-driven Humber car, in which Fedya had come from Cologne, parked in front of our apartment block. Cars were rare then and attracted attention, especially one with a military number plate from the British Occupation Zone. Fedya drove off that evening and I was about to meet him for the first time since then.

I made arrangements for the following Sunday. His house was modest, the downstairs apartment of a two-storey vanilla brick building. It had a small, rather neglected garden front and back. An elderly, white-haired man opened the door and at once recognised me as my father's son. I also immediately saw a family resemblance in him. He embraced and hugged me in the Russian manner and ushered me in.

'A long-lost relative', he exclaimed loudly. 'Richard, come and meet Evgeni, the son of Pavel Fyodorovich and Natalya Vasilievna.' A man in his late thirties introduced himself as Fedya's son Richard and immediately excused himself again, saying that he had work to do. The apartment was modestly furnished yet welcoming. I had expected to see more evidence of his Russian years but the general feel was of sober Englishness. Fedya spoke fluent English with only a slight Russian accent. He explained that he had grown up in St Petersburg speaking English as a second language and had received some of his schooling in England. He had not attended the Karl May *Gymnasium*. From that occasion until he died, two years later, I visited him regularly. He told me about the childhood he had shared with father; he commented on father's interest in electronics, his memories of my grandparents and life in St Petersburg. But first of all, he needed to explain the circumstances of the lost visas, clearly still pained by the memory.

'How could I have been such a fool? I am so sorry. I could have spared your mother so much pain and perhaps Pavlusha might still be alive.' He recalled his car trip to Frankfurt.

'It was so soon after the war and none of the services could be trusted. Oh my, what a mistake to make.'

His folly had haunted him and it seemed to do him good to speak of it.

'I will never forgive myself.'

Fearing that it might cause further pain, I refrained from asking him about the possible connection between father and US intelligence. Instead I asked him how he had escaped Russia. Like so many, he had walked and then swum the shallow section of the Gulf of Finland, the most easterly part of the Baltic Sea.

Mother had also written that she had news from Fedya's sister Alice that a memoir had been written by a Dr Swann, *Home on the Neva*, that included his experiences during the Russian Revolution and Civil War. The book described life in Petrograd before and during the Revolution and contained some details of Alice's experiences in Russia. I found a copy at the Public Library in Swiss Cottage and read that Alice had been a nurse in the Civil War, assisting Dr Swann, the author. It reminded me of Pasternak, the great Russian writer, who has his heroine Lara go through a similar experience in his novel, *Doctor Zhivago*. Alice had been with General Denikin's White Army and, when defeat threatened, she escaped with Dr Swann and others by boat from Sevastopol in the Crimea. I was later to learn that aunt Zinaida was at precisely the same time a nurse in the White Army and was also forced to flee via the Crimea. I fancy that Alice and she may even have met. (Dr Herbert Swann was the father of the entertainer Donald Swann, who with Michael Flanders composed and performed humorous cabaret songs.)

Lost Property

I had many setbacks in excavating this history, and locating the Sablino property offers one example. While frequently tempted to give up the search, I persisted as I was hopeful that important information would be gained, since this substantial property had been willed to Paul in such unlikely circumstances. The will was handwritten in Russian and referred to several localities. Frequent name changes in Russia following change in political power was frustrating. The indistinct handwriting did not help either. Eager to know more about the location, I asked a Russian friend about the name. She felt that the land would long ago have disappeared under concrete roads and housing developments. Despite my best efforts, I was unable to locate 'Sablino' on any maps and indexes, so I suspended my search. But I couldn't let it rest. Sometime later I examined the details of the will once more. It said that the property lay on the St Petersburg–Moscow railway line, some three and a half verst – about four kilometres – from the Sablino Station. I again looked for Sablino on every map I could find. I still owned father's meticulously detailed *Andrees Handatlas*, published in 1930, but it did not show Sablino either on a map or in the index. Time and technology moved on, and when it became possible I Googled 'Sablino'. Still nothing came up. Laboriously, I tried to decipher a few more words in the will, but in vain. Eventually another Russian friend deciphered another word, 'Trotsk'. Apart from its apparent derivation from the name 'Trotsky', this was a surprising name to emerge until she explained that it could refer to the name of a region. Still, despite further extensive searching I could not find it on any map. When next I mentioned it to an older Russian friend, he thought he knew of it and believed that it might be located a short distance south of St Petersburg. Recalling the reference in the will to the St Petersburg–Moscow railway line, I traced it along its entire length but still could not find Sablino. I resigned myself to accepting that Sablino had either undergone a radical name change or had disappeared under concrete. Another two years passed when, on the spur of the moment, with the expanded Internet at hand, I decided to Google 'Sablino' again. This time, dozens of pages seemed to explode at me. Why had I not found them before? Because, as I was soon to learn, they had only recently been uploaded. I printed every page, photos included, and began a careful examination for clues as to where Sablino was and what it consisted of. All the information was in Russian so it took time, but eventually I found the answer to why I had been unable to find it. The township had been renamed Ulyanovka after the Revolution, and was then in the region of Trotsk, a name which had also been changed when Stalin expelled Trotsky from the Party. Today only the railway station retains the name 'Sablino'; it is not shown on any map as such. Then an essay caught my attention – an account of a trip down the Tosno River from the town of Tosno to Sablino and beyond. The essay was written in 1923, the same year that the will had been made! I read the article carefully and at one point became thoroughly agitated. There in print was my family name. After I recovered from the shock of recognition, I concluded that this must have a connection with the property mentioned in the will. The author was identifying geological features as he guided other specialists and enthusiasts interested in the geology of the river valley. At one point I read: 'As you round the corner, you will see on the opposite bank the *dacha* which used to be known as the "Schlüsser *dacha*"'. My heart raced. After all my efforts, here was a new set of possibilities, thanks to an unknown traveller. Much of what had been surmise on my part now might be confirmed. An unknown eyewitness noted the existence of a Schlüsser property! I was overwhelmed by this discovery and immediately determined to go there. Perhaps I could find the property after all and what it consisted of. Perhaps it could give me some clue to why father had been made co-beneficiary with his brother Nicolai, and why the other brothers and sisters had been omitted. The faint hope also stirred, I confess, that somehow I might be heir to a stately home and estate, though the description given by the traveller of a 'Schlüsser *dacha*' suggested a more modest property.

I arranged my next trip to St Petersburg for the northern summer, and my Russian cousin-in-law Lev Samoilov agreed to accompany me. The plan was to find the Tosno River and walk along it if need be, from the town of Tosno to where it joins the Neva River. Luck seemed on my side when I learned that the train for Ulyanovka and its station Sablino leaves from Moscow Station, confirming information in the will that the property was on the St Petersburg–Moscow line. On the train, I speculated how often my father may have taken this journey. Arriving at Sablino Station – much diminished, I learned, since its heyday early in the twentieth century – we asked for directions to the river and were advised to take a bus. The will said that the property was about four kilometres from the station. The obliging driver advised us to alight at a bridge on the Tosno River. We reached the river and prepared to walk along it to look for evidence of the 'Schlüsser *dacha*'. But then we discovered a Visitor's Centre offering detailed information of the Geological National Park, which had been created around the Tosno River because of the many caves in the area. Surrounding the wooden building were stones with signs detailing the area's millennia of geological history. I wanted to learn what had happened only eighty years ago! I took out my video camera as Lev approached a man who identified himself as the director of the Park. In his usual uninhibited way, Lev asked him directly if he had any knowledge of or had ever heard of a Schlüsser *dacha* along the Tosno River.

'Schlüsser! Schlüsser!' The man repeated the name a number of times, pronouncing it in a way that suggested he might be familiar with it. 'It rings a bell … but I can't put my finger on it.' My pulse rate went up and the hair literally bristled on the back of my neck. 'No, I don't know.' After a few moments' further reflection, he said: 'I do know someone who will know'. He pulled out his mobile phone and dialled. (It says something about me that I was surprised that people in these parts would have mobile phones and that there would be coverage.)

'Tatyana Nicolaivna!' he exclaimed loudly and repeated the name, 'I have two gentlemen here who are enquiring after people by the name of Schlüsser.' He got no further but listened, occasionally grunting an affirmative reply. 'Can you be here in an hour?' He turned to us and said: 'Tatyana Nicolaivna would very much like to talk to you. She is in a car on her way to St Petersburg but will turn back and come if you can be here.' We would wait, we said, of course. She was true to her word. In less than an hour, she arrived. I had occasional trepidations about how I might be received as a Westerner. But the woman coming toward us now immediately allayed any fears. She was a friendly, handsome woman with large features and a distinctive mole on her left cheek. I didn't mention the will at this point.

'Yes, I can tell you quite a bit about the Schlüssers', she said, after we had introduced ourselves. Emotion swelled within me and I could barely prevent myself from shedding a tear. I had invested more emotional energy into my search than I had realised. I still can't quite understand it. It seemed as if all the resentment, all the defensiveness I had employed over the decades regarding our family name was rolling away when she made that statement. There were literally thousands of times that people had said: 'Say that again? How do you spell that name? German is it?' And that is when people were well disposed toward me. At other times, they would feign choking as they tried to pronounce a name with four consonants in a row. The worst experiences were when the speaker seemed to want to blame you, or to make you feel that you had been complicit in the Holocaust, World War II and the Pacific War, all in one. And here was this friendly, warm person, a total stranger, implicitly trusting me when I told her my story. It was a moving encounter.

'This is what we'll do. I'll tell you a little of what I know and then, if you wish, I can take you to where the Schlüsser *dacha* once stood.' As simple as that. We wouldn't have to trail along the river after all, looking for the landmark identified in the essay. I had found a person who knew some important details of my family's history. Incredible!

'There was a Schlüsser farm (*miza*, in Russian), a Schlüsser forest and a Schlüsser *dacha*', she began. 'There are documents and descriptions in various publications of members of the family over the years.' She explained that the road between Sablino Station and the farm was once called Schlüsser Street. It was renamed Sovietskaya Street after the Revolution, but people still referred to it as Schlüsser Street. Had it been renamed because of its German connotations or because of its bourgeois owners? Probably both. A horse-drawn tramway had run along it to carry people and goods between the station and the farm.

I was astonished by her detailed knowledge of my family. But how was it that she had all this information? She explained that she was a teacher at the local school and had established a museum of the district, housed in two of her classrooms. She had been collecting archival material for some years. I was welcome to visit the museum whenever I wished. I experienced an almost spiritual sense of calm. For the first time in my search, I could feel my father's spirit. It is difficult to explain, but my sense of him had been so dominated by the periods of tension and violence in our lives that he seemed almost a stranger. It was also as if I had constantly to explain, if not apologise, for the apparent mix that I was: a Russian in Germany but with a German name or a Russian in Russia with a German name, speaking both languages. That lack of a clear identity can 'mess with the mind'. But here, for the first time, was someone who knew of the family and spoke of them as people with integrity and learning, contributing to the community in money, in kind and in spirit. There is a record of the Schlüssers donating twenty roubles towards building the St Nicholas' church in Sablino – an amount that could have bought two good cows. The church was duly built but then destroyed during Stalin's rampage against religion and church property. Tatyana Nicolaivna Slepnova showed me sections of the foundations that can still be seen. Antonia Schlüsser, owner of the property, was actively involved in the development of Sablino; records show that she chaired the local planning council for four years, from 1908 to 1912. Tatyana Nicolaivna conveyed the decency and common humanity of these people, which I also believed my father had, and I felt I could take pride in who they were and what they did. I had my own sense of pride in my family, but this was always kept private because of the dangers of speaking about it. I remain grateful to Tatyana Nicolaivna for preserving that part of my past so that she could now share it and I could celebrate it.

The background to the property was that in the 1890s, Vasily Schlüsser, Paul's great-uncle, like many among the Russian middle class, bought a country property as an escape from the polluted city atmosphere – the result of rapid industrialisation – and to grow food. His daughter Antonia Schlüsser had retained the use of the property by providing a haven for a handful of *bezprisorny*, the homeless children victims of the 1917 Revolution and Civil War. An estimated seven to nine million orphans and abandoned children were then roaming the countryside, largely children of workers and peasants reduced to foraging. Lenin's decree stipulated that provided a property was used to assist the proletarian poor, it could be used by the owner. Antonia Schlüsser turned her property into an orphanage. With help from Paul and Nicolai, she gave some nine children at a time food and shelter, taught them to read, write and count, and to acquire farming skills. There were orchards of apples, pears, cherries and plums on the property. Of the original thirty-five hectares, half was wooded and logging timber brought some income though most of the wood was used domestically. Several large fishponds (Tatyana showed me remaining evidence of them, a site now used by locals to dump rubbish) provided protein all the year around. Granaries and stables flanked the two-storey *dacha*. Ploughing, hoeing, seeding and harvesting were done with two horses. Two cows provided milk for the family and some surplus to sell. Paul, after arriving at Sablino Station, would walk the four kilometres along a road flanked by the ubiquitous log huts, *izbas*. Sometimes, if the horses could be spared, he was picked up by the tramway. The location was a picture. The house stood on the higher, left bank of the Tosno River. The Tosno flows from above the town of Tosno through Tosno, Sablino – or rather, Ulyanovka – and several other localities before it joins the Neva River upstream from St Petersburg. It formed its own narrow valley, not extensive but wide and deep enough to provide slopes for skiing and tobogganing when the snows came. Paul and his friends could skate on parts of it when the river froze in the months from November to March. In summer, the water is a deep brown colour heavily laden with peat leeched from the upstream countryside. St Petersburg is at sea level while Sablino is at an elevation of almost a hundred metres. The clean water and stretches of forest ensure healthy, fresh air. Sablino became a desirable place for people to buy *dachas* to escape the city during the most difficult months. It attracted some notable people. Countess Alexandra Tolstoy, a cousin of the author of *War and Peace*, lived on a large estate nearby on the opposite bank. The Russian philosopher and theologian Vladimir Soloviev lived here; he was also a poet, pamphleteer and literary critic who played a significant role in the development of Russian philosophy and poetry at the end of the nineteenth century, and in the spiritual renaissance of the early twentieth century. Soloviev is said to have been the model for two characters in Dostoevsky's book *The Brothers Karamazov*, Alyosha and Ivan Karamazov, who debate the nature of God, free will and morality. I wondered whether father might have been aware of these cultural icons, and how the contemplation of deep human experience and reflection may have influenced him. Father, without a doubt, had grown up and been educated to become a complex, spiritual and practical man.

In 1923–24, Paul spent extra time in Sablino. He helped on the farm as a member of the family, not as hired labour, which remained illegal. In return, his cousin gave him food and other provisions which he took back to his room in Petrograd, renamed Leningrad in 1924. Here he provided for himself and his aunt Albine König, who had moved in with him in the communal apartment. She was the daughter of a past director of the Schlüsser Trading Company, Adolph König, and an aunt to Paul.

Paul's cousin Konstantin Bruni was also a regular visitor to Sablino. He used the occasions to make pencil and oil sketches of the farm and the surrounding landscape. On 14 March 1924 – the date on the painting – he completed an oil painting whose subject, mother said, was the view from father's room at the *dacha*, across the apple orchard to an outbuilding. The snow is about a metre deep and the shadows are long. Snow clings to the north side of the bare trees. Recent footsteps in the snow, leading to the wooden building, suggest regular traffic between the buildings: perhaps for milking and feeding the cows and horses, mucking out the stables or turning the dung heap. The scene is sunny, impressionistic in the use of colour and brush strokes – an uplifting scene. There is no suggestion of the difficult circumstances prevailing at the time. Is it too fanciful to suggest that Kostya, by depicting a winter scene, was symbolically seeing Russia as being in a slumber before the arrival of spring? Unreal as it might be, I like my fancy. The date on the painting is most probably when he completed it, by which time he was in Berlin or Paris.

One version of Kostya's life at this time is that, soon after the 1917 Revolution, he and his father's positions became untenable and they had to escape. They fled across the spit at Kronstadt in the Gulf of Finland to Kuokaala, then Finnish territory. There they joined the distinguished Russian artist Ilya Repin who, while a supporter of the Revolution, yet offered sanctuary to persecuted artists. He assisted them to move on to other cities in Europe. The specific cause for their persecution is uncertain, but in Kostya's case it may have followed his father's dismissal as teacher at the Academy of Arts when it was closed down by the Bolsheviks in 1918.

A few years later, Kostya drew a head and shoulder portrait of Natalie. Natalie gave the portrait to her brother Michael to take back to the family in Leningrad, and it hung in the family's apartment until the 1970s. Cousin Natasha remembers how much Michael loved his sister and how beautifully she was portrayed in the picture. When in later years the two families lost contact, the picture became part of cousin Natasha's inspiration to search for her aunt.

When Kostya prepared to defect from Russia, he asked Paul to come with him. Paul decided against it. Kostya could not recall the reason when he spoke of this in his studio to my brother William in Paris many years later, but perhaps Paul, as a patriot and in the hope of regaining the family property, felt an obligation to remain in Russia. With Repin's help, Kostya Bruni travelled to Berlin and then moved to Paris. He never returned to see the winter scene that he had painted so effectively. He gave the painting to Paul when they met in Paris, and now it is in my possession. I weave numerous stories around the scene as I imagine father's life in Sablino.

If Only

On a humid summer's day, I found myself sitting on the median strip of *Bolshoi Prospekt*, on the corner of the Third Line outside the building where my grandfather and his family had lived. A relief sculpture of Lenin fastened to the wall caught my eye. I read the inscription and was both intrigued and somewhat affronted to learn of the nature of the event commemorated by the plaque, which had taken place in the building. In 1895, five years before Paul's birth, the St Petersburg League of Struggle for the Emancipation of the Working Class was established here, with Lenin as a driving force. It eventually morphed into the Bolsheviks. What might have happened, I pondered, if my grandfather, the capitalist Frederick Schlüsser, had confronted Vladimir Ilych Ulyanov, as Lenin was still known then, on the landing in the building, each aware what the other represented? It is possible, though there is no evidence, that my grandfather may have had some part in the arrest of six members of the group a few months later, in December 1895, when Lenin was sent into exile.

Lenin established two principles with this League. First, a small group of activists well versed in Marxism was to be the vanguard of the proletariat, and second, violence was to be a legitimate weapon to instigate revolution. Acting on these principles, they agitated among the St Petersburg workers by distributing leaflets in factories and provoking the workers to express their discontent, if strategic, even striking. Armed struggle had begun. With this call to violence, Lenin set the pattern for decades to come. Violence was justified and made part of 'Leninism', the road map to establish Communism.

How should I respond, and what could I do to honour my parents' courage and resilience? I contemplated these questions as I sat on the nature strip of *Bolshoi Prospekt*, looking at the plaque. These plaques in so many places in St Petersburg, Moscow and in regional towns form a kind of 'Stations of the Cross' for Lenin, the Communist saint replacing the Christian saints. But the plaque also confirms for me that the actions of individuals can have big consequences, good and bad. I felt that I wanted to make a small gesture to honour what I had found and learned. The basement of the building housed a dimly lit bar. I took the few steps down and on entering it found that I was the only patron. I wanted to raise a glass to my discoveries and to the people who had been involved, not least my grandfather. I reflected on my modest connection with this history, aware that my contribution had been merely to discover a link. Nevertheless, I thought, what a loss it would have been had I failed to discover the connection. Writing this history is my contribution. Many more revelations were yet to come. As I headed back to the T-junction at the *Kadetskaya Linya*, I found a basement bookshop. There on a shelf was Mikhail Bulgakov's book *The Master and Margarita*, the story in the form of magic realism of life under Stalin as the author experienced it. Written between 1928 and 1941, it was not published in an uncensored Russian version until 1973. It was now 2000. It has inspired plays, novels, an opera and ballet even a ten-part Russian television series. I bought a copy and it forms part of my homage to my father and his father whose broken lives are somewhat reflected in Bulgakov's writings. In 2013, my son staged a successful version of the book as part of the Melbourne International Arts Festival. I like to believe that there is a certain continuity down the generations, conscious or not.

A statue of the Russian poet Anna Akhmatova had recently been erected on the banks of the Neva River. I visited it as soon as I was able. It is inspired by a drawing that the Italian painter Modigliani made of her and is a graceful, lithe figure placed there to commemorate her work, specifically the line from her poem where she is asked a question by a woman outside the prison, one of many waiting for news or bringing food to their incarcerated husbands and sons.

> ... (she) asked me in a whisper
> Can you write about this?
> And I said
> I can
> Then something like a smile came to her face
> looking for a moment as it had once done.

Akhmatova's husband and son were gaoled at one time or another. She looks across the Neva to where, on the other side, a forbidding sight meets the eye: Kresty Prison, a conglomeration of red brick buildings with the dome of a church rising from the middle. My companion Lev pointed out the hypocrisy of having a church in the centre of such a complex – a prison where thousands of innocent people were incarcerated, to be exiled to one of the gulags, or summarily executed. I didn't know then but would soon learn that father's cousin Artur had been shot there and perhaps other, yet unknown relatives. Lev and I silently contemplated the statue from all angles, while traffic was racing past on the embankment. Lev's own life had been blighted by the Soviet Secret Service. Two smaller bronze sphinxes (mirroring those outside the Academy of Fine Arts, a kilometre downstream), opposite each other with the side of the faces turned to the prison, sculpted as death heads, sit on plinths with inscribed lines from Akhmatova's poems and from those of her friend, Nobel Prize winner Joseph Brodsky: a memorial to those who died during Stalin's reign of terror. The sight left me numb and often comes back to mind to cause renewed distress. But what is most difficult for me to comprehend is why Kresty Prison, with its inhumane past, has been allowed to remain standing. Why hasn't it been razed to the ground and replaced by something as a redemptive gesture – a park, perhaps?

After a time, we walked in the direction of the Winter Palace. On the way, Lev pointed to a building and explained that Leningraders had for many years simply referred to it as 'the Big House'. It was the headquarters of the KGB, now called the FSB. I determined to make enquiries there. On the following day, a friend and I headed for the Big House. I was fearful of what might happen. We entered the building and were politely directed to another door. There in a crowded waiting room were dozens of people enquiring about arrested relatives and friends. The walls were covered with excerpts of laws and regulations relating to various crimes. There was an air of subdued desperation about the people, mostly women of various ages. I was full of inexplicable anxiety and was willing to give the enterprise away when a young man ushered us into a room from where a woman had just emerged. A man in his thirties in an immaculate dark blue suit, sitting behind a large desk, asked us to take a seat. As I did so, I noticed that behind him was a portrait of Felix Dzerzhinsky, the notorious Pole who was instructed by Lenin to form the secret service 'to protect the Revolution' and did so ruthlessly. For that, he became one of the most hated men in the Soviet Union, responsible for countless deaths. Lev had told me how, in the 1991 demonstrations through Moscow in support of Yeltsin and a reformed Russian Federation, the procession had ended outside the Lubyanka Prison, the hated red-grey multi-storeyed Moscow headquarters of the KGB. In the front stood a large statue of Dzerzhinsky. In a show of defiance, the crowd set about pulling it down, at first using any tools at hand. It took three days and nights, with cranes and winches and blowtorches, before the statue lay on its side. Masses of people had cheered the crews on and Lev was proud to have been among them. As an architect, he had some knowledge of how the statue was mounted and could help in dismantling it. (Today it remains in a sculpture park, though there are moves among some to remount it.)

The photo on the wall did not bode well. But the FSB officer was ready to be helpful. I explained what I knew of Artur Arturovich Schlüsser, referred to him as my uncle and stated that I was his nearest surviving relative.

'Where was he arrested?'

'Memorial* says it was in Novgorod.'

'Ah, in that case it is in the Novgorod jurisdiction and not ours. You'll have to address yourself to them.'

---

* An organisation documenting Stalin's victims.

It was unclear whether he was being helpful or passing the buck. In any case, he wrote down two addresses in Novgorod and explained: 'Write a letter both to the local FSB and the local office of the Ministry of the Interior. One or the other should have records of your uncle.'

I translated his Russian into English for my companion, stalling for time to think of more questions. But my eye caught the portrait of Dzerzhinsky again and I became uncomfortable staying any longer. I felt that I was pushing my luck. We said goodbye and let ourselves out. As soon as we were in the street, I asked my companion:

'Did you notice the portrait of Dzerzhinsky?' and explained who he was.

'Is that who that was?' she said, 'I thought he looked familiar'. She had seen the statue in the Moscow sculpture park.

I wrote to the address I had been given and soon received a one-paragraph reply with a one-page attachment from the Novgorod FSB. It gave some detail about Artur's arrest on trumped-up charges on two occasions. The second time he was executed in Kresty Prison. This was a revelation to me. The dates of his imprisonment, only weeks before Paul made his decision I now believe, were known to father in 1927 and became a major cause for his decision to leave Russia. But did he ever learn of his cousin's execution?

Tsunami Approaching

Ever more powerful forces were building up which would create conditions at odds with what Paul had been taught and believed. Communism appeals to two sorts of people, wrote Ellery Walter, author of *Russia's Decisive Year*, after an extensive visit to Russia in the early 1930s: the tyrant and the idealist. Lenin was a combination of both. Lenin's hunger for power and control knew few bounds. He had no patience for the laborious business of providing a useful service through a network of people who had to be motivated and directed to contribute effectively to the success of an enterprise. No need for him to try to understand human nature and work with it. He wanted to change human nature by changing the circumstances, especially those of the working class. He believed that he had the theory and it required only willpower to turn it into reality. (Hitler acted on a similar rationale.) In some sense, he never grew past being an impetuous teenager who wanted the world to conform to his idea of how it should be organised and operating. That way lies disaster for the young, and that way lay disaster for Lenin and his followers' aspirations. Paul and Natalie were innocent victims of the violence he unleashed.

Paul and Natalie's life was unfolding against the background of developing political and social chaos. Stalin's Soviet Union was daily becoming more repressive and Hitler's Nazism would soon envelop Germany. How could Paul assess and judge the situation and make decisions? How could anyone? In considering the conundrum, I recalled mother's dry conclusion about people – a conclusion held at age eighty-four, after having lived a full but precarious life.

'People are crazy! It's a funny world.'

But the word 'funny' wasn't said with any humour, rather with bitterness, after which she exhaled loudly and tapped the ash from her cigarette, the stained index and middle finger of her right hand evidence of her need for their sedative effect. The two fused golden wedding rings on her right hand remained a constant reminder of what she had lost.

Justus Friedrich Schlüsser, 1760–1840. Doyen of the Schlüsser family. Arrived in St Petersburg, Russia, in 1784. Founder of Schlüsser & Co. Trading Company. Painting shot at in 1917, with bullet hole visible in forehead

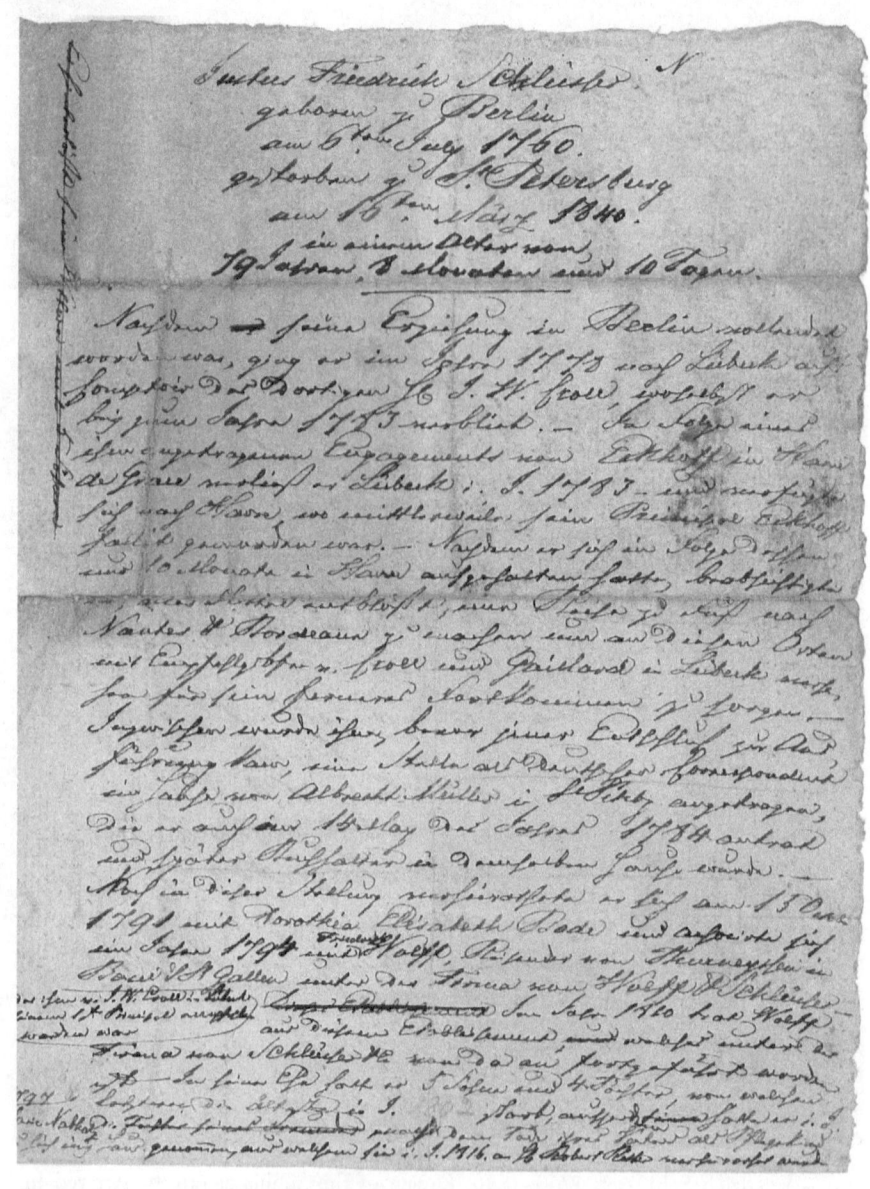

Eulogy for J.F. Schlüsser. Much-loved and respected businessman, member of the St Petersburg Stock Exchange, husband of Dorothea Elisabeth, née Bode, father of nine children, awarded title 'Honorary Hereditary Citizen of St Petersburg'

Centenary of Schlüsser & Co. Trading Company – commemorative artwork, 1905. The Latin inscription in the crest reads 'Nothing without toil' or colloquially, 'No pain, no gain'

Above

Natalie with her mother, brother and nanny. Tver, 1905

Left

Paul aged three with brother Vladimir aged six

Karl May *Gymnasium*, St Petersburg, 1913. Paul attends the school in the years 1912–17

Paul receives an excellent education, matriculating with a silver medal

Left

Natalie aged sixteen, 1916

Below

Natalie's graduating class, 1917. Natalie (back row, third from left) wins a gold medal and considers she received an outstanding education

Above

Paul's graduating class, 1917. Paul centre back row

Left

Natalie's favourite uncle, Nicolai Kamenzev, in a photo taken in Irkutsk in 1905. He will be gassed by the Germans in World War I

Petrograd House Committee issues ID to Paul, May 1918. His family apartment is nationalised. He is given permission to occupy one room

Left

Paul in Balaclava, Crimea, recovering from typhus, early 1920s

Below

Paul with friends skiing at the *dacha*, 1920s

Духовное Завещание

Находясь в здравом уме и твердой памяти завещаю свое имение и дома в нем находящиеся с движимым имуществом племянникам моим Николаю Федоровичу Шлюссер и Павлу Федоровичу Шлюссер. Из земли прошу их выделить по (1) одной десятине земли Артуру Артуровичу Шлюссер и сестре его Дагмаре Артуровне Шлюссер. Земля и дома находятся в 3½ верстах от ст. Саблино Н.Ж.Д. причислялось прежде к Детскосельскому уезду, а ныне к Троцкому уезду.

1923 г.
27 Ноября

Гр. Антония Васильевна Шлюссер

The Will, November 1923. Why, since all property has been nationalised by the Bolsheviks, is Antonia Schlüsser making a will, bequeathing it to Paul and Nicolai Schlüsser?

Above

Paul's room in Leningrad, with his aunt Albine König (right) and an unidentified woman

Left

Artur (left), Paul's cousin, with parents, sisters Dagmara and Margaret, c.1913. Did Paul know of Artur's later imprisonment and execution?

Vladimir Shuisky, Paul's fellow student and family friend, 1936. His phone call leads to revelations about Natalie's Russian family

Above

Natalie and Paul begin their honeymoon in Paris, with Paul's brother Nicolai, his wife and their children, Beatrice (aged 3) and Oleg (aged 2), 1927

Left

Marriage certificate, 1927. Allegedly lost, it allows Paul to falsify the date of marriage

Above

Zinaida and Vladimir, Paul's fateful sister-in-law and brother in Paris, 1927

Left

Paul and Natalie (right) share a meal at the 'rich, rich, rich' Berlin apartment of Paul's stepmother Theresa Vasilievna (third from left), with cousin Alexander Makarov and wife (left) and Mrs Makarova senior (seated centre), 1927

Left

Paul's cousin Konstantin Bruni painting in the streets of Berlin, 1927

Below

Paul's caption for this photo was "Fear women and thunder. French proverb". This 'turkey' takes Paul and Natalie across Germany, France and Switzerland.

Natalie captioned this photo 'The Lovers', taken while on their honeymoon, 1927. Paul wrote, "The heart is made to love, so then love. Christine, Queen of Sweden"

Natalie with her Swiss aunt, Anna Dupond, Geneva, 1927

Natalie at the famed Robert Koch Institute, identifying viruses, 1928

Natalie with colleagues studying for a higher degree at the Robert Koch Institute, Berlin, 1928

The faculty, with Natalie the only woman, Berlin, 1928

Transliterating Russian in a telegram from Leningrad on the birth of Svetlana: 'Congratulations mum and dad for daughter terribly happy good health'

And from Paris: 'Congratulations happy parents kiss daughter everyone'

Above

In the Bois de Boulogne, Paris, no hardship yet, judging by the furs. Paul's sister, Nadya (left), brother Vladimir (third from left), sister-in-law Zinaida (fourth from left), her mother, rear, Beatrice (front), sister-in-law Olga and brother Nicolai Schlüsser, 1929

Left

Natalie with brother Michael, exchanging confidences during his visit from the USSR, 1931

Natalie and Michael's father, Vasily Kamenzev (1870–1931). As Russian as Chekhov, c.1930

Paul and Natalie (left) welcome the new year, 1936, with their neighbours and colleague, Rudolf and Dietlinde Heiss

PART 2
STALIN

Saving Lies – Love Finds a Way – Preparing for Freedom – Full Swing in Berlin – The Rise and Fall of Evil

Saving Lies

I was dis-informed from the beginning. I was told that we were not Russian at all but Byelorussian, that is, from the state of Belarus, or White Russia. That thought appealed, with 'White' implying anti-Communist sentiments, although in fact there is no connection. I believed we were Byelorussians and tried to locate the borders with the intention sometime in the future to trace the fate of any relatives. I was also told that mother was born in the west Russian city of Smolensk. In fact I was to learn that she was born in the central Russian city of Tver. But Smolensk was close enough to the Belorussian border for me to wonder if the borders had changed since her birth. Borders in central Europe had been redrawn frequently during this period. When I made these enquiries in the 1950s, the Russian branch of the family had disappeared without trace and all were believed to have perished. As far as I knew, we were the only family with the surname Schlüsser or Schlusser, and mother's family in the Soviet Union had been wiped out – if not in the siege of Leningrad 1941-44, then in one or another of Stalin's repressive periods. When, from time to time, someone claimed to have come across the name elsewhere I dismissed those claims as misunderstandings of German-sounding names. Schlosser is common and other variants exist. I was wrong. Further, I was told that mother and father were married in 1924, not 1927. I possess signed documents from witnesses testifying that they were at the wedding in 1924. Added to this was another piece of dis-information. I was told that on graduating, mother and father had been offered a choice: work experience in one of the Soviet Republics or a scholarship to undertake postgraduate studies abroad. These options never existed for them. What was the purpose of all this deception? I took the opportunity on one of our annual visits to mother in Sydney to challenge her about the accuracy or otherwise of this information.

'Ugh, you're silly!' she grunted, 'What do you think? Of course we were Russians. Everybody had *falsche Papiere.*' She often used German when recollecting distasteful incidents and events, from the time she had lived in Germany.

'It was very simple', she continued with an ironic tone in her voice and exhaling as if to suggest that I was somewhat slow in grasping the obvious. In reality she was expressing weariness as she recalled the never-ending stressful circumstances.

'Nobody wanted us Russians after the war. The Americans had quotas and other countries took only whom they considered to be genuine refugees.'

'You mean we weren't refugees?' I asked in astonishment. 'But we were brought to Australia by the International Refugee Organisation!' Indeed, the IRO figured prominently in the family's postwar history.

'That fool Churchill gave in to Stalin on everything! You know what happened at Yalta!' I didn't know the details. All I knew was that there was a meeting between Stalin, Roosevelt and Churchill to decide the fate of postwar Germany, and Europe generally.

'That stupid man allowed thousands of our people to be sent back straight to Siberia. Awful! They decided at Yalta that we were not refugees.' Russians who had left Russia in the years 1924–27 were not classed as refugees. She agreed she wasn't being completely accurate historically but that the consequences were the same. If we were not refugees, why did father so desperately try to turn us into refugees? Another conundrum. I did eventually find the explanation for the two different marriage dates and the conflicting dates and reasons for their departure from Russia.

Paul had survived Lenin in what was now called Leningrad. Natalie had survived Lenin in Leningrad. Paul's future sister-in-law, Zinaida, with an estimated three million other Russians had escaped abroad – in Zinaida's case, to

Paris. All three had survived by avoiding attracting attention as best they could.

Paul applied himself to his electrical engineering course. Natalie studied for her medical degree. The course was demanding, leaving her little time to do anything other than concentrate on her studies. Her brother Michael, three years younger, also attended what was by then known as the Lenin Electrical Engineering Institute. (Michael would go on to specialise in high-temperature ceramics.) I felt those years of 1924 and 1927 had more secrets to be uncovered. Thus when I had access to the family documents, I was keen to establish the truth about Natalie's career as opposed to the version she had wanted me to believe. I was able to draw a fairly accurate picture with the help of the ever-expanded Internet. To do so, I needed to improve my written Russian to decipher the documents. One document shows that Natalie graduated in May 1924 and on 15 July was appointed assistant at the Dzhennera Institute in Leningrad, where she undertook research in identifying various viruses. Relatively few viruses had been identified at that time, since Louis Pasteur had begun to classify them in the 1880s. This started her interest in microbiology. It was routine to send professionals from Leningrad and Moscow on *komandirovka*, a period of time to work in the provinces. Natalie was sent to Odessa, in Ukraine, to the Mechikov Bacteriological Institute. There she acquired technical experience in virology, a part of which was the preparation of rabies vaccine. A reference made out to her on 9 April 1927, signed by a Professor Tashalgu, is effusive about her abilities. In the course of this work, she may have become familiar with the research being done at the Robert Koch Institute in Berlin, one of the foremost laboratories in the world for the control and prevention of disease, and perhaps this was the time she first thought she might like to further her skills there.

Paul's experiences had made him more earnest than he otherwise would have been. Natalie's lighter presence compensated somewhat for that. But his periodic brooding became the cause of disagreements. He had no other way of dealing with his anxieties. It didn't help that he had a 'one chance only' approach to solving problems in comparison to Natalie's pragmatism, which allowed her to adapt more easily to changing conditions.

Natalie and her brother Michael were close. Michael would name his only child after her. It was family lore that while Michael approved of Paul's courting his sister, when it came to discussing marriage or a period abroad he was so against it that they almost came to blows. He was unwilling to lose his sister but also had real faith in the socialist experiment and wasn't sure that leaving Russia was the right thing to do. Nevertheless Natalie was soon to be separated from her family, and, tragically, except for Michael, would never see them again. We believed that they died in the Soviet Union during World War II. Mother accepted this difficult reality for forty years but a series of accidental events decades later, starting with that phone call from Vladimir in Sweden, brought me and my Russian cousin together. Cousin Natasha (the diminutive of Natalie) studied to become an engineer like her father. On one occasion, a teacher at her Institute recognised her family name and enquired about her aunt, Natalie. The teacher was keen to learn what had happened to her, as he had courted her but had been sidelined in favour of 'that German', as he referred to Paul. I was surprised that father was described as such, since he was pure Russian for me. All Natasha could tell her teacher was that her aunt had married Paul, moved to Germany and there had been lost, presumed killed, during World War II.

Paul and Natalie attended the theatre and went to concerts. Natalie did not care for ballet, but the plays of Gogol and Ostrovsky amused them both. They probably saw the long-running production of *The Government Inspector* with Erast Garin in the role of the Inspector and directed by one of the great innovators of Russian theatre, Vsevolod Meyerhold. Or the young playwright Bulgakov's controversial *The Days of the Turbins*, chronicling how the Turbin family survived the Civil War in Kiev as both sides of the conflict ravaged the city. The Commissar for Enlightenment, Lunacharsky, had approved Bulgakov's plays, however Stalin would later ban them for their 'formalism'. This was Stalin's way of controlling the arts. Bulgakov was accused of putting form above content and the content was not using the theatre as Stalin decreed, to celebrate the achievements of the proletariat and educate them in the work of the Communist Party.

Paul and Natalie shared, too, an interest in poetry, particularly the work of the flamboyant Yesenin. Yesenin had initially supported the Bolshevik cause but soon became a disillusioned critic of the regime. At one time the husband of Isadora Duncan, he succumbed to alcoholism, had a severe nervous breakdown, and hanged himself in the Hotel Angleterre in Leningrad. The romantic aspects of this Byronic figure have appealed to generations of Russians. Banned for many years under Stalin and Khrushchev, he is popular again in Russia today.

Natalie was intrigued by Paul's background and that of his extended family. He told her of his connection with the artistic family, the Brunis, about the century-old family business confiscated during the Revolution, the Seviers with their banking and insurance background, and of some of the distinguished alumni from his school. He introduced her to his aunt, Albine König, the daughter of a former director of the Schlüsser firm.

Stalin now established a pattern. Certain categories of people came under suspicion and were targeted as a way of strengthening the power and authority of the Communist Party. One group were people who had travelled abroad or had relatives abroad. Travel between Western Europe and Russia remained possible during the Revolution, the Civil War and several years following it. Then the policy was changed and more restrictions were introduced, putting under suspicion those who had been abroad. Travel abroad or contact with people abroad could lead to charges of 'espionage for a foreign power' and be punished by exile, imprisonment or even execution. Bureaucrats were another group targeted. Bukharin and Trotsky, members of the Politburo, became alarmed at the 'bureaucratisation' of the Party and government. Decisions were being made by disinterested, uncommitted apparatchiks for reasons of convenience rather than to implement Communist ideology. Lenin had begun to take more decisions personally and Stalin in turn refined his control, further centralising power. Bureaucrats were instructed to implement decisions dictated to them. On the other hand, if errors, misjudgements or false accusations were made, it was easy to accuse subordinates of sabotage and punish them by removing them, where they were unable to testify against

---

* Yesenin, it is believed by some, may have been assassinated

those who had given the inappropriate orders.

Paul saw his circumstances deteriorating. It showed in the way he was treated at his university and by his house committee. They had never completely lost their suspicion of him because of his bourgeois background, nor could he hide that he had relatives abroad. His documents were checked more often and he was questioned about his family. He saw acquaintances harassed and arrested, causing many to emigrate to a Western capital such as Prague, Berlin or Paris. It was only a matter of time, he feared, before someone found it to their advantage to inform against him.

Paul had a kind nature. His aunt Albine, who had come to share his room, was elderly and in need of help. With the persecution of her social class, she had reasons to be frightened. Though she was a Russian citizen, her German name and her bourgeois background made her a potential target for being accused as an 'enemy of the people'. Fearful that they could be victims of capricious accusations, Paul made preparations for a possible – perhaps even inevitable – raid by the secret police. Should such a raid occur, he instructed his aunt to signal him by placing a lamp in the window. Such precautions might seem laughable in normal circumstances, but the secret police was clearly dangerous. On returning home one February evening in 1927, he saw the lit lamp in the window. He acted immediately, avoided his room and, as planned, headed for Natalie's apartment. Mother was agitated as she recalled how pale he was when he arrived at her room but she calmed him down and persuaded him to stay the night. It was courageous of both and the shared experiences brought them closer together. Yet, I wonder whether in later years mother ever wished that she had not become intimate with a person of father's complex, potentially dangerous background. Judging by her character, I think she recognised the folly of regrets. When Paul returned to his room in the morning, he found his aunt distraught.

'They were so rude and common', she exclaimed. 'They didn't believe a thing I told them. Awful people!'

'Did they take anything?' Paul asked. They may have been searching for 'evidence'. He'd been careful not to keep records of the money he had been receiving from abroad.

'I wanted to tell them of the family and the firm, but I could see it was a waste of breath. They had no respect for anything. One of them called me a hysterical old *baboushka*, cursed me and told me to shut up', bemoaned Albine. It became clear to Paul that neither of them was now safe in Leningrad. It had been ten years since the Revolution and the return of the Schlüsser property was a forlorn hope. His family in the West could not expect him to risk imprisonment when waiting for speedy change was futile. He discussed his options at length with Natalie and was reassured by her calm analysis of his choices. It seemed to them that if trends continued, there would come a time when he would have to leave the country – even if, he hoped, only temporarily.

I am a little ashamed to admit that for me at the time, mother's account of the ruthlessness of the Soviet regime was difficult to accept. It seemed exaggerated. Why would you hunt down your own people? Why would you create a prison population of so many hundreds of thousands, even millions of people? At various times I had seriously attempted to understand the origins and achievements of Soviet Communism, and its promise. In my teens, living in Western Australia's capital city of Perth, I would occasionally sneak into the Socialist bookshop in East Perth to read *Soviet Union*, a magazine published in Moscow – the Russian answer to America's *Life* magazine – extolling the virtues of life there, and I accepted as true the accounts of the industrial and social achievements reported in it. In the West, there was great disaffection in the late 1960s and 1970s, especially among my generation, about the direction that capitalism was taking. What mother tried to make me understand about the true nature of the Soviet regime seemed to be the attitude of a person out of touch. I said so, making mother fear that I had turned Communist. My Estonian-Russian brother-in-law tried to get a rise out of her by mocking me as a 'Red'. With greater knowledge, I came to accept that what mother had understood about the horrors committed in the name of 'building Communism' was true. Freedom and equality never existed and were never contemplated. It was a tyranny cemented by fear.

Decades later, I grew anxious that my children, nieces and nephews had little understanding of why they were born in Australia when they had a Russian and German heritage. This strengthened my determination to write this memoir and record the facts as I knew them. An opportunity to convey the political, historical context came when I found a short book titled *Communism*, written by the American historian Richard Pipes. Pipes summarised the history of the rise and fall of Communism so succinctly and convincingly that I bought a copy to give to each member of the family.

The book helped me to answer a question that had troubled me for a long time, of how Stalin could acquire such power as to be able to lead the people willingly to commit atrocities and eventually go to war. I had seen references to a group of people in the Soviet Union collectively known as the *Nomenklatura*. Stalin, as part of the bureaucracy under Lenin, learned that power lay with – for want of a better description – 'middle management'. He saw their strategic role and that, if he controlled appointments to this level of administration in government and industry, he could have total control. Stalin ensured that officials owed their position to him, and through his power to hire and fire he cemented their loyalty and allegiance. He exercised this power ruthlessly, dealing violently with anyone who didn't adhere to the rules he set. The stories are legion of transgressors and their fate. Fear and intimidation were Stalin's main weapons, but he knew he had also to offer inducements and rewards. Stealthily, a 'new class' evolved whose members were all appointed by the Communist Party, presided over by Stalin, and who were beholden to it for their security. Once you became a member of the *Nomenklatura*, you received privileges such as higher salaries, better housing, and much else besides. A chain of shops was established, known as *Beryozka*, where the *Nomenklatura* could buy foreign and rationed goods not available to others. The elite were freer to travel within the Soviet Union and – a great privilege – could travel abroad. The majority was excluded from this class and, while generally aware of its existence, relied on rumours for an insight into how the system worked. You became a member of the *Nomenklatura* once your name was on a list from which all important appointments to positions in

Soviet society were made. Many people were ideologically committed Communists, otherwise the system would not have worked, but many others were opportunists who accepted the Faustian deal offered to them in exchange for these benefits. Those who belonged had what has been called a 'patron–client relationship'. They owed their position to a patron, someone higher in rank, and would therefore do everything to remain in the favour of that person. These were the people who often acted in an arbitrary way as they tried to interpret their patron's wishes. These were the people to be feared the most, mother had warned. The lack of independent judicial oversight gave licence to this system. There was no recourse to the law. Policies, attitudes and actions could change from one day to the next, with little accountability to the people but total accountability to the patron. I found a detailed analysis of the system described as early as 1934, in an obscure book titled *Das Land ohne Sonntag* (Country Without Sunday), by Ludwig and Elfriede Kummer. While travelling widely through the Soviet Union, they had first-hand experience of the nature of Stalin's power. Everyone had obligations to someone of greater authority, so everyone did – even thought and believed – as they were commanded. The system has been referred to as a form of twentieth-century feudalism, a form of slavery, and Paul recognised it as it developed. It was a frightening prospect for a man brought up to think for himself, to use his own capacities and abilities to assess his circumstances and to make decisions based on experience. The idea that a new 'tsar' knew best and demanded his subjects follow without questioning went against everything that he had learned to value. Paul reluctantly came to the conclusion that he may have to leave Russia even before completing his engineering degree. The authorities might also move against him once he was no longer bringing foreign currency into the country to pay for his fees. Where to go and when? He made discreet enquiries among firms in Leningrad, affiliates of German companies, seeking to gain work experience abroad. The Schlüsser firm may have had dealings with the Leningrad branch of Berlin's Siemens-Schuckert company. This may be how he gained a place for work experience in their Berlin plant. September 1927, the beginning of the academic year in Germany, seemed a suitable time. He had no plans to leave Russia permanently, only to keep out of danger until the system changed, which he firmly believed it would. When he confided his plans to his aunt Albine, she pleaded with him to take her too. This suited him, as he could use her as a further justification as to why he should be permitted to go to Berlin: to reunite his aunt with her relatives. As an elderly woman, she would have been seen as merely a drain on scarce Russian resources. Paul did not keep secret that he had relatives abroad, but fortunately it did not prevent him from receiving an exit visa. Given the circumstances, this remains puzzling – though very likely, bribes could have been involved.

Love Finds a Way

Paul faced further challenges. He and Natalie were in love and he would not leave Russia without her. But how was she to get permission? Natalie had thought about undertaking postgraduate study abroad, so why not work in Berlin at the eminent Robert Koch Institute? She was in the second year of her internship in a laboratory in Odessa. She had become interested in preventative medicine and this could take her further into the field. When Paul discussed temporary exile in Berlin with her, she agreed to go with him.

The Communist regime had become wary of its citizens having contact with Western Europe and trips abroad were vetted by one man. The Commissar for Enlightenment, Anatole Lunacharsky, was an erudite man who valued education. Natalie took the train to Moscow as she had been requested to do following her written application. As she recalled the interview, in the last year of her life, Natalie felt no rancour towards Lunacharsky, and remembered him as a pleasant, well-informed man. When questioned by him, she expressed a sincere desire to return to Russia to help her country in whatever capacity she could. All members of her family remained in Russia, so she was at a low risk of defecting were she ever to think of it. In all, she made a favourable impression and he gave her his permission.

The Soviets had a system to prevent defections. As recently as the 1970s, Soviet citizens were prevented from travel abroad unless they had a husband or wife, or another close relative, remaining in the country as a kind of hostage. This was the case with my cousin Natasha, who had married a man with the right to emigrate from the Soviet Union on account of his Jewish background. US President Carter had insisted that Jews be granted permission to migrate in exchange for providing grain to relieve the famine which was threatening the Soviet Union. As soon as she left the country, her previous husband was dismissed from his work as an interior designer/architect for Trade Fairs. He had already been abroad to such places as East Germany and Japan with his wife back in Russia, the lure to ensure his return. But as he told me without a wife in the Soviet Union as hostage, he might be tempted to defect. He lost his job, and his life and career never recovered from the adverse record he now had.

How could Paul and Natalie receive permission to leave the country together? They applied independently and were issued with travel documents. But there remained a problem. So far, they had not spoken to Natalie's family of their plans but, with arrangements in place, they needed to confide in them. Her mother had come to Leningrad to work in a dental clinic in the Petrogradsky district. Her father remained in Smolensk as a company doctor.

'Your father will never allow it', Evgenia Trofimovna said emphatically on hearing of their plans, meaning that she herself never would.

'We didn't bring you up to bring shame on this family! You'll get married properly or you will not travel with Paul nor will you any longer have a place in this family.'

Natalie's mother was not making an idle threat. Every fibre in her body revolted against this breakdown in moral behaviour. Whatever social and political changes were being made, her daughter had to have a legal husband who was able to protect her, care for her and support her. Natalie's brother, Michael, fell in line with his mother and was equally as determined in his opposition.

'Think of your family!' he accused her unfairly. 'Go away and have a good think about it before you do something that you'll regret forever.'

As subsequent events unfolded, mother may have pondered often about this reprimand.

Sexual mores had changed in the Soviet Union since the Revolution. The Bolsheviks regarded fidelity as a bourgeois notion, and in 1920 they legalised abortion on demand. Alexandra Koltai, the sole woman to become a member of the Politburo, the highest decision-making body of the Communist Party, was seen by many as the model of an emancipated woman, free of bourgeois values. She believed in open relationships and 'free love'. (Lenin rejected free love as a moral code, but this was hypocritical. For many years he had a lover while married to Krupskaya.) But my grandmother Evgenia Trofimovna Kamenseva did not embrace the new mores. She was as intolerant of the moral changes as she was of the political and social ones. They lowered standards and she would never sanction such arrangements. Natalie would not think of alienating her parents nor did Paul wish to do so. The Catch 22 of the situation was that if they married, one or other of them would have to remain behind, to ensure the return of the travelling spouse. But if they remained unmarried, her mother would not sanction the trip. The solution they found was worthy of one of Gogol's scathing satires on Russian society. The challenge, as in many of his stories, was to outwit officialdom. The Bolsheviks had declared church weddings unlawful, had confiscated church properties and were determinedly dissuading Russians from practising their religion – the 'opium of the people', as Marx had designated it. Despite being persecuted, many of the older generation did not forsake their religion. Evgenia certainly hadn't compromised her spiritual life. She was too intelligent and too well informed to defer to a secular authority which relied on violence to force citizens to comply. Then a way was found. The ingenious solution agreed on was for Natalie and Paul to have a church wedding. This would satisfy Evgenia's moral code and, as there would be no legal requirement to register such a marriage, the bureaucrats would remain ignorant of it. Natalie and Paul were married in Krasnoe Selo, thirty kilometres southwest of Leningrad. The relatively remote church was chosen to minimise unwanted attention. Only the immediate family and a few close friends attended. Natalie's father and brother were witnesses for the bride, and the groom's witnesses were his cousin Michael Nikolayevich Bruni and a certain Sergei Afrikanovich Binchenkov. The traditional ritual was followed. At one point of the ceremony, the two best men stand behind the couple holding gold crowns over their heads, elevating bride and groom to 'royalty' and signifying endorsement of their union by the King of Heaven. An altar boy carries an icon at the head of the wedding party as they circle the church three times. This icon travelled everywhere mother did and now is one of my treasured possessions. It is of the Virgin Mary with the Christ child, gold metal embroidery forming a halo around their heads. Two candles, carried by the bride and groom at the wedding, flank the icon. The image is contained in a carved wooden box with a hinged glass front. Around the icon are other religious talismans from different occasions in Natalie's life. Her life's experience would make her reject religion, but she treasured this reminder of her marriage and the time with her family. They helped to sustain her in the difficult years that followed. I have clear memories of the icon's being prominently displayed high in the corner of a room wherever she made a home for us, often with a burning candle in front of it: a beautiful memento. It has pride of place on my glass shelves of family heirlooms.

I have also a marriage certificate signed by the officiating priest. But how did I come to have a second one? One is in Russian, issued on this occasion, 27 March 1927; the other certifies that the marriage took place in 1924, in a different place and with different witnesses, Pavel Feodorovich Ivanov and Lydia Feodorovna John. To be accurate, rather than another certificate I have a statutory declaration by the two witnesses, in which they declare that they were present at the 1924 ceremony. Paul, in an affidavit, declared that in the turmoil of the subsequent years the original certificate had been lost and this declaration replaced it, sworn before a legal councillor, A. Segelins in Frankfurt, on 24 August 1949, as his signature and a rubber stamp show. Which marriage date is the correct one? For many years, I believed that the 1924 date was the real one, which is what my parents wanted me to believe. I recall mother's gruff response when I questioned her about the discrepancy.

'A marriage in 1924 and departure from Russia in that year put us into the category that the League of Nations had decreed as Old Immigrants', mother used the Russian *Stariye Immigranti*, meaning people displaced by the 1917 Revolution. 'By 1927, with the New Economic Policy in place [not for much longer], the League declared such people to be 'immigrants' not 'refugees'. Can you understand?'

'But who benefited from that?'

She sighed: 'After the 1917 Revolution, the people who escaped it and settled in Prague, Berlin or Paris became known as Old Immigrants and were classed as asylum-seekers. That made them eligible to migrate to third countries.'

'So you lied!'

'Everybody did!' she said impatiently. 'Thankfully the Americans were so young, naive and inexperienced that our deception worked. We were lucky!' She meant it and was not ungrateful. She had great admiration for Americans and their way of life. The last trip she undertook in her life was not to Russia, although that had become possible again, but to the United States. In her letters, she praised the 'marvellous Americans' and gave a special salute to the Statue of Liberty and the Lincoln Memorial. She visited old family friends who had made successful homes in the USA. Americans were the freest people in the world, she concluded after her seven-week tour. Her husband had aspired for his family to share such a free life, but it was not to be. I believe that with that trip, Natalie completed something that had been left incomplete. With her fused ring on her right hand, she brought Paul's spirit to the real destination which was denied him in life.

Since they were not legally married, they each retained a passport in their own name, mother explained.

'After the wedding', Natalie recalls in the video interview made in her last year of life, 'he went back to his apartment and I to mine to avoid arousing suspicion'.

Few knew of the marriage. Six weeks later, on Friday 13 May together with aunt Albine, they both left Russia. The marriage may not have been consummated until after they left Russia. Mother, always somewhat prudish, as befitted women at the time, understandably did not comment on this.

The sequence of events described so far fits all the details that mother had given me, and I believed them to be true. But there was one piece of evidence that came to me after my enquiry to the FSB in Novgorod, and I am certain that mother knew nothing about it. Not even her husband had confided this information to her. What I discovered, I believe, was the real and urgent reason why father left Russia when he did. He had cause to be anxious, which led to his sudden departure from Russia. Overnight it became more urgent and potentially a matter of life and death. He had not told Natalie of the terrifying event only three weeks before the wedding, on 20 March. Mother never referred to it, which makes me believe that she knew nothing about it. No one in the family had any knowledge of it until I found a reference to it on a website, two years ago. The website of Memorial, an organisation dedicated to recording the victims of Stalin's terror, showed that one of Paul's cousins, Artur Schlüsser, was arrested in Leningrad on 20 March 1927 by the Cheka, Stalin's secret police. They found Artur guilty of 'engaging in espionage for Germany and Estonia since 1925'. He was sentenced to three years' imprisonment, to be served in the notorious penal colony of Solovetski, in the Arctic Circle. Paul was terrified that he might be next. Perhaps it was even a warning to him. He knew his cousin was innocent. He also knew that people were being arrested for not reporting 'subversives' and 'enemies of the people'. Even if he might not be arrested in his own right, he could be arrested for not reporting his cousin. He feared that if he told others, they would be in the same danger. He told neither Natalie nor any of her family, nor even his own, of the arrest. I believe that Natalie never knew of it and Paul took the secret to his grave.

Preparing for Freedom

Mostly for Paul but also for Natalie, each day was filled with fear, and camouflaging their plans was important. Whether for political reasons or out of personal spite or jealousy, any number of people might find a pretext to report them. They still planned to be away for only a year. They made separate arrangements. Paul kept to his story that he was accompanying his elderly aunt Albine abroad and that he would stay as an intern at Siemens-Schuckert, part of his studies. Natalie could truthfully declare that she was going abroad for postgraduate studies. A stay of six to twelve months abroad required careful preparations. Albine gave Paul the pretext to take more luggage than would otherwise have been possible. It included two trunks, which had been used on the annual migration to the family *dacha*. One was allocated to Paul and his aunt, and the other to Natalie. At that time, you needed to be largely self-sufficient when travelling. Bed linen, cushion covers, serviettes, tea towels, cutlery and crockery were needed. Many decades later, I still own some of the bed linen and kitchen utensils that they took with them, embossed with the initials of grandparents on both sides of the family. This includes two sets of cutlery engraved with the respective family's initials and wrapped in soft cloth, embroidered with the date '1927'. They took them for their own use, but they might also be needed to barter with. Foreign currency could be difficult to obtain legally, and black market rates could be better value. Prices were unpredictable, with inflation, varying exchange rates, bribes and 'inducements' to be considered, besides food, accommodation and other living expenses. They brought writing material and a selection of their professional books. Natalie included a volume of Pushkin's *Collected Works*. She would have liked to take some sheet music, especially some of Chopin's work – she was a very competent pianist – but had to limit herself to taking a lithograph of her favourite composer. Custom inspections and duties payable at the border would be rigorous, so they would have to justify each item and prove ownership. They were prepared to pay incentives to the customs officers and border guards as needed. Paul was also fearful that valuables left in Russia might be confiscated at any time. In the event, Paul and Natalie, with careful management, were able to keep some family heirlooms even during the most chaotic years. Today, their value lies in the history they embody, the journeys, revolutions and wars during which they were used. Several times they were hidden to save them from revolutionary mobs, Russia's invading armies, and in Germany from desperate individuals. In future years, in Frankfurt, the *Gute Besteck* (good dinner set), was brought out on Sundays for family lunches. As I used them, even as a child and especially during the leanest and hardest years, I was reminded that the family had once been affluent, that the cutlery had come from Russia, where it was hoped it would return some day. In the 1970s, when Natalie had given up all hope of returning to Russia, she was tempted to sell the silver cutlery. At the time, the West with its disdainful excesses, as she expressed it, was in the grip of 'silver fever'. Hoarding had driven the price of silver so high that she was tempted to sell. I found it difficult to believe that she would do this and dissuaded her. I feel that she was attempting to clear out the past with this action, or perhaps thumbing her nose at her children for taking so little interest in her family history (in justification, we were preoccupied with raising our own children). I still have the cutlery. Many of the items came from Natalie's 'glory box': linen and towelling that Natalie, with the help of her mother, had collected over the years in anticipation of marriage. The glory box was the last remnant of a dowry system that survived into the 1960s.

The thirteenth of May 1927 was a Friday. 'Black Friday' Natalie remembered it as and referred to it every time it came around. They departed late in the evening from the Warsaw/Byelorussian *Vokzal*. Only Natalie's family came to see them off. It had been a hurried last few days to get the luggage to the station. Everything had to be minutely listed, checked at customs and the requisite duty paid. Papers were checked and rechecked by uniformed officials who were afraid of making mistakes. Finally the two trunks and a number of suitcases were stowed in the luggage van at the rear of the train. Natalie and Paul took two packed suitcases each to their *wagon lit* (sleeping carriage), still occupying separate compartments, where they hoisted them onto the luggage rack. There were tearful farewells and expressions of hope for a speedy reunion all around. It was heartbreaking but necessary, everyone agreed.

With a whistle and a profusion of steam from the engine, after a mere half-hour's delay, the train pulled out of the station, picked up speed on the flat country through Novgorod, through the marshlands where, in a few years, Paul's brother Vladimir would die, and past Smolensk, the Kamenzev family seat, and Brest-Litovsk where Lenin had signed the Russia–Germany Peace Treaty in March 1918. Here the railway gauge changed. Passengers waited in the café while the luggage was transferred to another train on a parallel, narrower track. The crew changed from Russian to Polish and the train continued through to Warsaw, where Natalie's mother had been born, and through the Polish corridor which separated East from West Prussia and had been ceded to Poland at the Treaty of Versailles after World War I. Claims on this land would become the pretext for Hitler's invasion of Poland and the start of World War II, twelve years later. Soon they pulled into the main station of the German city of Stetin. Here their passports were inspected and visas issued for their stay in Germany. A further full day's travel and they arrived at the Silesian Station in Berlin, commonly known as the *Ostbahnhof* (East Railway Station).

Leaving Russia soon proved to be the right decision. The year 1927 was the lull before Stalin instigated his first purge. His main rival for power, Trotsky, was expelled from the Communist Party in October 1927 (which soon led to the renaming of the region of Trotsk, that so frustrated my search for the property at Sablino) and collective farms were created as part of the first Five

Year Plan. When Stalin met determined opposition to his plans to collectivise farmland, he starved the peasants and *kulaks* into submission. Years of terror and famine followed, during which a reported ten million people starved to death. Stalin, the ideologue, believed that it was the 'right road' and if the plan failed then people – 'enemies of the people', spies and saboteurs – were to blame. He felt no need to check the plan against the reality of people's experience.

The Germany that Paul and Natalie were coming to in May 1927 was going through great changes, with Berlin attracting the most dazzling artistic and scientific talents of the century – Einstein, Schoenberg, Brecht and Gropius, to name a few. The Great War had been the 'war to end all wars' and the League of Nations, formed in 1919 (though the USA refused to join it), negotiated the Treaty of Versailles and oversaw its implementation. Many unintended consequences of that Treaty were being addressed and it seemed that, with the technical and industrial progress leading to rising prosperity, another war was unlikely.

The Pact of Locarno was signed in October 1925, securing the until then disputed borders of Germany and France, and with it fears of revenge eased. Not yet evident were any signs of the economic depression to come. What was remarkable to me as I read about it was that Germany, in a very short time, had become a functioning democracy. It had abolished the monarchy in 1918 and established elected parliaments in every regional state, with a Federal Parliament in Berlin. The move towards this had begun years previously, with the political upheavals of 1848, when the first freely elected German parliament met in Frankfurt. Nevertheless, it seems an astonishing achievement of negotiation and compromise that a constitution could be agreed on and signed in Weimar (hence Weimar Republic), and power sharing between the states and central government could be exercised peacefully. But perhaps it was too fast after all. When in a few years Hitler characterised all this as a 'conspiracy' to rob the people of their rights and entitlements (they were going through the Great Depression), they began to fear the change and became vulnerable to the rhetoric of the demagogue. The tragedy for Paul and

Natalie was that, in escaping one tyranny, they were soon to become captive to another.

Berlin was at the crossroads of East and West, where ideas and ideologies clashed visibly. The capital city was the centre of intrigue and espionage. Agents of many governments came to Berlin to spread disinformation and spy on their own citizens and those of other countries. Soviet agents were sent immediately after the 1917 Revolution, as detailed in Schlögel's book, *Das Russische Berlin* (Russian Berlin). One of their tasks was to persuade, urge and not infrequently threaten *émigrés* to return to the Soviet Union. Paul and Natalie seem not to have been in this category. They succeeded with some, such as the author Alexei Tolstoy and poet Anna Akhmatova, but failed with others, writers like Nabokov and Bunin. The case of the poet Marina Tsvetaeva was particularly tragic. Her poet husband, Sergei Efron, was later exposed as a member of the Soviet Secret Service, by then known as the NKVD. He spied on *émigrés*.

Having escaped death or imprisonment in Soviet Russia, Paul would, it seems, become somewhat blinded to the threat that fascism presented. His fear of the Soviet State and Stalin would prove greater than the danger posed by Hitler.

'I thought he was a clever man', mother says on the video, referring to father, 'but he wasn't clever at all when it came to Hitler. He thought soon there would be National Socialism in Russia', she exclaimed and sank into a silence. I let her reflect for a moment and then posed the obvious question.

'He'd read *Mein Kampf* (My Struggle), as you had, where Hitler condemns all Slavs as subhuman. How could he ...?' I didn't complete the question but let it hang there. As it was over fifty years after the event and momentous changes had taken place in between, perhaps it was impossible for her to think back to those times. But maybe the opposite was in play, and perhaps she saw the past clearer than she could at the time. Perhaps no one had asked her such a question over all the years. Could she now see the flaws in decisions made when under such stress? She had repeatedly said that the primary task and achievement in those years was survival. Any other consideration was a bonus, even perhaps decadent. My intuition is that Paul was a man with definite opinions, who held them so strongly that he was less able – or even unable – to deal with ambiguity. (I think I sometimes see the same trait in my brother.) I believe that his life had been too fraught to allow for half-measures, and that was part of the reason for the angry quarrels in the kitchen. Natalie would proffer alternatives, which Paul would hear as contradictions to his ideas. That surely is the inherent danger in fascism, when individuals are threatened and lose the power to choose. The result is a rigid compliance to a pre-determined worldview. I believe that my father may have been subject to that and suffered the consequences.

When Natalie and Paul arrived in Berlin at the *Ostbahnhof*, they knew precisely where they were going. A telegram to Paul's stepmother Theresa Vasilievna had informed her of the details of their arrival, and another telegram was sent to the hotel to reserve a room. They left most of their luggage stored at the station, took their two suitcases and boarded the *S-Bahn* (fast rail), one of Berlin's marvels, to *Friedrichstrasse* Station. From there it was a short walk to their hotel, *Der Russische Hof*. Once settled and freshened up, they took the *S-Bahn* again, this time to *Tiergarten* Station, and walked to 123 *Würtemberger Allee*, Charlottenburg, the address of Paul's stepmother. Charlottenburg was known as 'Charlottengrad' (echoing Petrograd) as so many *émigré* Russians had settled there. She was living in affluent surroundings, perhaps even suffered somewhat from a delusion of grandeur which made her believe that she would return one day to Russia and the lifestyle she had previously enjoyed there. When she left there in 1918, she took her two youngest children – Olga aged eleven and Raymond aged eight – as well as money and items of jewellery, porcelain and other valuables to make life in Berlin comfortable for herself. Apparently she took little interest in *émigré* politics or the politics of Russia, except how they might immediately affect her. When she had married Paul's father, Fyodor (Friedrich), in 1906, she knew his wealth. She also knew that there were assets spread abroad and she was keen to claim her share. Paul brought news from Russia and, without mentioning the arrest of his cousin, he told her that things were getting worse. She was keen to meet Paul's bride and Natalie made a suitably good impression, though Natalie for her part was not taken in by her mother-in-law's pretensions. They felt the difference between Berlin and Leningrad immediately. Berlin was efficient, bustling and bursting with confidence. It was May and spring and the city was at its best. The linden trees in the grand boulevard *Unter den Linden* were basking in light green foliage and, Natalie recalled fondly, they strolled through Berlin's Central Park, the *Tiergarten*, between the *Reichstag* (Parliament) and *Potsdamer Platz*, together with the stream of Berliners freed to go outdoors after hibernating through the winter. The freedom to breathe the spring air reflected their feeling of ease. That didn't stop Natalie from feeling homesick, though she consoled herself believing that she would see her family again soon. Mother never mentioned the darker side of Berlin. Certainly, hyperinflation of the early 1920s had been checked and many of the worst consequences of World War I had been resolved. But Berlin had large districts of the very poor, and organised crime and drug-dealing was widespread. Perhaps Paul and Natalie were too preoccupied with their own issues to take much note of this side of Berlin. Perhaps it compared so favourably with Leningrad that it didn't warrant mentioning. Perhaps as young people in love, they allowed nothing to cloud their optimism for the future.

They found a reasonably priced apartment, on the ground floor of 145a *Kantstrasse*, within walking distance of Theresa Vasilievna's more lavish apartment. They bought furniture and organised for their trunks to be delivered. Natalie completed the application forms for her postgraduate studies; her German was adequate though she called on Paul to help when needed. She was duly accepted into the Robert Koch Institute and would soon start work under a Professor Gins, testing the effectiveness of vaccines when trialled on animals. Meanwhile, Paul sought advice from his older cousin, Alexander Makarov, who had come to Berlin three years earlier and was teaching at the prestigious Humboldt University. Paul took Makarov into his confidence and Makarov was gratified that he was able to help his considerably younger cousin Paul using his own network of contacts.

Paul and Natalie were atypical of Russians abroad. They had a purpose sanctioned by the Russian authorities, their work colleagues and their social circle, and they were not politically engaged. Paul neither received nor sent mail to Leningrad, knowing that to do so could endanger the recipient, especially in the light of Artur's imprisonment. (He would not have known of his sentence.) Natalie received mail regularly from her mother, father and brother. Though the letters and postcards were reassuring, Natalie still felt concern for them. That anxiety and uncertainty may explain why she made few friends among the Russians in Berlin. She did form a close friendship with a Fräulein Elfriede Paasch, the registrar's assistant at the Robert Koch Institute. Perhaps each appreciated the solidarity with the other, as they were heavily outnumbered by male staff and colleagues. They spent leisure time together and Fräulein Paasch accompanied Natalie and Paul on several vacation trips. They wrote to each other for some years after Natalie had left Berlin, in words that reflect a warm, trusting friendship.

Natalie and Paul did not avoid the Russian community altogether. There was the family John, a family of two brothers and three sisters. One of the sisters had married a cavalry officer, Pavel Fyodorovich Ivanov (I would later be page-boy at their daughter's wedding) – the same man who would certify that Paul and Natalie's marriage had taken place in 1924. The father of the John children had become one of three accountants who ran the Schlüsser firm between 1912 and 1917. Lydia, the youngest of the sisters, made no secret in later years that her father had acquired certain assets of the Schlüsser firm to which he was not entitled. Natalie says in the video interview: 'Lydia John urged Pavlousha [her affectionate diminutive for her husband] to claim the money which rightfully belonged to him, for the sake of his family'. But he didn't and Natalie later recalled it with recrimination in her voice, describing father as being incapable of taking responsibility for his actions. A harsh assessment of her own husband. Yet, based on some of my experiences with him as a boy, she may have been accurate in her judgement. He undoubtedly had a volatile temper, perhaps stirred by self-recrimination and a feeling of powerlessness – a legacy of his experiences in revolutionary Russia.

However the John family came to the money, they spent some of it in Berlin organising events at their apartment, which was large enough to host what mother referred to as 'balls'. Masked balls were the rage and a photo shows Natalie dressed in the multi-coloured costume of 'Harlequin'. Natalie and Paul were excellent dancers and made an attractive couple on the dance floor. Paul loved to see his new wife dressed in the latest fashions, especially on festive days. Photos show them celebrating Easter, Christmas and – so important in the Orthodox calendar – their Name Day. These photos were regularly sent to Natalie's family in Leningrad and gratefully received, as attested in return letters.

Natalie was a modern woman: attractive, well educated, witty and sociable. No wonder she had admirers. A family friend, Dr von Füner, would later recall that 'everyone was in love with Natalie'. As Marina Makarova, Alexander Makarov's daughter, told me in Heidelberg: 'My mother loved your mother, Natalia Vasilievna. She adored her.' In the manner of the day, the men expressed their admiration and affection in verse and flowers. These relaxed, happy times were, without a doubt, Paul and Natalie's salad days. Despite the uncertainties of their future, 1927–29 were their best years, to be recalled with pleasure ever afterward and sadly never to be repeated. Had they known that this was as good as it would get, what might they have done differently? Paul, as an idealist, might have made the same decisions but Natalie, the pragmatist, might have urged them to leave for England or America where they had good opportunities for successful careers. For the moment they were enjoying the freedom, street life and entertainment of Berlin, even taking pleasure in their relatives, as difficult as Theresa Vasilievna could be. They would have to return to Leningrad all too soon. It was difficult to assess what was happening there as all mail from Russia was read by the censor, so communication was very circumspect. They had justified fears that their actions in Berlin could make trouble for the family in Russia. Paul took care to whom he spoke and what he said. The closest acquaintance could be an informer. He maintained contact with the Soviet Embassy only to keep their registration and visas current. Stalin's first Five Year Plan was launched in 1929, aiming to industrialise the country and collectivise agriculture. There were those in the West, such as playwright and polemicist George Bernard Shaw and authors and activists Beatrice and Sidney Webb, who welcomed these plans as a mark of a new dawn in human evolution, a new civilisation built on scientific principles of social development. For years, they played down the cost in human terms. But there were also those who saw it for the tyranny it was, among them George Orwell, the future author of *1984* and *Animal Farm*, both merciless satires on the Soviet experiment. Stalin's plan was achieved at a cost in lives and human misery rivalled by few in history. But using propaganda and strict censorship, he convinced doubters that present hardships would be rewarded. Not everyone was taken in by the propaganda. In truth, we now know Stalin's policy of confiscating land and food from the wealthier peasants the kulaks, together with a series of droughts led to millions of deaths. Some scholars have designated it genocide. Several million people died, twenty five percent of the population by some estimates. A lack of records makes it difficult to be precise about the number of deaths. Ukraine's population and economy were decimated and other parts of the Soviet Union also suffered. Natalie's father, Vasily Ephimovich as a doctor in the regional city of Smolensk would have dealt first hand with people suffering from Stalin's ruthless policy.

While Paul applied himself to further his education, his oldest brother, Nicolai, chose to enjoy the high life of the Russian community in Berlin, and fathered a second child: their first, Beatrice, had been born in Leningrad in 1924 and the second, Oleg, was born in 1925, in Berlin. His wife, Olga, aspired to be a professional dancer and actress and felt that her chances would be greater in Paris. Paris was alive with Russian artists and culture, Sergei Diaghilev and Igor Stravinsky had galvanised the ballet world and *émigré* producers and directors had established a flourishing film industry. Olga had a contact there through Konstantin Bruni, who was designing and painting scenery for a Russian film studio. Olga used Nicolai's money to establish herself as a performer and succeeded to some extent, reputedly with the help of the many lovers she had. She was not without talent or success, as her daughter Beatrice told me. She danced with the prestigious Ballets Russes and later toured the United States with the De Cuevas Company, on that occasion leaving Nicolai behind in Paris with the children. Not surprisingly perhaps, both her children, Beatrice and Oleg, became ballet dancers, and Oleg married a dancer who would work at the New York Metropolitan Opera.

The lifestyle of Paul's next oldest brother, Vladimir, had dangerous consequences. Vladimir married Zinaida Demianovna Kungurzeva, the Siberian-born nurse who had served with the White Army and escaped to Paris via the Crimea and Turkey. I am glad that I never stopped asking why she had been so badly thought of, why she was never mentioned and why I was never given any answers when I asked mother about her. She was a 'wayward woman', washed up in Paris by chance. At one unguarded moment, mother even referred to her as a *prostitutka*. Long after mother's death, I discovered a photograph which identified Zinaida together with her brother and mother. That struck me as anything but wayward: somehow she had succeeded to bring them to Paris, presumably around the time she escaped Russia herself. Vladimir Schlüsser was a suitable, even desirable husband and she may have genuinely loved him. But he was too naive and weak to curb her profligate lifestyle, and lacked the will or stamina to complete any qualifications, perhaps as a result of his disrupted life. He had graduated from the Karl May *Gymnasium* and enrolled at Petrograd University in mathematics and physics. After escaping from Russia, his cousin in England, Robert Sevier, advised him to take a mining engineering course in Cornwall, where he himself was studying, but Vladimir failed to complete the course. Instead, he resettled in Paris to join his sister Nadezhda (Nadya) and brother Nicolai. Since he had money, they were able to enjoy the pleasures of that city. 'Tomorrow will take care of itself' was the attitude of so many Russian *émigrés*, who believed that a return to Russia and their former privileged lifestyle was imminent.

Such were the circumstances when Paul and Natalie arrived in Paris on their honeymoon, in the summer of 1927, six weeks after settling in Berlin and after putting their study plans into place. They arrived by train at Paris's

Gare du Nord and were met by Nicolai and his family. Nicolai had bought a car and they drove to their home in Neuilly, a fashionable part of the city, adjoining the Bois de Boulogne. It was a cordial visit but Natalie was a different personality from her sisters-in-law. Natalie considered that a career on the stage not a serious profession, especially when their lives as *émigrés* were so uncertain. They should either be working for an eventual return to Russia or be establishing themselves in Paris in a more substantial way.

It was another sunny day in Sydney as I spoke with mother on this subject. She was smoking, as usual. The cigarette seemed to inspire her thoughts. Her consistent criticism of the Paris relatives reflected her upbringing. She came from a family of professionals for whom education and service to the people were valued almost above everything else.

'There was the working intelligentsia and there was the leisured intelligentsia', she explained. The working intelligentsia was progressive and committed. The leisured intelligentsia squandered the advantages that their education, privileges and money had given them. Instead of putting them to use for the country, they indulged themselves with trips abroad, distractions and entertainments, dalliances with the so-called nobility, and squandered their assets.

Mother despised the characters of the playwright and short-story writer Anton Chekhov, especially Madame Ranyevskaya in *The Cherry Orchard*, who seems incessantly to yearn for her childhood or her life back in Paris, rather than living in the present and dealing with the changes taking place in her home, her relationships and in Russia.

'Can you imagine' – a phrase that she used repeatedly and in Russian, *Prestavlay tyebe* – 'they had virtually no income, were living on their inheritance but still insisted on living in the best part of Paris and, instead of giving them a good education, they sent their children to ballet classes. Can you imagine? Silly people! Did they imagine they were back in Imperial Russia? Noooo, that could not last', she concluded with a vigorous shake of her head.

Paris was Paul and Natalie's opportunity to regularise their marital status. They went to the Soviet Embassy to register their marriage at last. Paul explained that they had met in Berlin, though they had known each other in Leningrad, had fallen in love and now wished to become husband and wife. The embassy staff did not query their story, merely established the genuineness of their names, place and date of birth, addresses of relatives in Leningrad, Berlin and Paris. With declarations approved, they were now legally married and would shortly continue their honeymoon. They were young, they had each other and there was sufficient money to enjoy the attractions of Paris and rural France. Soon they would return to Berlin to pursue their professions. Life was good to them and full of promise. Opinion among *émigrés* in Paris supported Paul's own belief that in the long run, the Soviet regime could not last and *émigrés* would return. Paul was also aware of the vigorous politicking among the *émigrés* suggesting that change in Russia might be possible. Hindsight tells us that just as the people of the Soviet Union were blinded by Stalin and his promises, so the exiles saw what they wished, blind to the reality. The wheel of history was not turning in their favour. The iron will, genius and sadism of Stalin would prevent them from returning to their homeland in their lifetime.

Since family members were apparently leading a lavish life, how, I wondered, had they managed to retain such wealth? Hadn't they lost almost everything after the 1917 Revolution? My cousin Beatrice spent those years in Paris. On a visit in the 1990s to her home in North West Germany, I asked her how to explain that the Schlüsser family still had money, but she was unable to throw any light on the subject.

'*Ich weiss nicht*', she said in her attractive accented German mixed with her native Russian and French. 'I don't know where they had their money from. From the Schlüsser firm, I had always presumed.'

Her forty-something son, Richard, and my brother William were also there discussing the subject.

'When I first heard about the Schlüsser fortune', Richard contributed, 'I was determined to recover it'.

It was a fancy that most of us have at one time or another, to find from somewhere in the family a lost fortune.

'*Ich weiss nicht*', his mother repeated, 'but I do recollect one recurring incident in Paris. Whenever father took me to see uncle Kostya [Bruni] and aunt Anna in the *rue Tourlaque* in Montmartre, father refused to go past a certain building, instead insisting on crossing the street and walking on the opposite side at a particular point in the *rue Coulancourt*.'

'Any idea why?' we asked, I from behind my video camera.

'*Keine Ahnung* [no idea], but he did so every time, without fail!'

Her comment made me recall that mother had told me of a further reason for going to Paris in 1927, namely to secure some money owed to Paul and his siblings. One of the three accountants who had run the Schlüsser firm until it was confiscated had resettled in Paris – a certain Monsieur Huvalet. He was rumoured to have taken a large part of the Schlüsser assets without having any legal claim to it. In the video interview, mother says rather insistently that she wished father had been stronger. He had not confronted Huvalet on their visit and yet that had been the intention when they were coming to Paris. Huvalet had made himself comfortable, she recalled, in a large house with domestic servants and other trappings of wealth. He and his second wife and their two children entertained Paul and Natalie, but not a word was mentioned of the missing money. I connected Beatrice's observations with mother's and concluded that Monsieur Huvalet must have lived in the *rue Coulancourt*. I tried to follow that trail but my efforts to trace Huvalet have so far been in vain. Neither Nicolai nor Vladimir nor any other member of the family ever confronted Huvalet about the money either. Nicolai's only form of protest, I now learned, was to cross the road to avoid passing the house of the presumed embezzler.

Perhaps they had no urgent need for money in 1927. Paul and Natalie went to the International Paris Exhibition and bought an 'Indian' motorcycle direct from the floor, together with a side-car and the appropriate outfit: knickerbockers and leather jacket with cap and goggles. Natalie laughed as she recalled how, on their first run, Paul had failed to judge the side-car's ability to corner. Turning one corner, the side-car and motorcycle parted company, with the motorcycle rounding the bend and the side-car with Natalie in it carrying on in a straight line. Fortunately traffic was light and the side-car and Natalie came to a safe halt. They reconnected the two parts and, with that experience behind them, continued on their journey.

It was exhilarating to be in the city of early modernism, of Balzac and Maupassant, of Napoleon and the French Revolution, the Place de la Concorde, the Arc de Triomphe, the Eiffel Tower and the *risqué* nightlife of Montmartre. They shared sightseeing and dining excursions with cousin Kostya and his wife Anna. Together they applauded the performance of the black American 'exotic' dancer Josephine Baker. Baker embodied the essence of the 1920s: personal freedom, true sensual feelings and acceptance of the exotic as part of life. As in Berlin, to many it formed part of a search for a new meaning in life, with more liberal attitudes following the horrors of World War I. To others, it spelled decadence and despair. But in mother I could sense the power and force that these occasions held, as she was energised even by the memories of them.

Kostya and Anna Bruni lived at 8 *rue Tourlaque*, a few streets from Montmartre's *Sacré Coeur* Cathedral and quite close to the presumed address of the Huvalets. I visited them there in 1956. Kostya was a committed artist working in a studio that he said had once belonged to Toulouse Lautrec. His oils and watercolours of Paris streetscapes sold intermittently in one of the many private galleries in the area. But selling paintings in Paris was never easy in such a crowded market. He was seduced – or forced of necessity – into the film industry to design, construct and paint studio sets for a Russian film production company. He later regretted having undertaken this work and blamed it for his compromised talent.

Both Paul and Natalie qualified for a motorcycle licence. Photographed in her full outfit, Natalie epitomises the sophisticated, emancipated woman of the time: carefree, modern, affluent, confident of the future. She took delight in speaking French, the language she had learned from her Swiss grandmother. French fashion, manners and sophistication lived up to the expectations that her mother had raised in her. Evgenia Trofimovna had believed that Russian culture was inferior to Western European culture and refused even to read Lev Tolstoy, devoting herself exclusively to French and German authors and reading them only in their original language.

There remained big differences between Natalie and Zinaida, who was loud and brash with none of the refinements possessed by Natalie. Zinaida had lived too long among soldiers, partisans and rootless *émigrés* to retain any social polish. Her experiences had made her a pragmatist, cynical of any pretensions or idealism. She had known men at their worst and retained little respect for them. She could be coquettish at one moment and wildly abusive the next. Still, she could be affectionate and what she didn't lavish on her lovers she did on her dachshund. She never wanted children.

'She could be great fun', recalled cousin Beatrice, who gave me much of the information I have of her.

'She was a lively person', was how Beatrice's brother Oleg remembered her. They had known Zinaida and their mother Olga at their most extravagant. Natalie, over time, grew wary of her. Zinaida, a flirtatious woman without children, in Paris, could be as much of a challenge as a single woman.

Zinaida may also have been politically active. Certainly her previous and subsequent behaviour suggest that she was. She advocated for the defeat of Bolshevism and among her men friends there would have been a number involved in *émigré* politics, publishing and propaganda. These 'enemies of the people' outside Russia were considered by Stalin to be as dangerous as any within the country, and Paul and Natalie knew that. Stalin's agents stalked *émigrés* in Prague, Berlin and Paris. In a few years Miller, the head of the *émigré* organisation in Paris and very popular among the Russians there, would be betrayed by a fellow *émigré* and abducted in broad daylight from a street in Paris; he died as a consequence. Paul was wary of political activism and Zinaida's views and attitudes made him uneasy.

Natalie and Paul continued their honeymoon through rural France, heading for Switzerland. The name of their 1,000-cc 'Indian' motorcycle reminded them of the Russian word for a turkey, *indus*, so they always referred to it as their 'turkey'. Paul's photos of the time show French country houses and inns where they stayed. Natalie inscribed the album 'Travels on Our Honeymoon'. I was able to trace their route from the dates on the photos, some correspondence and a map of France. On 3 August 1927 they bought the motorcycle from a Monsieur Arnot, who delivered it to where they were staying with Nicolai's family in Neuilly, at *9 rue de Quatrefage*. After travelling a hundred kilometres they reached Montargis in the Auvergne, where they spent the night. From there they rode along the Loire River, past Clermont-Ferrand to La Bourboule, where their hosts were a Monsieur and Madame Royat. Paul had a passion for innovative technical developments and he took Natalie to see the French World War I flying ace, Monsieur Sardier at an airshow in La Bourboule, demonstrating parachute jumping. Parachuting was still a novelty. From there they went to see the Vernière waterfall. Here Nicolai, his wife Olga and children Beatrice and Oleg joined them for a few days. They travelled in convoy to Lyons, where they stayed at the Hotel Verdun. From there, they journeyed to Charlanes and Lake Servière, eighteen kilometres from Clermont-Ferrand, and then on to Lake Pavin. They rode the funicular to the top of the mountain, bought a souvenir – a small, inscribed copper pot (which remains in my possession) – and visited the basilica of Fourvière. On 8 September, after nearly a month of travelling, they arrived in Geneva. There they met up with Natalie's great-aunt Anna Dupond (her Swiss grandmother's sister) and took a boat across Lake Geneva past Lausanne, landing at Montreux to catch a bus to Bulle, the birthplace of Natalie's grandmother Louise Dupond, and home of the Dupond family. A fair was being held in the town square and they lunched at the restaurant *Cheval Blanc* (White Horse). My brother and I visited Bulle trying to trace any remaining relatives. Unaware that our parents had lunched there – a fact I learned much later – we also ate at the *Cheval Blanc*. Our enquiries drew blanks. It seems that none of the Dupond family had survived in the district. Aunt Anna, the last known surviving member of the family, had returned from Russia after the 1917 Revolution and lived in Geneva, where she later died. The view across the Swiss Alps was magnificent. Keen hikers, Natalie and Paul walked across mountains from one village to another, notably Gruyère, famed for its cheese. The farms, meadows and villages looked a picture. From Bulle, Natalie and

Paul returned to Paris, where a photo shows them meeting up with Vladimir, Zinaida, Paul's sister Nadya and an unknown couple identified as Ekaterina Kor and her husband Michael Evgenovich Voildo. In early October, they returned to Berlin.

Full Swing in Berlin

The newlyweds applied themselves to their work with their customary commitment while still able to enjoy Berlin. William Shirer, author of a seminal book *The Rise and Fall of the Third Reich*, first visited Berlin at this time. He wrote ecstatically:

> A wonderful ferment was working in Germany. Life seemed freer, more modern, more exciting than any other place I had ever seen … The arts were lively, the young optimistic and pacifist … with an enormous zest for living to the full and in complete freedom.

Paul and Natalie experienced that exhilaration and euphoria. Here, it seemed, was the future that the rest of the world would want to emulate and, all going well, soon would. Freedom of choice in a democratic country was working. People in the Soviet Union would become aware of this and over time would evolve into a democratic state. At least that was their hope.

Natalie believed that to be good at something you had to have a passion for it, and she had it for her work. (She would talk disdainfully of friends and acquaintances whom she considered 'dilettantes'.) Natalie caught the *S-Bahn* at seven-thirty every morning, six days a week, from *Tiergarten* to *Friedrichstrasse* and walked across the River Spree to the Institute, the Charité Hospital's teaching division. As an outgoing, sociable person willing to learn, she made friends with the other doctors as she progressed working for one department then another. On occasions Paul visited and took photos of Natalie with her colleagues. She had a promising career ahead of her and might have made a significant contribution to medical science had she been given the opportunity.

I was in awe of the thoroughness of her training and subsequent experience. She was eventually even given accreditation by UNESCO. After completing an introductory course in hygiene and bacteriology, Natalie was accepted as a research assistant and took part in research and analysis. Working closely with Professor H.A. Gins and another assistant, H. Hackenthal, they published their findings in the *Zeitschrift für Hygiene and Infektionskrankheiten* (Journal for Hygiene and Infectious Diseases). Natalie took pride in her contribution and I still have two copies of their published research. I imagine in her later, sometimes troubled, years that she took comfort from having once been a considerable person in her profession.

She next worked in the maternity section of the hospital, while also attending lectures by Professor Adalbert Czerny. Czerny was founder of the International School of Pediatrics and made an important contribution to the study of childhood illnesses. He studied the relationship between a child's nutrition and illness, and between nutrition and a child's behaviour. His influence has been felt ever since and it certainly influenced Natalie in how she raised us, and in her medical practice.

Paul's progress was more erratic. It took him almost a year to gain entry as a *Praktikant* to the firm of Siemens-Schuckert. (The firm had been dismantled after World War I as part of Germany's reparation payments, but by 1928 it had regained its pre-eminent position in manufacturing.) Once established, he worked in various departments of the communications and electrical engineering conglomerate, gaining experience in many facets of the company's work. According to his reference, between 1 April 1928 and 16 March 1929 he spent time in the workshops where electric motors for new applications were being designed, developed and built, materials tested, and small-scale manufacturing undertaken. Later he worked in the lighting/illumination laboratory where vehicle lighting was assembled. All good preparation for his future work at Schanzenbach & Co.

Paul was full of praise for the training he received at Siemens-Schuckert, my brother William recalled. In part it was because they insisted that he become familiar with every trade involved in manufacturing, such as carpentry and metalwork. It gave him a practical grounding for his work in development and design later on. Paul taught his son William to become proficient in constructing toy electric trains, moulding tin soldiers and – his proudest achievement – constructing a working microscope. William in turn passed this emphasis on to his own son Paul, who applied these skills in order to design and construct electronic equipment.

On 31 August 1928, a seminal event occurred in the history of modern theatre. *Die Dreigroschen Oper* (*The Threepenny Opera*), the reworking by Bertolt Brecht and Kurt Weill of Gay's *The Beggar's Opera*, opened on that day at the Schiffbauerdamm Theatre, only a few hundred metres from Natalie's teaching hospital. This theatre would, in 1949, become Brecht's base for his Berliner Ensemble. The opera was revolutionary in form and content. Paul and Natalie saw a performance early in its run and they may have experienced it less as the critique of capitalism – as Brecht had intended – and more as an *exposé* of the methods of the Bolsheviks under Lenin. The musical certainly lends itself to that interpretation. What hope, they must have thought, for change? Having grown up to value cultural expression, they enjoyed all that Berlin had to offer in the performing arts, graphic arts and architecture. Several blocks away from the theatre was the Adlon Hotel, where they attended afternoon tea dances, with music provided by Marek Weber's band. The Charleston had hit Berlin in 1925 and was still in vogue; Paul and Natalie danced it at the Adlon. The hotel was also the meeting place for celebrities, politicians, diplomats and artists. It is surrounded by foreign embassies – the Soviet Embassy was nearby, as was Hitler's soon-to-be Chancellery – and it served as the venue for many significant moments then and throughout the Third Reich. The Adlon formed part of Berlin's grand boulevard, *Unter den Linden*, with its neoclassical buildings, Opera House and Humboldt University, with the Imperial Palace at one end and the Brandenburg Gate at the other. The British, French and American diplomatic corps were also housed on the boulevard. There were picture palaces, too, and Natalie recalled seeing the 1925 Hollywood version of *Ben Hur*, marketed as the most expensive silent film ever made. Some sequences were in recently developed Technicolor. Perhaps with an eye on Soviet atheism, the distributor, Metro Goldwyn Mayer, advertised the film as 'the picture every Christian ought to see'. Mayer was of Russian Jewish birth and an ideologue intent on providing American audiences with virtuous, morally upright films.

The Rise and Fall of Evil

Forces were now at work in Germany, Russia and around the world, which undermined the confidence of Berliners. Where Stalin's megalomania in Russia led to greater repression as he pursued his plan to 'forge New Man', in Germany, Hitler was soon exploiting disaffection with exaggerated law and order issues while busily creating an organisation poised to take over the main institutions of the country.

Hitler, confident in his own powers, believed that this would come about soon. Yet in 1927–28, his Nazi Party was still struggling to remain viable. It had fewer than a thousand members in Berlin – so few that Paul and Natalie may have been unaware of their activities. But not for long. As a sign of things to come, the Nazis, under Göbbels, formed the *Sturmabteilung* (*SA*) – Stormtroopers or Brownshirts – to disrupt opposition meetings, protect Nazi meetings and generally to bully and intimidate the public. They spread distrust and fear by distributing propaganda leaflets and posters, and with highly publicised public brawls. In this way and by capitalising on the devastating effect of the Depression, by 1931 the Nazi Party had recruited 800,000 members, and industrialists like Hugenberg, Thyssen, Kirdorf and Schroder were supporting the Party financially. These industrialists were onside when Hitler declared ideological war on Marxism. Was this the act that so impressed Paul that he became convinced Hitler would be able to free Russia? Within two years Hitler became a seemingly unstoppable force. By 1933 he had dictatorial powers, and had built the first concentration camps.

Paul's year as a *Praktikant* at Siemens-Schuckert was to end in October

1928. His visa was due to expire then. What thereafter for himself and Natalie? What fears did they hold about returning to the Soviet Union? Whatever choice they made, how would that affect their relatives in Russia? The only legal way to avoid returning to the Soviet Union was for one or the other to continue studying. To this end, Paul enrolled for a PhD at the respected Karlsruhe Technical University and informed the Moscow authorities accordingly. Had Paul received help and advice from his cousin Alexander Makarov, perhaps? One man who appears in several photographs of the time remains a mystery, a Mr Kutepov. There is a Mr Kutepov listed as a graduate of the Karl May *Gymnasium*, only two years younger than Paul. Was he an old school friend now in a position to help? Mother identified him in the photo once as the Third Secretary at the Soviet Embassy in Berlin and referred to him as 'uncle' Kutepov, but to my knowledge he was not a relative. Perhaps Mr Kutepov used his influence in their visa renewal? To their relief, they received a one-year visa extension.

Natalie finished at the Robert Koch Institute in March 1929. This interruption to her career proved permanent. A perhaps unplanned but nevertheless welcome circumstance brought this about: Natalie was pregnant with her first child. Paul's choice of university was not accidental. Other graduates from the Karl May *Gymnasium* and Electrotechnical Institute had preceded Paul at the Karlsruhe Institute of Technology. On 23 May 1929, they received permission from the German authorities to live in Karlsruhe. Paul's five years at the Electrotechnical Institute were accepted as a precondition for completing his Engineering Diploma, to be followed by studies for a PhD. Records I hold show that in September, at the beginning of the new semester, he undertook a course in spectrometry, the behaviour of light, and voltaic instruments. He joined the Association of Electrical Engineers for the small fee of six *Reichsmark*. In July 1931, he was awarded the Diploma of Engineering (comparable to a Master of Science degree) and was given permission to continue research for his doctorate.

News from Russia remained disturbing. The power struggle between Stalin and Trotsky had come to a head: Trotsky was expelled from the Party and soon afterward from the country. With hundreds of Trotsky's followers arrested, Stalin's control over the Soviet Union seemed total. With increasing confidence he silenced his critics, including those in the arts. Theatre director Vsevolod Meyerhold, whose productions Paul and Natalie most likely saw in Leningrad, the poet Vladimir Mayakovsky – a favourite with Paul and Natalie – and the fantasy writer Zamyatin were all convinced Communists who devoted their talent to the success of the revolution. But through his paranoia, Stalin began to see them as rivals to be silenced.

For Natalie, a difficult period now began. The heady days of Berlin became a thing of the past. She became immersed in domesticity in the provincial city of Karlsruhe. While it has a proud history going back to 1715, it was very small compared to Berlin. They moved into a duplex house built from designs developed at the renowned art school, the Bauhaus, using the new building material, reinforced concrete. In line with Bauhaus principles, every part of the house was functional, with the latest fittings and facilities in the laundry, bathroom and kitchen. The architecture and services were visionary, but the house was unfinished and Natalie was shortly to give birth. Births then were routinely home births supervised by a midwife. To Natalie's consternation, construction work was still in progress when she gave birth, on 4 November 1929. For a reason not known to me, they were expecting complications and so decided that Natalie should give birth in a hospital. When the time came, Paul took Natalie to hospital in the 'turkey'. Once she was admitted, giving birth proved more difficult than anticipated. The doctors consulted among themselves but, to Paul's dismay, failed to ask for Natalie's opinion or wishes. Paul grew more agitated as he waited outside her room. To try to contain his anxiety, he wrote down a record of events and his feelings, hence I am able to recount these details here. Without her or Paul's consent, they gave Natalie a cocktail of drugs to induce a state of sleep which would leave the mother without any memory of the birthing experience. After a further delay, the delivery was completed using forceps but not before, Paul records, he fears for her life. With great relief he writes, 'Natalochka, I congratulate you and kiss you fervently, kiss, kiss, kiss', before he is permitted to approach his unconscious wife and give her a kiss. The baby girl was registered in the name Svetlana. Russian custom is to use a patronymic, which serves as a second name. Svetlana became Svetlana Pavlovna, daughter of Paul. Paul's happy task was to let relatives and friends know of the event. Congratulatory telegrams soon arrived from Leningrad and Paris. From Leningrad, Natalie's mother Evgenia wrote of her hope that they would soon have a chance to hold their first grandchild in their arms. She repeated that hope in many letters and regretted that she was not able to see Svetlana grow up. But she clung to her view that the time would come when they would be reunited and could share the joy of the baby. Neither grandparent ever saw their granddaughter.

Natalie was a practical woman and could improvise in the home, but she was a career woman and being a mother was an entirely different experience. In letter after letter she received advice from her mother about what she should do at this or that point of the child's life. Paul employed a *Schwester* (children's nurse) to help. This became necessary because of a totally unpredictable, potentially lethal complication in Svetlana's health. To mother's dismay, Svetlana, the doctors discovered, had a malfunctioning kidney. Natalie immediately felt that she was to blame. Had her trying circumstances caused the issue, at least in part? She was living in an alien culture without the support of any family member, the house was still a building site, and she didn't have the satisfaction of working in her profession which she had enjoyed until recently. There was little left of her self-esteem and now she had given birth to a sick child. How quickly her fortunes had changed. An operation became necessary. The malfunctioning kidney was removed. Or so it was thought. I have the *Röntgen* (X-ray) images, and checked with a doctor friend. He examined them and explained that, at such a young age, a baby's two kidneys are very close together and mistakes can easily be made. Indeed, in a few years Natalie learned that the wrong kidney had been removed. This left Svetlana permanently vulnerable, with periodic health problems that eventually meant she would remain childless. Should she attempt to have a child, the single kidney would most likely not sustain baby and mother, and she could die while giving birth.

Svet is the Russian word for 'light' and Paul thought it a good omen to name his daughter Svetlana as his research was in lighting technology and illumination. There were three more children to come, and their names were chosen in part so that the initials spelled the word *SVET*: Svetlana, Vasily, Evgeni and Tatjana. While underlining Paul's obsession, the choice of Russian names suggests that neither parent had stopped being Russian in their thinking and sensibilities.

The upstairs apartment of Paul and Natalie's semi-detached house was rented by a Rudolf Heiss and his wife, Dietlinde. Years later, I searched for Dr Heiss at an address in Munich that I am unlikely to forget: 8 *Im Eichgeholz*. I found it in mother's address book. It included a phone number. Mother had died a few years earlier and I was almost sure that Dr Heiss and Dietlinde would also have died. I had some troubling information which I wanted to confirm, so as not to risk misrepresenting the doctor in my writing. On impulse, I dialled the number hoping perhaps to get a lead to where any of his three daughters might be contactable.

'Excuse me, but this number used to belong to a Dr Heiss. I was hoping …' I said in my best German when a man answered.

'This *is* Dr Heiss.'

'I was hoping to make contact …' I then registered what I had heard. 'Is this Dr Heiss?' I asked incredulously. He must be close to a hundred years old, I thought.

'Yes, this is Dr Heiss.' Showing surprise would be impolite, I thought, so after a moment's hesitation I explained that I was Paul Schlüsser's younger son and brother of William. He remembered me (I had met him once in 1956) and immediately enquired about mother. I told him that she had died some time ago. When I asked him his age he replied,

'Ninety-nine.'

I allowed myself an expression of delight to find him alive, but he remained matter-of-fact. We spoke some more but I did not get to ask the question that I was bursting to ask and that had prompted my call: Were you ever a member of the *SS*?

I let my brother know that Dr Heiss, who had been a mentor to him, was alive and we immediately made plans to visit him at the address where he had been living since 1940. We flew to Munich, booked into a hotel, and after making arrangements by phone took a suburban tram. On the tram, William, ever organised, read me the last letter that he had received from Dr Heiss some years earlier. To a query from me he replied: 'He admired our mother's heroism in taking her brood to Australia in 1950'.

He read some more: 'The extent to which I could help you to find work I was honouring your mother and father for all the help they gave us, particularly in the early 1930s'. This was when they were neighbours in Karlsruhe and Natalie had helped them with their daughters.

We walked about a kilometre from the tram stop in Munich's humid summer heat before reaching the address in the oak forest. An old man with a walking stick stood in the open door of the garage. Dr Heiss, it turned out, was inspecting damage he had caused to his car in a minor accident. Our jaws dropped as he explained that he was still driving at ninety-nine! His three daughters together with their families had moved to other cities, he explained, and his wife Dietlinde had died some years previously.

Rudolf Heiss was Paul's fellow student at the Karlsruhe Institute of Technology. He was also studying for an engineering degree and, as they were also neighbours, they became friends. Dietlinde was grateful for Natalie's medical expertise and whenever she was uncertain how to treat a child, she called on Natalie's help. Her first child, called Margarethe, was a difficult birth and had a troublesome early infancy. She had another two girls and Natalie helped Dietlinde with each of them as a medical professional and as a friend. Despite their friendship and mutual regard, Natalie felt uncomfortable with Rudolf. He was a German nationalist and willing to proclaim it by giving his daughters ancient Germanic names: Dietlinde, Roswitha and Svantje. Mother once expressed her suspicion that he had been a member of the *Schutzstaffel* (*SS*), the 'foremost agency of surveillance and terror within Nazi Germany and German-occupied Europe'. My questions about Dr Heiss's role in the war were eventually answered, but not on this occasion.

Svetlana was to be baptised and the nearest Russian Orthodox church was forty kilometres south, in the spa resort of Baden-Baden – in earlier times frequented by Russian royalty, writers and intellectuals: Turgenev and Dostoevsky were visitors. As it was a place the Imperial family had visited, an Orthodox church had been built there. The spa resorts of Bad Homburg and Wiessbaden were similar summer destinations for the Imperial family, and Russian tourists followed in their wake, as would members of my family. The spa towns tended to be in the western part of Germany where the climate was more moderate all the year around, and where the spring waters were valued for their healing qualities. Svetlana was baptised in Baden-Baden a few weeks after her birth and before her operation. Two godfathers and godmothers were nominated, members of the Orthodox faith. The baptism followed the Sunday Mass, when the priest spoke and sang the short service and then wet the baby's head. Svetlana did not protest, much to Natalie's relief, as she was a contented baby. After the baptism, the guests were invited to the manse to celebrate. These occasions provided opportunities to share information in the *émigré* community: stories of hardship, luck and successes in dealing with bureaucracies, and speculation as to what was happening in Soviet Russia. At the end of 1929, at the birth of Svetlana, the new parents were looking forward to a happy and peaceful future for their daughter, who smiled radiantly at the world from her wicker basket. Her father took numerous photos and sent them to relatives in Paris and Leningrad.

Then came the collapse of the US Stockmarket, signalling that the Great Depression was only a month away.

Paul continued his research during 1930–31, at the same time becoming an *Assistent* (tutor). He became a valuable member of the faculty, while enjoying family life as a counterpoint to his intense work. Once a year he wrote to the Department of Foreign Affairs in Moscow to extend their visas, describing the progress that he was making in his studies. He informed them of the birth of his daughter, and by default she became a citizen of the Soviet Union. Ministry officials did not raise any objections to renewing the visas.

Life in Russia was hard but at the same time many held out hope for a better future once the revolution had fully succeeded, which they expected to be in their own lifetime. As incongruous as this may seem, by the 1930s the people's sacrifice had been of such magnitude that failure was inconceivable. Natalie's brother Michael may have had such faith in the Soviet project.

'My father survived in the Soviet Union because he never joined the Party and he never spoke badly of anyone.' My cousin Natasha was answering questions about her father Michael. I was having one of many conversations with her about her experience of how the Soviet Union operated, and how and why it failed.

'He was liked and trusted by everyone. He formed a choir at his place of work, organised sporting events and ensured his workplace was harmonious.'

He believed in Stalin's programme and was genuinely committed to the industrialisation of the Soviet Union. In a letter to his sister Natalie after one of his visits to Moscow, Michael wrote in glowing terms of the excavation that was taking place to build a skyscraper. The site in central Moscow was that of the Sacred Heart Cathedral, the former seat of the Orthodox Patriarchate. For believers in communism, there were many successes widely trumpeted in the Party organs, on film and in agitprop theatrical performances. Programmes were created to inform even the illiterate that industrialisation was proceeding even faster than the Five Year Plan had envisaged; for instance, iron production increased by 200 per cent and electric power output by 335 per cent. There were other significant achievements as well to support the acolytes and confound the critics: free universal education, free medical care, free pre-school education and workplace nurseries to encourage women to return to the workforce, and low-cost travel within the Soviet Union though movement was greatly restricted once Stalin introduced an internal passport system.

I had a minor experience of the way the system of rewards and punishment worked in the Soviet Union. In 1977 I had an acting role in the BBC television serialisation of Tolstoy's novel *Anna Karenina*. The outdoor sequences were filmed in Hungary's capital, Budapest, then still under Communist rule. Crew and cast were accommodated at the Volga Hotel, the most prestigious and comfortable hotel in Hungary and among the best in the Soviet bloc. (It no longer exists under that name.) Foreigners were given no choice but to stay there. The day after arriving, I found myself in a lift with a group of Russians who, judging by their clothes and behaviour, were from rural Russia. I tried to strike up a conversation but was met with total silence. Further attempts to be friendly failed completely. I found this disconcerting until I realised that they had probably been told they would be approached by 'foreign agents' who would urge them to defect or become spies. On asking the desk clerk, I learned that these people were prize-winners in a competition for the most successful state farm in their region. Their reward was two weeks in Budapest. Their commissar, a KGB operative, had control over the group and decided where they should go, what they should see and with whom they might talk. 'Inappropriate actions', such as talking to a foreigner, would be censured and the person might even be sent home. None of this was unusual to them, as they had been indoctrinated at school and through the media. Such forms of control and variations on them operated throughout the Soviet system. We weren't surprised to learn that every room in the hotel was wired for sound, and we took great pleasure in rattling our cups if we wanted to annoy whoever was listening, or stepped outside to frustrate their attempts to monitor our conversations. Other incidents and direct confirmation from several disaffected Hungarians confirmed that it wasn't paranoia on our part, that indeed there was an ubiquitous system of surveillance and control.

Paul's life would surely have been easier and longer if the Western press and apologists had made more courageous, insightful, accurate and honest assessments of the appalling circumstances in the Soviet Union, and if politicians had had the courage to act on that information. There were notable exceptions, but in general it is difficult for me to understand why people ignored the reports of so many *émigrés* of their experiences under Communism. How and why were Western governments allowed to collude, albeit perhaps unwittingly, in the death and misery of so many people?

Unexpectedly, Natalie's brother Michael came to visit them in Karlsruhe.

'My beloved Misha, your uncle', mother reminisced. She always referred to him as our uncle not as her brother, and always used the affectionate diminutive.

'We cared for each other so dearly', she recalled ruefully. With his doubts about how to proceed, it helped Paul when he heard a first-hand account of life in Leningrad and the political situation there. His friend and brother-in-law Michael had been given permission to visit Germany to learn about new applications for high-temperature ceramics. He first went to Berlin, where Natalie arranged for her friend Fräulein Paasch to introduce him to the appropriate people and to tour industrial plants. From there he came to Karlsruhe, ostensibly to acquaint himself with the facilities at the university but mostly to visit his sister. Natalie recalled fondly how she interpreted for him. What heartache that meeting must have created! She was grateful for the opportunity to be with Michael and to introduce him to his niece, Svetlana. They took Michael on their 'turkey' for trips to the Black Forest and Heidelberg, with its famed university and castle. Paul, as always, recorded the trip on his camera.

What confidences did Michael pass on to his brother-in-law about their circumstances in Russia? They were close friends and trusted each other, but were aware that they were living under antagonistic and competing political systems – though at that time their respective governments were not openly hostile to each other, on the contrary closely cooperating in a range of areas. What the two friends revealed to each other remains speculation, but it is likely that Paul took what he heard from Michael very much into account when he made his next decisions.

Paradoxically, considering that the Great Depression was overwhelming or about to overwhelm liberal democracies, Paul may have spoken of his optimism for his prospects in Germany. Michael, on the other hand, saw many good prospects in the Soviet Union where the Five Year Plan brought great expansion in industrial activity. His mother and father were employed, and Michael could look forward to getting married and starting a family. But what might they have communicated regarding political attitudes and their consequences? They both knew that Michael would be debriefed on his return by the OGPU (predecessors to the KGB); his career and the safety of his family could depend on the report that he would make. Understandably, they avoided the most sensitive topics. But, mother suggested, they may have spoken in a simple code. A conversation may have gone like this: 'How are people with foreign qualifications or of foreign extraction treated?' To which the answer may have been: 'Foreign qualifications are much sought after. The Soviet Union is very keen to learn from the industrialised West and we welcome foreign experts.' He might then have added an apparent digression: 'We've had some rough weather in Leningrad, so anyone planning to go there must consider how the climate might affect them'. He might have added: 'I've learned a great deal in Berlin and Karlsruhe, and I've been lucky with the weather'.

Paul understood the inference that there would have to be significant changes before it would be safe for him to return to Leningrad. Regarding the family, Michael was free to speak about his brother Sergei, who had qualified as an accountant and also remained unmarried. He conveyed the sadness their mother felt at not being able to see her granddaughter grow up, and her concern for Natalie's and Svetlana's health.

In the end, judging by Paul's actions, he was left in little doubt what Michael was conveying. But Michael also expressed hope that life in Russia would improve rapidly, rewarding the people for years of deprivation and hard work. He believed that a relaxation of social and political constraints would follow in the next few years, not decades. He had faith that he would see his sister back in Leningrad, reunited with her parents. Sadly, this was the last time that brother and sister met. Had they known that this would be so, might they have made other decisions? Did they contemplate that Michael might defect? Unlikely. There was something of the idealist in Michael, who with so many other Russians believed that their first loyalty should be to their motherland, right or wrong. Besides, his parents would suffer badly.

Did Evgenia Trofimovna regret the day that she had agreed to her daughter's marrying Paul? Did Paul agonise about his decision to marry Natalie when there were such consequences for her? Did they consider using bribes to help the family in Russia? Did it not matter whether an action was legal or not, or was the fear of reprisals so great that there was no option but to conform? Perhaps the response was altogether more hopeful. After all, Michael had been able to come to Karlsruhe. Was this a sign of better times to come? Perhaps the questions were just too awkward to deal with and best suppressed. You 'got on with it', as mother put it, 'there was nothing else to do'.

Paul remained convinced that the Communist government would fail or be radically transformed, despite Michael's optimistic attitude. Earlier attempts in Berlin and Munich to foment Communist revolutions had failed and the movement was dealt a severe blow when Stalin declared his aim to be the achievement of 'communism in one country' as opposed to a world revolution. Trotsky continued to agitate for world revolution and his followers were accused of 'Trotskyism' and ruthlessly persecuted by Stalin. For Paul, these were signs of increasing Soviet failure.

Michael was a keen sportsman and ice-skating was very popular in the winter months. Natalie wanted to send him home with a present of the best pair of skates she could find. She found a pair where blade and boot were one, of good quality brown leather, laced to just below the knee, giving good ankle support. Michael could use them to skate on the ice-bound Neva River. Paul had bought a magnificent set of drafting tools for his brother-in-law – dividers of various sizes, protractors etc. But when Michael came to customs at the border, there was trouble. Under no circumstances was Michael allowed to take these gifts into the USSR. Aside from any other consideration, mother believed, customs officers refused to allow anything into the country which might reflect badly on Russian goods or even create envy. Michael continued to Leningrad without the skates or instruments, but he was able to post them back to his sister. Natalie had bought herself a matching pair and when skating must have been reminded of her brother. Svetlana, when old enough, inherited those skates, while Paul skated in Michael's pair. My brother, as an engineer himself, still has the drafting tools in their pristine lacquered box, while I have the skates hanging on my wall.

A year after Michael's return to Leningrad, on 24 November 1931, their father died. Vasily Ephimovich had continued to practise in Smolensk. He had regularly written affectionate letters and postcards to his daughter in Berlin and Karlsruhe. He wrote of his fishing and swimming in the Dnieper River, where he had spent idyllic times with his daughter. He enquired after Svetlana's health and gave advice on treating her for various minor conditions. He never mentioned hardships. He was only sixty-one years old when he died of stomach cancer, possibly as a result of a poor diet, or his smoking habit, or the difficult conditions that he had endured when his world changed from pre- to post-revolutionary Russia and then to Stalinist Russia. Mother had lovingly preserved the letters and cards from him, which remain in my archive eight decades later.

Natalie's origins as a Russian with Polish and Swiss ancestry were now clear to me. Also clear was the dilemma that Paul and Natalie faced, divided by distance and ideology but joined to the family in Russia by love and care. Stalin's drive, like Lenin's, was to destroy families and personal loyalties: loyalty belonged and was to be shown to 'the state', he maintained. Hitler encouraged the family but demanded that loyalty be given to him personally as *Mein Führer* (my leader). Paul had to choose between these competing personal and social forces, or to seek a third way. That might be to leave Europe altogether. Yet his instinct was not to flee further from his homeland but to engage. His whole upbringing and experience had led him to this understanding and he felt the need to commit himself. As Churchill noted in 1935, in his book *Great Contemporaries*, many were yet to see the really dark side of Hitler's rule, so Paul can't be blamed for retaining his optimism about regaining his homeland if he remained in Nazi Germany.

The Russian film director Mikhalkov in his film *Burnt by the Sun* tells the story of a trusted general who comes too close and is burnt by Stalin's 'sun'. Paul had to be clever, cunning and on alert to stay outside Stalin's lethal orbit. The greatest threats were yet to come.

PART 3
HITLER

Another Fascist Sun Rises – Naughty Zinaida – Paul Schlüsser PhD? – Diminishing Options – The Arsonists – Focus on the Innocent – Closer to the Sun – Preparing the Fire – More Lost Fortunes – An Idyll in the Sun – Eclipsed

Another Fascist Sun Rises

Paul and Natalie were not entitled to vote in the elections, on 5 March 1933, which brought Hitler to power. With his election, Paul and Natalie entered a new period of uncertainty, contradictions and fear. With the Enabling Act passed soon afterwards, Hitler claimed for himself dictatorial powers, making the *Reichstag* (Parliament) impotent. He was acting on his belief – as he wrote in *Mein Kampf*, drawing on the ideas of Nietzsche and Schopenhauer – that only powerful individuals can bring about meaningful change. Democracy, he wrote, was a sham and Parliament 'appeared as a monstrosity of filth and fire'. Ranking people along racial lines, Hitler classified Russians to be *Untermenschen* (subhuman). How did my parents react to this? Admittedly, there was some confusion about whom he meant. Did 'refugees' from the 1917 Revolution, and *émigrés* (frequently referred to as 'White Russians'), belong to this category?

'Your father was so keen to have Svetlana join the *BDM*', recalled Marina Makarova, referring to the *Bund Deutscher Mädchen* (Hitler Youth movement for girls). 'I couldn't understand why. Kira [her older sister] and I never joined!' We were lunching in a café in Heidelberg, in the year 2000 within sight of the castle ruins. My cousin spoke fluent English, her accent suggesting that she had learned it in England. She was an imposing, immaculately dressed and groomed woman. It was the first time that I had seen her since I was a ten-year-old in Frankfurt, in 1949. It had taken time to arrange the meeting and there were moments when I felt that she didn't wish to meet me. I was keen to speak to her about her memories of my father. She was ten years older than I, and her family had close contacts with mine. Her father and Paul were cousins and father looked to Alexander Makarov as a mentor. After the introductions, it was evident that Marina preferred to speak about my mother rather than father and I was about to learn why.

'My mother loved your mother. Your mother was so beautiful and such a generous, kind person. My mother loved receiving letters from her. And then your mother died and nobody told us! We didn't find out until a couple of years later!'

This was embarrassing. I immediately recognised and acknowledged the error that I had made. After mother's death, I went through her address book and made lists of whom to inform. Somehow the Makarov family was overlooked. A grave oversight indeed. Then she posed a question that shook me.

'Why did your mother leave?' Marina was referring to the time when we left Europe in 1950. 'We all advised her not to!'

'It was thought too dangerous to stay, with the Soviets threatening to overrun all of Germany', I offered as an explanation.

'But my father and our family didn't run away! And it made our mother so sad to lose contact with your mother like that.'

She was so emphatic that it made me uncomfortable, though I was naturally pleased that they thought so highly of mother. It was flattering. But that question disturbed me as it had been asked by other family friends and it firmed my view that father had extra reasons to get out of Germany when others in a similar situation had felt no need to do so. What were those reasons? She went on to speak of my father's strictness.

'I was really shocked that he would do such a thing. Your father had come to have a meal with us in Berlin before the war. I had just been to the bathroom to wash my hands and, when I returned, your father demanded to see my hands, front and back. He then declared they weren't clean enough and promptly sent me back to wash them again! I was so affronted, but I obeyed.' She shook her head as if she couldn't believe the memory. Her comment brought to mind my experiences of father, often so strict. But I had not known or imagined that he had treated others like that also. I felt that this anecdote showed his anger and frustration went deeper than I had known. It was this and other revelations during the conversation with Marina that strengthened my resolve to find answers.

Had Paul been blinded by Hitler's expressed intention to defeat Bolshevism? Mother mumbled darkly as she pointed to a photo with a large swastika in the background. In Russian she said, in an ominous tone: 'Here is where it all begins'.

'What was the occasion?' I asked, hoping to draw her out. She had never spoken of this period. This was one of the few photos in the album showing a swastika, or any other Nazi insignia.

'Must I explain?' she said through clenched teeth. It was self-evident, surely, was the implication. I thought I had pushed my luck with her and, with a gesture of impatience, I turned the page. But she insisted on returning to the previous page. We were looking at a photo of a packed hall at father's university with a giant swastika draped along the rear wall.

'You can see what that is!'

'Yes, a swastika', I said as casually as I could. Feeling that she now wanted to talk about it, I asked if she had ever seen or heard Hitler in person.

'Yes, once. Papa and I went. They made such a fuss, built a huge tent for ten thousand people or so, put in lights, everything. He was there. It was full, full, and he spoke. He was a marvellous speaker. They compared him with …', she grasped for the name, 'this old man here … Churchill'.

'Was Churchill known to the Germans?' I asked to encourage elaboration.

'Yes, he was well known but he could hardly speak compared to this Hitler, a born speaker. He spoke of politics, nothing but politics', she replied to my original question.

What did she think of him?

'I thought he was a good propagandist … what's it called, more than propaganda, what's the word?' She kept searching for the right word but we never found it. Perhaps she was comparing Hitler's single-mindedness to that of a crusader, or an evangelist, which would seem appropriate. Hitler saw himself as a knight astride a horse, holding a staff, as in Hubert Lanziger's infamous

1935 painting of him. But perhaps she was referring to his ability to mesmerise his audience. Others have commented on this quality. He certainly appeared to hypnotise the German people and many beyond Germany's borders. Ian Kershaw, in his biography of Hitler, emphasises his subject's power to rouse audiences, and William Shirer, who heard him in the flesh, refers to Hitler's oratory as 'spellbinding'.

'At any rate', mother continued, 'the people went just crazy. They were in his spell with what he was saying and how he was saying it.'

'What sort of things was he saying?'

'Well, we Germans, we are the best, we'll do this and that. The others don't know anything! And … have you read *Mein Kampf*?'

'Yes', I lied, but quickly corrected myself and admitted that I hadn't.

'You must read it', she said. It was the first time she had spoken of any of this. I hung on every word, especially as these were words which had been filtered through the events of half a century, a distillation of her experience. And I was hoping perhaps that, for once, she would hold nothing back.

'Everything east of here is manure for the German race. And the German race is the best: blond, big, blue eyes and everything good. And so on, and so on. And the German people [she used the German word '*Volk*', so often invoked by Hitler] believed it and they went just crazy!'

How did she react?

'He was a good propagandist but he will flop … you can't do these things … He wrote it in black and white: Slavs are manure for the German *Volk*.'

How did that make her feel as a Russian in Germany?

'It made me feel really very good, can you imagine! No, I thought, this can't survive.'

The first-hand account of an eyewitness to the murderous tyrant was chilling, but the next part of the conversation shocked me more.

'Papa was so enthusiastic! "Everywhere will be Nationalism. In Russia, it'll be Nationalism."'

This confused me. Nothing of what I knew of father, his words or actions, suggested that he was a fascist. Nor, I believe, did mother mean that. So perhaps by 'Nationalism' father may have had Russia in mind, as opposed to the Soviet Union – a Russia with a strong central government within her legitimate borders, and speaking a common language. Might he have misunderstood Hitler's intentions, or was he blinded by his desire to see Russia freed of Communism? Hitler's Nationalism was based on allegiance to one person: himself, with his much-vaunted slogan *'Ein Volk, ein Reich, ein Führer'* [One people, one country, one leader].

Mother spoke in a tone of exasperation as she recalled the confusion of those years.

'Oh, everybody is silly. I thought at first that Papa was clever. He wasn't.' Since mother had to piece together her life and that of her children after it all went tragically wrong for her, this was not a surprising response.

'I thought at first … then things got worse and worse, until he was completely schizophrenic. He was so frightened the Soviets would come to Frankfurt. We know that the Soviets were planning to occupy France! All of Germany and France too!'

'Why was father so desperate?' I kept pressing the point, reminding her that many of her contemporaries remained in Germany, convinced that the Soviets would be contained by the Americans and the Western Allies. What convinced father to believe the opposite?

In 2008, I had the pleasure of meeting Marina's older sister, Kira Makarova, in Stockholm. She asked bluntly: 'Why did your family leave Germany?'

As she insisted on an answer, though she didn't necessarily believe I had one, I voiced my vague feeling that father may have worked for American Intelligence. I had no evidence for this, but I offered it as an answer and only that possibility satisfied her.

'That would explain it, of course, I see.'

With the photo of the swastika in front of us, why did I not ask mother about any possible connection between father and American Intelligence? I didn't, for whatever reason, and I never again had the opportunity to ask her. Had I done so, it may have saved me much anguish, heartache and research. As it was, I didn't learn the truth until long after her death.

Mother continued: 'Papa had been arrested once and he didn't want to ... his family was decadent and left him as the youngest back in Russia while they all fled the country ... he didn't want to repeat that experience'. Her judgement of the Schlüsser family seems harsh, but understandable when the consequences for her had been so dire.

Paul's apparent sympathy for National Socialism came at a time of financial and social collapse in Germany. Following the 1929 Wall Street crash, by 1932 six million Germans – out of a population of sixty-five million – were unemployed, and twenty-one million were living wholly or in part on state or charitable support. Hunger or the fear of it is a great motivator. The people embraced the extremes of politics that claimed to have the solution and be able to bring order to society. The country was split between those who advocated socialism, and even Communism, and those who believed the rhetoric of Hitler's National Socialists. Each promised to end the financial crisis and create full employment. But only Hitler undertook to redress the humiliation heaped on the Germans, as it was perceived, with the Versailles Treaty, and only the National Socialists vowed unequivocally to destroy Bolshevism. Paul had been working in Germany for six years and had experienced the good and the bad of German life. With his overwhelming desire to return to his homeland – a homeland free of the Communist tyranny – he may have been persuaded by Hitler's rhetoric. With hindsight, I believe, it is a legitimate position that he took in those early Hitler years. What might await him if he was forced to return to the Soviet Union was unthinkable. Logically, he would support all the forces for 'regime change'.

Paul kept applying for extensions to their visas to remain in Germany. On each occasion, he felt the same apprehension as to whether he would be given these vital documents or be forced to return to the USSR.

In Berlin, clashes between Communists and National Socialists became more frequent and more violent. As social and financial circumstances deteriorated, and not only in Germany, the Nazi programme looked ever more attractive to many inside and outside of the country. By January 1933, when Hindenburg appointed Hitler as Chancellor of Germany, an incredible 92 per cent of the electorate was in favour of the Nazis. But rather than ease up on the violence, as many apologists had expected, Hitler was ruthless as he consolidated his power. To ensure loyalty, people needed to fear the alternatives. The German historian Joachim Fest recalled in his autobiography that there were hosts in the 1930s who insisted that no guest was welcome unless they had read *Mein Kampf*. Fest stressed that there was no hint of irony in this. Both Natalie and Paul had read it. As a blueprint for Hitler's plans for a '1,000 Year Reich', the book spelled out his motives and the methods which he was to employ to achieve his objectives. Reduced to its simplest, he wanted to reverse the 'humiliating' (and financially largely impossible) terms imposed on Germany with the Versailles Treaty following Germany's defeat in World War I. Beyond that, he claimed the need for *Lebensraum* (living space) for the 'superior' Aryan race that he was leading. That space was to be found in the east of Germany, in the rich lands of the Ukraine and of European Russia, as far as the Ural Mountains.

Natalie's dislike, almost disdain, for Germans increased over this period. She was a woman without guile, pretence or affectations. Above all she valued independent thought, not slavish acceptance of what some 'authority' might put forward. She had learned to be open and honest. The behaviour of many Germans repulsed her. She carried this resentment to her grave. At the same time, she depended on many kind-hearted Germans to assist her and her family – Germans with compassion who offered help even in the darkest days of World War II.

Natalie gave birth to a second child in 1933, a son whom they named after her father, Vasily. It translates as 'Basil' but his parents decided to Germanise the name to 'Wilhelm'. While this was common and there had been others with that name in previous Schlüsser generations, was this nevertheless an effort to disguise their Russian roots? The relatives in Paris sent congratulations and Natalie's family in Leningrad sent telegrams and postcards. Even the head of Paul's Institute of Technology in Karlsruhe sent a congratulatory card. Letters in and out of Russia continued to be delivered. This surprised me. All correspondence had to pass the censor, which is probably why many letters sound contrived. Letters from Natalie's relatives in the late 1930s carried only good news. This despite newspaper reports of the Moscow Show Trials, the period remembered as the *Yezhovchina*. Yezhov was then head of the Soviet Secret Service when a thousand people a day were shot for 'sabotage' and other crimes against the Soviet State. I can empathise with Paul and Natalie's state of mind as they read of these events, fearing that their relatives may get caught up in them at any moment. Yet, in the midst of it all, in a letter dated 6 April 1937, Paul's brother-in-law Michael wrote to him happily outlining his plans for a holiday: 'I'll be playing tennis. Our organisation [meaning: his union] has bought a yacht so we'll be going sailing', he announced proudly. He gave details of who was holidaying in which *dacha* and when. Was this true or a code of sorts, or even both at once? The Soviet censor would have been pleased to read that Michael was sharing news of happy events. I've come to believe that Michael's description of mundane events was his way of being best able to convey the circumstances of their day-to-day life. It was meant to reassure Natalie and Paul to read homely details such as these. In an earlier letter, written in 1936, he describes a business trip to Moscow. He took time off to go sightseeing, where he came across the site for the planned 'Palace of the Soviets' where the Cathedral of Christ the Saviour had been demolished on Stalin's orders. It was to become a Palace of the People, he wrote, with a gigantic statue of Lenin crowning it. He described the project in some detail because he believed that Paul, as an electrical engineer, would be interested. He commented on the challenge to install adequate illumination for such a huge building. It was also a plausible way of keeping the censor from blacking out the information, as there was no reference to any political implications. Michael continued in his letter that he had walked along a road from the building site when a NKVD officer stopped him. Unwittingly, he learned, he had taken the road leading to Stalin's *dacha* and was promptly stopped. Had he taken a risk in mentioning the episode? I think that my uncle Michael believed in the future of the Soviet Union. Like so many, he saw the shortcomings but believed them to be temporary and necessary before the benefits of the revolution could be fully enjoyed.

Naughty Zinaida

When Paul's family in Paris sent congratulations on the birth of Vasily (William), Vladimir included a photo of his wife Zinaida and their sister Nadya. Zinaida is with her dachshund while Nadya looks somewhat dourly into the camera. The photo is the last photo of Zinaida.

'Zinaida was great fun!' My cousin Beatrice surprised me with this comment. I'd always heard Zinaida referred to as an evil presence, though no one had ever explained why. I now know why.

'She was full of life and anecdotes. She often made us laugh.'

I had my video camera running as she spoke. We were in her home in Münster, northwest Germany, a rather 'brutalist' building but with plenty of space. It was the home where she had reared her three sons, only two of whom were then still alive, and where she had coped with her abusive husband, a former German fighter pilot. My mother was a sympathetic soul to her, to whom she could open her heart and mind. She sent her copious letters for many years, written in French.

'Zinaida and my mother were thick as thieves and, I suspect, confirmed each other in the rather wild lifestyle they led in Paris.'

I pressed Beatrice about this innuendo but she only hinted that there had been an array of men friends, apparently with the acquiescence of their husbands.

The way she faintly smiled, I felt that Beatrice was rather impressed by the bravado that her mother and aunt had displayed in those circumstances.

'It was common knowledge that aunt Zina had a lover at the time the photo was taken. She could hardly hide it. He lived in the apartment above theirs in Neuilly.'

The revelation almost took my breath away.

'In the upstairs apartment?' I mumbled.

'Yes', she insisted as she glanced at me, in part because of the memory and in part a reaction to my incredulity.

'She was so much fun! And she had so many stories to tell.'

Whether Beatrice thought that I might be indiscreet or whether I found other questions more pressing, I never got to hear any of those stories. How at odds was this picture to the one that I had formed of her! I had deep reasons to recall this side of Zinaida's persona later.

Beatrice, whose own life in Paris had been so full of promise, reminisced wistfully.

'There were always people coming through the house: artists, musicians, dancers. It was like living in a Dostoevsky novel.'

'How did Zinaida's husband take it?' I asked Beatrice, expecting to hear about Vladimir's outrage.

'He was a dour man. Quite different from her. Not many laughs with him.' She paused while she took another drag at her ever-present cigarette (just like my mother). Beatrice clearly thought him a weak man, colourless compared to the others in the *émigré* community in Paris.

I couldn't tell Beatrice that my mother disapproved of her mother Olga, her mother's career choice and the way that she was raising her children, and the extra-marital affairs that she was conducting. Beatrice's niece Patsy recalled many years later that her grandmother had a friend by the name of Dima (Dimitri), who was purportedly an uncle. She treated him as such only to learn years later that he had in fact been her live-in lover. Perhaps I should have been shocked but I admit that, like Beatrice, I rather enjoyed the idea that my family had such feisty women in its ranks during a much less permissive era than today.

Beatrice was now sifting through the photographs and newspaper cuttings, which she had scattered over her large writing desk. Pointing to individual photos and cuttings, she fondly recalled those times. She had good reason to do so. Those were the best years of her life, with the subsequent years blighted in many ways.

'I danced at the Paris International Exhibition of 1937', ran part of her commentary. I was impressed, even more so when she added:

'I performed in *Petrouchka* and Stravinsky himself came to see it!'

After expressing my admiration, I asked her whether Paul and Natalie had seen her perform, since they had been in Paris to attend that Exhibition.

'I don't recall, but I don't think so. The Exhibition ran from May to October, whereas we only performed on a few select dates.'

Also, Natalie's dislike of ballet and disapproval of Olga's children learning ballet may have meant that they avoided attending a performance.

'Mother had her own studio', Beatrice continued.

Who financed it, I wondered, though I didn't ask, and surmised that her husband Nicolai must have done so.

'I got the bug when I was allowed to watch rehearsals in mother's studio. I sat at the back and watched all these marvellous people go through their routines. It was exhilarating. That was when I first met Stravinsky. They were rehearsing his *Firebird* when he turned up to a rehearsal and I was introduced.'

Beatrice explained that *Firebird* had been Stravinsky's first successful ballet. It had been part of the dance and art revolution brought to France by Diaghilev and his Ballets Russes, around 1910, which had so profoundly influenced all the arts.

'I found him very easy to talk to. Not at all the formidable man that he appears in photos.'

Through my own film work and interest in modern dance and contemporary culture, I have learned to appreciate the influence that Sergei Diaghilev had on the twentieth century, and I wonder whether mother appreciated the quality of Stravinsky's work and that of the Ballets Russes. Might she have responded with greater understanding of the choices made by her sister-in-law and niece had she done so? I did not get to discuss this with Beatrice. But I understood why mother held her opinion when Beatrice referred to her mother's studio in words implying that it was also a place for more intimate meetings. That would have been Natalie's sore point: she did not approve of artistic licentiousness, which was apparently rife among the friends and students of her Parisian sisters-in-law.

Paul Schlüsser PhD?

The life of the family in Paris seemed frivolous to Paul and Natalie, viewed from their middle-class enclave in Karlsruhe. For them, life had a more serious purpose. Paul was studying for his doctorate while also a tutor, with his focus on research. What sort of research? Strangely, I've learned little of that. One story, however, has persisted and was frequently repeated in the family, though I have long wondered whether it was true or instead formed part of our parents' disinformation.

'Papa was unhappy with the quality of his work and so abandoned his doctorate', my sister Svetlana explained to me on more than one occasion.

'Why would he do that?' I asked, somewhat disbelieving.

'Papa told me himself.' She said it as if, by quoting the source, she would confirm its truth. 'He just felt it wasn't good enough.'

Since then I have discovered, among the family papers, a part of what appears to be a newspaper weekend supplement – a glossy publication consisting largely of photo essays. One of the photos shows my father in a laboratory coat, although he is not identified by name. His assignment, the report said, was to study the diffusion of light using a variety of materials, and experimenting with different ways of shading light. The article explains how the direction of the light source can affect how an object is perceived. This has application in aerial reconnaissance and mapping. Considering the times, it seems to me that its potential military application would have been of first importance. Here, perhaps, is the explanation why Paul dis-informed us about his doctoral studies. Information after the war of Paul's participation in this programme could have been dangerous. He was also testing different gases in lamps, determining their luminosity and durability. Cool lighting was used in mines and importantly in the manufacture and storage of explosives. He worked on developing automobile and lorry headlights that could be shaded so they were not visible from certain angles, particularly from an aircraft for instance. The research might have had many applications, but he must have known that this work was part of Germany's war preparations. Hitler in *Mein Kampf* had nominated 1943 as the date for Germany's invasion of Russia. Paul may have begun to feel, and perhaps even to hope, that it might come sooner.

How did Paul react to Hitler's tightening grip over the German people? German historian Joachim Fest, in his memoir *Not I*, traces the steps by which the Nazi regime turned the population into willing or unwilling collaborators. After Hitler was appointed Chancellor in January 1933 by President Hindenburg, he began his programme of 'racial purification'. To do this and implement other measures of his manifesto, all organs of the state were placed under the control of members of the Nazi Party – including law courts, education and the churches. Hitler's methods were so effective that only a few months later, to quote Fest, 'you knew who to trust and who not to trust'.

I believe that Natalie could sense the danger of the developing Nazi dictatorship. Paul, she felt with hindsight, was blinded by the hope that Bolshevik Russia would be destroyed. Was he the one who, in a few years, would encourage his brother Vladimir to join the German *Wehrmacht* (Armed Forces)?

With the *Reichstag* fire in early 1933 and the Röhm *putsch* in June 1934 – two staged events to incriminate them – Hitler eliminated his rivals. All youth organisations such as scouts and church groups were banned, while the 'Hitler Youth' was created in their stead. Membership was made compulsory for all young Germans. To my distinct discomfort, I learned that 'racial studies' were introduced into the school syllabus and teachers who were not members of the Nazi Party were either dismissed or severely constrained in what they could teach. By autumn 1936 it was noticeable, Fest observes, that more people openly supported the regime because this was rewarded with privileges denied to the less enthusiastic. Every apartment block now had a *Blockwart* (warden), a member of the Nazi Party who informed on 'misdemeanors' and nonconformity, large or small. Individuals were reprimanded and ordered to adhere to the party line. Under the mounting pressure, care for a neighbour or concern for each other disappeared and was replaced by suspicion. As in the Soviet experience, family loyalties were destroyed, replaced by the 'superior' loyalty to the leader, in this case, Hitler.

Paul and Natalie, now with two children and a third on the way, lived in such a neighbourhood in Karlsruhe. While father was studying and tutoring, Natalie was confined to being a mother and housewife, a role that she neither wanted nor ever really enjoyed, though her affection for her husband meant that she would not deny him his wish for a substantial family. But she was a qualified woman keen to work in her profession. She, too, was subject to Hitler's new policy to confine women to *Kirche, Küche, Kinder* (church, kitchen, children). To implement it, the regime restricted the number of women teachers and doctors to 10 per cent of the total. Her dealings with neighbours and other mothers were formal and superficial. Natalie stood out among her neighbours with her appearance and Russian accent and her attitudes. She resented the middle-class conformism forced on her in everything she did: dress, child-rearing and toys. She remembered the free atmosphere in Berlin where she could wear fashionable clothes and was able to express her own personality. She may have aspired in time to return to work at the Robert Koch Institute, and she kept in touch with and had visits from her good friend Elfriede Paasch, who sent her photos, including a group photo of the Institute staff in 1939.

She had an ambivalent relationship with her upstairs neighbours, who nevertheless remained lifelong friends. But Rudolf and Dietlinde Heiss were open supporters of the Nazi regime. The nanny whom Paul had employed, Elizabeth – known to the children as Lilibeth – was helpful with domestic chores and child-minding, but she too was a supporter of the Nazi regime. Natalie never fully trusted her: she might be an informer. Her presence did, however, free Natalie from full-time mothering and she was then fortunate to be given permission to work a few hours a week in a nearby medical practice, though she worked as an unpaid volunteer to circumvent Hitler's restrictions.

Diminishing Options

Natalie never stopped being anxious that remaining in Germany could have dangerous consequences for her family in Russia. And the time was coming when they would have to make a decision whether to return to Russia or seek asylum in Germany or somewhere else (France, for instance). What dilemmas did this create for Paul and Natalie? Surely, the only way to cope with them was to hope that Bolshevism would either collapse or be destroyed from without. You would put your heart and soul into any effort which would help to bring this about. I doubt that too many high-minded, idealistic debates would have taken place. Hope and the day-to-day struggle determined their actions. Paul was in a high-wire act hoping to get to one end or the other before falling off: one end was a liberated Russia, the other a despotic Germany.

One typed, foolscap-sized letter already looks ominous on its letterhead: '11 Gorky Street, Moscow, at the Hotel National'. I located the address in 1993, and found that the street had returned to its original name, *Tverskaya Uliza*. The hotel was located within sight of the Kremlin, a few blocks from the Lubyanka KGB headquarters and prison. The Soviet elite had favoured it as a place to stay, with Lenin, Trotsky and Dzerzhinsky among those who frequented it. Intourist, the Soviet travel agency, had been headquartered there since Stalin founded it in 1929, and it was staffed entirely by NKVD (later KGB) personnel. When I visited it in 1993, it was still staffed by secret service personnel and was extensively bugged. Each floor had a *dizhurnaya* sitting at the end of the corridor. Ostensibly she was there to offer help, clean rooms, even provide a cup of tea from the samovar over which she lorded. In fact, her main task was as a KGB informer instructed to learn as much as she could about each guest.

The fateful letter which sealed Paul and Natalie's fate is dated 16 February 1935. Until 1935, Paul had obtained annual permits to remain outside the Soviet Union. He knew that this would come to an end, as it was now almost seven years since they had left Russia. I assume that his request to extend his visa was finally refused in 1934. He was obliged imminently to return to Leningrad. He knew very well that anyone who had spent time in the West came under suspicion and could be charged with spying. It alone would have made him hostage to the authorities. They could be accused of having been to places where they revealed information valuable to a foreign power; they might have books in their possession or letters that 'betrayed' them. They might bring back belongings that could be used as evidence that they were 'profiteers'.

Paul had three choices. The first was to return to Leningrad. On brief reflection that was unthinkable. Second, he could try to emigrate legally; third, he and his family could defect. Whichever they chose, what would be the repercussions on the family in Russia?

He tried the legal route first, and this document from Moscow was part of the process. The form listed the conditions under which a person could emigrate. There is a heavy emphasis on fees to be paid. A German law then recently promulgated, stipulating that people wishing to return to Russia from Germany would need an exit visa, further complicated matters. The purpose of this law was perhaps to prevent political and industrial espionage. Would Paul's education and experience be considered industrial espionage? Laws and regulations, not for the last time, put him into a no-win situation. Which way could he turn? He reasoned that if you gave the appearance of complying with the law, you might evade the consequences for a time, perhaps long enough to see changes in Russia. Intourist, headquartered at the Hotel National, handled such matters. He could be given permission, provided he paid an exit fee of 1,100 gold roubles for the children and 550 gold roubles for the adults. He would also have to pay a commission of 10 per cent to Intourist and a fee of 59 gold roubles per person for the cost of travel from Leningrad to Karlsruhe (although they had paid for it themselves). Payment could only be made in an approved currency, at the exchange rate prevailing on the day.

I believe that my sister Svetlana had not seen this letter. Years earlier, I was on a visit to her home in Northam, in Western Australia. As so often on these occasions, I had questions about our family history. We were sitting in deck-chairs outside the house that she and her husband had built. It was a hot day in February. Her border collie, Daisy, was lying panting at her feet.

'Why did the Soviet authorities let our parents leave Russia just like that?'

It was a naive and ill-informed question, but I was still under the impression that our parents had been free to leave Russia as students, quite legally.

'They didn't. They tried emigrating from Russia but the cost was too high', she informed me. 'That's one way they discouraged, even prevented, people from leaving Russia. In no way could Papa afford it.'

Father probably did have the means to pay but chose not to. Why had he dis-informed Svetlana again? Perhaps this rationale was easiest for Paul to justify and least dangerous if that information fell into hostile hands.

How had the authorities calculated that sum of money? They considered it compensation, I believe, for what the state had spent on education and social services, and as reparation to the Soviet people. Paul thought about the ramifications and then took the step that would be his final break with his homeland. He decided not to reply to the letter. This decision meant that his name was henceforth prominent in the list of the Soviet secret service, if it wasn't already. With this action he was now both illegally outside the Soviet Union and illegally in Nazi Germany. Stalin hated nothing so much as an enemy abroad. Such enemies formed a threat almost greater than the enemies within. Outside the country, they were free to criticise the regime and speak of the conditions in the Soviet Union. Russians in exile self-evidently disliked and feared the Soviet regime. Communist Party members and sympathisers abroad were actively discrediting such people, as father knew, even using violence. How could father deal with being an illegal immigrant and an illegal emigrant? His strategy included emphasising his German background. He could not totally disguise his Russian side, but from now on he made his German heritage paramount. He had chosen to teach Svetlana Russian as her first language. By the time his second child, William, learned to speak he taught him German first. That would apply to the third child, Tatjana, and his fourth child, myself. He chose to register my sister in her name spelled in German and my name also, Eugen. The nanny and wet-nurse they employed were German.

The Arsonists

Natalie's antipathy towards Germans would only have deepened as she observed how people began to treat each other. The historian Fest describes how you never knew whom you might make into an enemy. People justified their actions on ideological grounds in National Socialist terms of 'unity of purpose' and 'German solidarity', which Hitler was implementing with his programme of the *Volksgesellschaft* (national community) with citizens of *Volksgenossen* (national comrades). But, says Fest, in reality the regime created envy and provoked a natural meanness. Tolerance was framed as weakness to be condemned and, conversely, Hitler's hard, uncompromising attitudes and decisive actions, as remedies to be supported. Fest talks about a 'wall of silence' that was built up so certain topics were never mentioned. This distrust extended so far that it became common for people to cross the road rather than engage in even a 'good morning' with anyone who might be the 'wrong' person. Natalie may have been treated as one of these 'wrong' persons, but she had too much pride ever to talk about this. It would have legitimised those insults. But the strain of watching your every word and action, and suspecting every individual including your own children's nurse and your neighbours, left a lifelong habit of suspicion.

A revealing item came to me after my sister Svetlana died. As her executor, I was left to sort her private papers. Among them I found the order of events on Svetlana's first day at school. It was decorated with swastikas, made more prominent as Svetlana had coloured them. Apart from the swastikas, the running order is decorated with a boy and girl dressed in Hitler Youth uniforms and standing to attention at a flagpole. Svetlana had coloured the figures. The ceremony was held on 15 April 1936 – three years into Hitler's dictatorship – and commenced at 3 p.m. It began and concluded with the parading of Nazi banners in and out of the assembly. There were some songs and poems and an address, an oath of allegiance to the Nazi flag and a prayer for 'our *Führer*'. The occasion concluded with two songs, *Deutschland Über Alles* and *The Horst Wessel Song*. The words of the Horst Wessel song, lacking somewhat in poetic subtlety, sung by Svetlana and her six-year-old classmates, is the expression of an aggressive regime:

> The swastika is looked up to by millions full of hope;
> The day for freedom and for bread is dawning;
> The final call to arms has sounded,
> For battle we are all prepared,
> Hitler flags fly high in every street,
> Our time of slavery is about to end.

The song was the anthem for the notorious *Sturmabteilung* (Stormtroopers) and was sung on every opportune occasion. Groups of youths hiking through the mountains sang it to keep in step. It was constantly played on the radio, and I recall my brother and his friends singing it. In 1934, a regulation was introduced requiring everyone to maintain the Hitler salute while stanzas 1 and 4 were played. Loyalty had now to be demonstrated in a very public way. Dissent became more dangerous.

Focus on the Innocent

Nazism was anti-religious and anti-Russian. Paul defied them both. They baptised their children, still standard practice then, and Svetlana was taught Russian as her first language. With the language came an introduction to Russian culture, through its stories, poems and art. 'Uncle Misha', Natalie's brother Michael, had brought presents of Russian children's books, among them the rhyming stories by Chukovski. Svetlana learned her mother tongue reading these stories. Paul took his daughter to church in Baden-Baden, where she had been baptised. He explained to her the intricacies of Russian Orthodox religious art on the altar, the iconostasis and in the body of the church. She listened to the church music sung by singers with careers in Russia behind them. Svetlana, an intelligent and inquisitive girl, learned about the history of Baden-Baden and its Orthodox church. Above all, Svetlana learned to love Pushkin's poetry and stories as all Russian children do, learning a number of them by rote. She was getting a thorough introduction to Russian history, language and culture. What would she be taught in the Nazi schools? How would she reconcile what her father was teaching her and what she was reading? How did Paul and Natalie reconcile the contradictions? These were matters of life and death, not only for his own family in Hitler's Germany but for his relatives, scattered across Europe, and Natalie's family in Russia. Both regimes had imposed a morality which Paul challenged through his actions.

To counter the self-serving rhetoric and actions of the Nazi regime, Paul initiated afternoon walks with his daughter.

'He took me into his confidence, as the eldest. We would talk about things he may not have talked about to anyone else.'

She took pride in the trust that he showed in her. They would stroll through the nearby fields in Ginnheim, a suburb of Frankfurt where father had a job by then, returning after an hour. Father avoided politics, Svetlana recalled, and focused on the personal: what was expected of her, particularly as the eldest; what she might expect from relationships with others; how she should relate to her mother. Paul encouraged a private morality in her, independent of that taught in school.

'Blood is thicker than water. There are times when you can trust no one except your closest family', he would repeat on these occasions. He stressed loyalty to family and friends, uprightness, good manners and consideration to others – values opposed to those promulgated by the regime. Father explained what the Orthodox church meant to him, stressing the symbolic and metaphoric lessons of love, sacrifice, redemption and service to others. He was careful to express these thoughts in such a way that, if his words were repeated anywhere, it would not compromise Svetlana. He emphasised that their conversations were confidential. I now believe that father also used these occasions to selectively misinform her.

When the time came, Paul enrolled Svetlana in the youth organisation for girls, the *Bund Deutscher Mädchen*. Membership was compulsory. In my meeting with my cousin Kira Makarova in Sweden many years later, she echoed her sister's surprise that father had taken this step. Her own father, she maintained, had kept her out of the organisation. I am unclear where the truth lies. When William turned ten in 1943, father enrolled him in the *Jungvolk*, the junior version of the Hitler Youth Movement compulsory for boys aged ten to fourteen. I recall how mother made his uniform: black corduroy short pants, and a brown shirt. Normally William wore *Lederhosen*. She bought a belt with an iron buckle depicting a swastika and made a black kerchief to put around the neck with a wicker bind.

The aim of the youth organisations was to teach young boys all about National Socialism. Once a week they went to a meeting where they were taught about the political, racial and ideological ideas that Hitler was pursuing. Members were expected to inform on anyone, including their parents, if they saw any anti-Nazi behaviour. When World War II began, they were trained in military skills including target practice with small-bore rifles.

Every boy had to take the oath:

> In the presence of this blood banner which represents our *Führer*, I swear to devote all my energies and my strength to the saviour of our country, Adolf Hitler. I am willing and ready to give up my life for him, so help me God.

Closer to the Sun

In 1937, a request was made to Paul's Institute of Technology in Karlsruhe by a Frankfurt firm, Schanzenbach & Co. (the firm which would 'dismiss' him after the war). They asked that Paul be released from his PhD studies to work for them in Frankfurt. Encouraged by his supervisor, Paul accepted the invitation and in a letter of offer the company expressed gratitude to the head of the Institute, Professor Weigel, for releasing him for this work, giving Paul the option to return to the Institute at any time. He postponed his PhD – in fact, abandoned it – and resettled the family in Frankfurt. Schanzenbach manufactured electric motors, transformers and lighting equipment: lamps of various shapes, sizes and applications. His duties were to research, develop and expand the lighting technology section. They were eager to have him start and gave him just a month to relocate. As a foreigner, he could not choose his place of work and needed his employer to apply for a permit. They obtained a *Befreiungsschein* (release form), which gave him authority to work in Frankfurt, to be renewed every year.

Father rented an apartment in a newly built housing estate in Ginnheim, within a bicycle ride to his work. It is now known as the *Dichterviertel* (Poets' Quarter), as many streets are named after poets and writers. There were signs of economic progress everywhere, a result of Hitler's policies. Rows of new apartment blocks built and equipped with the most modern appliances and conveniences virtually unknown before then: large kitchens, a separate laundry with hot and cold running water, a cellar to store coal and potatoes, and an attic for storage and clothes-drying in wet weather. Ominously, by this time it had become mandatory that every apartment block be built with a *Bombenkeller* (bomb shelter). This was a large bomb- and gas-proof underground space with a single shock-proof door, a gas mask for every person in the building, and emergency rations. The purpose of such spaces was clear: preparation for aerial attacks, with anticipated use of poison gas bombs.

A period of appeasing Hitler began in 1937, when Lord Halifax became Foreign Minister of Great Britain and came to Germany to meet Hitler. He confirmed the Anglo-German Maritime Agreement, signed two years earlier, which aimed at limiting the development of the German naval forces (Kriegsmarine). Nevertheless increasing signs of a military build-up were evident to Paul not least as his firm was manufacturing equipment suitable for military purposes. His friend and neighbour in Karlsruhe, Rudolf Heiss, had completed his PhD and was appointed head of a newly created Food Technology Institute in Munich. From him, Paul learned that military rations suitable for supplying a large army on the move were being stockpiled in large quantities. From what he had read and heard, Paul believed that England would not now attack Germany, so war preparations could only mean the invasion of Soviet Russia. Germany, Italy and Japan had signed the Anti-Comintern Pact, declaring thereby that the Soviet Union was to be contained in Europe and Asia. Paul faced many unknowns if hostilities commenced. As a foreigner, how would he be treated once war broke out? What would happen to his wife's family in Russia? Would they be interned? Would he and his family be interned in Germany? What help would other members of the family need? What could he do to secure some financial security for his family?

Paul's cousin Robert, one of the Sevier brothers, childhood friends from St Petersburg, was a senior employee at the Schroder merchant bank in London, which had in part prospered with the expansion of the Schlüsser firm in St Petersburg. Alexander Schlüsser of St Petersburg and Henry Schroder of Hamburg had combined to build a successful merchant bank in the city of London, through which the St Petersburg firm conducted its business in the English-speaking world. In the 1850s and 1860s, Schroder and Schlüsser turned J. Henry Schroder & Co. from a modest Anglo-German trading company into a prominent merchant bank in the same league as firms such as J.S. Morgan, the Baring Brothers and even the Rothschilds. By the time Alexander Schlüsser was in his sixties, he was *'riche comme un prince'*, as Heinrich Schliemann noted in his diary after visiting him in 1866. Robert Sevier was therefore, in a sense, working for the family firm, and any money entrusted to it could be considered safe. Paul's work at Schanzenbach, and Hitler's aggressive policy toward Czechoslovakia, Austria and Poland, convinced him that he should secure his remaining assets outside Germany.

Where had this money come from? I had been misled into believing that all money had been lost during the 1917 Revolution or had been 'stolen' by the firm's accountants. It turns out that considerable sums had remained in the family's hands. The money, I learned, had come from insurance policies that Schlüsser & Co. had taken out and somehow it had been possible to redeem them, possibly via the 'thieving' accountants. Perhaps also there had been some prudent selling of merchandise which was outside Russia at the time of the Revolution. The sums involved were enormous. It was Fred Sevier, Robert's brother, who persuaded me that the figures he quoted were credible. They amounted to an astonishing £8 million sterling. If the figures are anywhere near correct, then Natalie was justified in referring to the 'Schlüsser fortune', and the family could wonder what had happened to the money. The widow, Theresa Vasilievna Schlüsser, Paul's stepmother, was legally entitled to half the estate and would have received the equivalent of £4 million sterling and the children close to £700,000 sterling each. Using conservative figures, in today's terms this amounts to £200 million sterling for the stepmother and £20 million sterling for each of the six children. I was confused.

Cousin Marina Makarova told me that when she visited Theresa Vasilievna in her Berlin apartment, 'her flat was very rich, rich, rich'. Father's cousin Fedya Sevier who visited my step-grandmother in Berlin reported being wide-eyed with the affluence. There must be money somewhere to which I might be entitled, he believed. He could not credit that the money had been spent and encouraged me to do some searching and find out where it might be.

Paul moved to find a safe place for the money. By the time he set out in 1937 to bank the money in London, with inflation and living expenses, his portion, I estimate, had been reduced to a not inconsiderable £300,000 sterling. Paul travelled to London by train and ferry via The Hague. He stayed with the Sevier family. Robert Sevier drew up the appropriate deed and it was signed on 28 May 1937. For reasons that are unclear, the deed was drawn up not between Paul Schlüsser and the bank but between Robert Sevier and the Schroder bank. One reason may be that Paul, coming from Germany, could not sign such a deed. In fact, the question arises: on what passport and visa did Paul travel to get into England? These remain unanswered questions. But it would be consistent with Paul's actions and beliefs to ensure that the money could not be claimed by either the German state or the Soviet state. The money would earn a fair dividend, but it would also be safe from government authorities. Paul had confidence in Britain's economy and rule of law, and a war between England and Germany was only a distant possibility. The British currency was as 'safe as the Bank of England', as the expression went. The Trust invested the money in a range of stocks and shares. Far-reaching conditions stipulated in the deed included that the money could not be accessed until Paul's youngest child was thirty years old. This suggests that Paul believed the confrontation to come might last until 1966. Paul's stay in London was brief and he returned to Frankfurt. Apart from Fedya, he would never see any of his English cousins again.

Preparing the Fire

Preparations for war were now being made overtly. Some time early in 1939 (before the German–Russian non-aggression pact was signed), Paul was given confidential information – presumably by his employer, Schanzenbach – about plans including him among the Germans [sic] who would take control of factories, infrastructure and installations in the Soviet Union, once the country had been conquered. Paul told Svetlana that he had been designated to head an electrical plant in the Ukraine, presumably under the aegis of his firm Schanzenbach. This plan may have been anticipating things, but Paul shared the confidence generally held that Hitler's armies would triumph, leading to a rapid collapse of the Soviet Union. The Western powers appeared so aggressively opposed to Bolshevism, in words and deeds, that Hitler – and perhaps Paul also – could believe that they would support him in his plan to destroy Stalin. The least Hitler expected was that they would not hinder him. We now know that this was a fatal miscalculation.

Hitler and Stalin were opportunists. While they gave the appearance of negotiating for security and peace, in fact they were negotiating for war. On 23 August 1939, Germany and Russia appalled the Western powers when they signed a non-aggression pact, the Molotov-Ribbentrop Pact, with a secret agreement to partition Poland between them. A week later, Germany invaded Poland, and Russia did so on 17 September, and as agreed both invaders carved the country into two, intending to wipe Poland from the map forever. This was the trigger for the democracies to finally respond to the threat that Hitler posed, and on 3 September Britain and her allies declared war on Nazi

Germany. It was a fortnight to Bill's sixth birthday (he had recently started school), Svetlana was completing *Volksschule* (primary school), Tatjana was a boisterous four-year-old and I was seven months old.

Hitler had not expected opposition from the Western powers, but even if they did oppose him, he believed in Germany's invincibility. The German people had indications of this when Hitler annexed Austria and marched into Czechoslovakia without significant opposition. Hitler's Air Force and ground troops had already gained battle experience in Spain, in General Franco's Civil War. Göring's *Luftwaffe* carried out the infamous bombing of civilians in Guernica, immortalised in Picasso's mural. Germany had the largest standing land army in the world.

Cooperation and collusion between the two arch-enemies, Germany and Russia, surprised and dismayed Paul. What would it mean for the plans to invade the Soviet Union? Natalie urged Paul at this time to leave Germany, perhaps for England or the United States. The English relatives might help. But Paul remained stubbornly persuaded of the strength of the Nazi economy and war machine and the inherent weakness of Stalin and his hold on power. He wanted to be well placed to return to Russia once Bolshevism was defeated – a fact often repeated in our family. He did, however, share his wife's apprehension and at least twice, fearing being caught in a war zone, evacuated his family to relative safety. The first time was in September 1939, when Germany invaded Poland. Paul feared that France would invade from the west, with Frankfurt as one of the targets. As a precaution, Paul took his family to the spa town of Bad Worishofen in southern Germany, in the foothills of the Alps. Depending on how events unfolded, he was close enough to the borders of Switzerland and France to be able to take his family across the border. In France, he could join relatives; in Switzerland, he may have been able to become a legal migrant, since Natalie's grandmother had been a Swiss citizen and, according to Swiss law, Natalie as a granddaughter could claim Swiss citizenship. If these reasons failed to get him out of Germany legally, he could perhaps bribe his family's way into one or the other country. When Britain and France declared war on Germany on 3 September, tense months followed in fear that France would invade across the Rhine into Germany. They didn't and by spring 1940 Paul felt that it was safe to return the family to Frankfurt.

I had not known of the drama of these flights to safety in Bad Worishofen. On the contrary, I used to look enviously at photographs of the family in their idyllic surroundings and was keen to visit. It took until 2001, but finally my brother and I went. While superficial things had changed, the essentials had remained the same. William still remembered his way around the town and surroundings, so we set out to follow the 'spa' route, a walk of several kilometres across open fields, pastures, and through forests. The sun was shining, making it pleasantly warm but also humid. Elderly couples ambled past and disappeared out of view between the trees. Summer light filtered through to the forest floor. At intervals, we came across wading pools where we took off our shoes and socks, rolled up our trousers and waded back and forth through the cold spring water, following instructions given on a nearby notice. A metal railing helped to steady the less sure-footed. Wading in water and the forest air were said to cleanse the lungs, the blood and the body overall.

Encouraged and refreshed by our walk and wading, William and I decided to revisit the *Pension* (guesthouse) where the family had stayed. We were astonished to find that it was still managed by the same people who had done so during the war, nearly fifty years earlier.

'Do you recall the Schlüsser family staying here in 1940?' William half-shouted at the woman over the noise of her vacuum cleaner. She turned it off and thought a moment.

'Yes, I do. A very distinguished man, a professor I think, and a doctor for a wife. Yes, they had four children', she reminisced.

'One of them was me', William eagerly informed her, 'and this was my young brother who came with us on one occasion'. We expected a warm recognition and welcome, but instead she merely nodded.

'Is that so? Yes, I do remember the family, they lived on the first floor, in two rooms with a balcony.' She searched her memory some more but that seemed all she could recall.

'You'll have to excuse me now, I've got to get this done.' With that she switched on her vacuum cleaner and attacked the wall-to-wall carpet again. We said '*Guten Tag*' over the noise and left the building. I was disappointed, as I would have liked to have seen other parts of the building and perhaps encourage other memories in the woman now disappearing around the corner with her vacuum cleaner.

Bad Worishofen's reputation as a spa town was due to a Kneipp, an ordained Catholic priest, who started his career as a healer by offering hydrotherapy to the monks at the Worishofen monastery. His 'water cures' consisted of participants 'purging' their bodies in the clean, wooded environment and in the open fields. Kneipp's methods became fashionable and widely practised. Paul was so taken by Kneipp's method that he took photos of his children standing at Kneipp's statue in the town square and photos showing us doing our water-treading exercises. Paul believed in them strongly and did the exercises himself. His health had been of concern to him since he had recovered from typhus twenty years earlier, and life in Nazi Germany was never without its stress.

Paul hurried the family to Bad Worishofen again in May 1940, when Germany overran Holland and Belgium, forcing France to capitulate. This time I was taken along as a two-year-old. However, Svetlana remained behind in Frankfurt so as not to interrupt her schooling. Father returned to work in Frankfurt once he had settled the family in the *Pension*. I was too young to have memories of this visit, but there are photos which confirm it.

More Lost Fortunes

While Paul had taken his money to England, his siblings in Paris had made a poor decision when they agreed to invest in a leather goods shop in an upmarket location near the *Champs Élysées*. Perhaps they thought that since they came from a merchant family, they would know how to conduct a retail business. They may have chosen leather goods because the Schlüsser firm in St Petersburg had dealt in leather, among other commodities. According to his daughter Beatrice, Nicolai teamed up with an unemployed Cossack he had known and put him in charge of the business. It seems that they expected it to earn an income without any personal input. They were wrong. Business went from bad to worse and finally the Cossack pocketed what was left of any money and disappeared. The venture ended in bankruptcy. Before long, the two brothers became that cliché of Russians in Paris: taxi drivers. Both had previously bought cars and now they turned them into taxis. As foreigners, they were barred by French law from gaining other employment, Nicolai ended his working life as a taxi driver and Vladimir started the ride to his death in his taxi.

Life in Nazi-occupied Paris was no easier. Hitler had accepted French surrender in the same railway carriage in Compiègne where, in 1918, Imperial Germany had been forced to sign its unconditional surrender to France. Hitler felt that Germany's humiliation had now been erased. Paris became an occupied city and Nicolai and Vladimir became drivers for the German Occupation Forces. They may even have shared Paul's optimism and hoped that the Germans would soon liberate their homeland. Their wives, Olga and Zinaida, fraternised with the occupying forces and cousin Beatrice coyly admitted that they acquired German lovers. This would prove dangerous for them and their families, but for now Zinaida used her charm and connections to get Vladimir the job to chauffeur a German officer. On one of the first trips, the officer asked Vladimir:

'Where are you from?'

Vladimir explained and the officer said in surprise:

'But you speak absolutely fluent German! How's that?'

Vladimir gave some details of his German-speaking stepmother and German heritage, as well as life in St Petersburg. He always refused to call it 'Leningrad', the name the Bolsheviks had given it. He also talked of his time spent at Sablino, south of St Petersburg. The officer recognised the value that a man with Vladimir's expertise and local knowledge might have for the German Army, at that time laying siege to Leningrad.

'You should volunteer for duty on the Russian front', he urged Vladimir. 'They pay, you'll be doing something for your country and, who knows, you might be back home sooner than you think.' The officer may have been Zinaida's lover. Did the officer believe it convenient for the husband to be out of the way? Stranger things have happened. Perhaps Vladimir made the decision to escape the compromising situation in which he found himself. He volunteered for the German Army, was given an intensive training course and, with some allowance made for his experience in the Russian Imperial Army, was given a rank. As I learned decades later from the archives of the German War Graves Commission, he was assigned to join the *Ost Bataillon* 667, 16 *Armee* – part of Army Group North – which was blockading Leningrad. Officially, Vladimir became an interpreter. Zinaida may have been pleased to see her husband at a safe distance. Olga's actions and circumstances during this period are unclear, but the negative consequences are known. Nicolai could not bear the humiliation of his wife's sleeping with the enemy. It was one tribulation too many and he took to alcohol.

I saw my uncle Nicolai only once, on my visit to Kostya Bruni in Paris in 1956. Uncle Kostya insisted that I should meet Nicolai. From his home in

Montmartre, we took one of Paris's unique buses with their rear platform, to which the ticket collector and boarding passengers clung precariously while the fares were collected. We found Nicolai in what I took to be a boarding house, but he was in no state to recognise me. Kostya tried to rouse him but, even though it was only mid-morning, Nicolai had already obliterated his worries for the day with alcohol and lay curled up in a foetal position on his bed.

Olga's actions had another unfortunate consequence for their daughter Beatrice. Towards the end of the war, Olga introduced her twenty-year-old daughter to a German officer, a handsome Dutchman who was serving in the German *Luftwaffe*-airforce. No doubt Olga meant well, believing that her daughter would find a suitable protector in him, someone who had the right connections to survive the dangerous times. Beatrice married Robert den Ouden in Paris and the unfortunate, violent consequences of this union reverberated down to at least the third generation. Robert was violent to Beatrice and their three sons.

With the political landscape so confusing for the extended Schlüsser family, I can only imagine what fears Paul felt. It became clear to him that only a German victory over the Bolsheviks could save the family in Germany and France. Whether this was rational, emotional or a combination of the two, or a convenient or inconvenient truth, was now a minor consideration. Fate and Paul's own choices (to the extent that he had them) had placed him into dangerous and compromising circumstances not experienced since the Russian Revolution and Civil War. He had a brother in the German Army, family in occupied France, and his wife's family in Soviet Russia. As well, he and his family were illegally outside Russia with unpredictable status and he was working for a German firm assisting the war effort.

The psychological pressure on Paul and Natalie, I fear, must have been near to unbearable. Paul endlessly turned things over in his mind debating what he could do to avert the dangers that they were facing. It didn't bear thinking about whether Natalie's relatives had survived the invasion and remained alive through the ongoing siege. And there was another tightly held secret in the family: details of Natalie's sister-in-law in Leningrad. It was not revealed to me during mother's lifetime but only came to light later, when my cousin Natasha told me about it. Her mother, Natalie's sister-in-law, *was of Jewish descent*. What would be the consequences if the German authorities discovered this? Michael had married a teacher, also called Olga, in 1937. I don't know when Natalie and Paul learned about this, but whenever, Hitler's nonsensical demand for 'racial purity' of the German race made it dangerous to have Jewish relatives. It was another secret to keep, yet worse was to come.

Increasingly father was concerned with what his daughter was being taught at school. Svetlana had passed the entrance exam to the *Ziehenschule* (an academic state secondary school with accelerated learning opportunities) in the nearby district of Eschersheim. It was a school with a good reputation that prepared students for matriculation to university. However, the National Socialists had introduced their ideology into the curriculum. 'Racial studies' and 'preserving racial inheritance' became part of biology. Paul must have baulked at Hitler's instructions now taught to his daughter: 'Marriage is not an end in itself, it must serve the greater end of preserving and increasing the race and the species. Therein alone lie its significance and its high purpose.' 'Shooting' became part of the sports curriculum, and athletics included 'defence skills'. Studies of 'aerial attack' and 'gas attacks' plus air-raid drills all confirmed that the Nazis were preparing the population for an even wider involvement in war.

Tatjana attended her first day at school in September 1941. Our apartment was in the catchment area of the *Holzhausenschule* (a desirable state primary school). She received the traditional decorated *Schultüte* (school cone – a large paper cone) filled with sweets, games and school materials. Here she recalls being taught by an esteemed teacher, Fräulein Veitel. Thinking of the Nazi-inspired order of Svetlana's first day at school, I asked Tatjana:

'Were you made to sing Nazi songs at your school and to give the Nazi salute?'

'Fräulein Veitel was a very decent person. She may have had instructions to do so, but she never, never made us do any of that.' My sister was adamant about this when I queried her. Why is this important? Perhaps it throws some light on the feelings of a six-year-old, or at least how she remembered that time over half a century later. Perhaps, despite everything, she felt that the drill of 'saluting' Hitler in verse and song was, at the least, artificial. Or had her father encouraged scepticism? Perhaps my sister sensed the decency in her teacher. Fräulein Veitel, in her memory, was someone not readily included among those others accused of the unspeakable atrocities that were revealed later.

Among the family's memories there are few more potent than what happened next. Not long before the German invasion of the Soviet Union, on 22 June 1941, Paul and Natalie received a postcard from Leningrad, written by Olga Shapoval, Natalie's sister-in-law. It was cryptic and the message in Russian unequivocal: 'Please no letters or postcards until we write to you'. That was all. The 'until we write to you' never came. It was the last communication that Natalie ever had with her Russian family. The fine balancing act that both sides of the family had performed for fourteen years had come to an end. But what had caused them to write this postcard? There was no end of speculation and yet all that could be done was to accept the instruction and remain hopeful that a letter would come. None did, and the exact reasons that prompted the postcard will never be known. The German attack on the Soviet Union was largely a surprise to the Russians, yet the timing of the postcard strongly suggests a connection. After all, until the invasion commenced, Germany and the Soviet Union had a non-aggression pact. In very short time, the German war machine rolled over the plains and marshes of Russia, from the Baltic to the Black Sea. Natalie and Paul were devastated when they learned that Hitler planned to raze Leningrad to the ground. I can just imagine mother pacing in our apartment, fighting off tears and despair, thinking of her family while father tried to reassure her. Angry, resentful outbursts could justifiably be expected.

Their worries increased when they learned that Vladimir had been sent to join the 16th Army Group North on the Russian front. He would be attacking his own city and perhaps even fighting his own relatives. It was September

1941, only three months into the invasion. Fighting on the Russian front has become synonymous with the greatest brutality ever inflicted by one army on another. Vladimir's first tour of duty was during the early successes, when all three Army Groups raced towards their objectives. Army Group North reached the periphery of Leningrad. Army Group Centre was on target for Moscow, and Army Group South was fast advancing on the oil-rich Caspian Sea region. Details of each successful battle were widely broadcast and frontline footage filled much of every newsreel shown in cinemas around Germany. Conflicted as he was, Paul felt vindicated in his belief that he would soon return to Russia. As the siege of Leningrad was grimly prolonged, horror stories began to circulate about the population starving to death. There were even reports of cannibalism. Paul and Natalie feared for their family. Vladimir, ironically, may have come close to returning to his city of birth. As a member of Army Group North, he may have been sent to the area he knew best, near Sablino, the idyllic vacation destination where he had spent time with family. German troops had overwhelmed the enemy positions around Sablino and encircled Leningrad. As the Sablino historian Tatyana Slepnova told me, Sablino became a German safe haven behind the front line. She also took me to a memorial site. It was a misty day and the graves were barely visible from a distance. On approaching, it was clear that they were well cared for. Ms Slepnova explained that every year she brought a class of school children to this site to tend the graves and with it teach them about the Great Patriotic War, as it is known to Russians. The approximately 200 graves were those of soldiers who had died fighting during the siege, and she felt it was urgent to inform the young students as there was a danger that the tragedies of World War II were being forgotten. She even expressed support for President Putin, invoking the spirit of Stalin as a World War II war hero, if it meant that the sacrifices of these local soldiers would be remembered.

Vladimir was aged forty-five and, after his first tour of duty in Russia, he was not obliged to return for a second one. But as the winter set in and became more severe, and as Soviet resistance stiffened, reports reached him of the many Russians who were being executed by the Germans, on suspicion of being partisans. His Company had been sent where partisan activity was particularly strong, in the marshes of western Russia, in the area between Novgorod and Kholm. German troops executed villagers on the slightest suspicion of collaborating with the partisans. Many were killed, unable to prove their innocence because they did not speak German and the German soldiers did not speak Russian. Interpreters were needed to save lives. Vladimir felt this strongly, and personally. These were his people, people he knew. He knew how they had suffered under Stalin and that many were ready to support the Germans, who were seen as liberators at first. He wanted to use his Russian and German language skills, and his knowledge of local geography and culture, to prevent unnecessary deaths. Consequently he sought a second tour of duty. Before departing for the Eastern front, shortly before Christmas 1942, he brought his wife Zinaida to Frankfurt to spend a couple of restful days with Paul, Natalie and the family. This was the only occasion when I saw my uncle. I retain a vague image of a man in boots and army greys, but best remember the big Alsatian dog that he had with him. In future, I would agonise over whether he had been a member of the *Einsatzgruppen* (operational groups) who were notorious for using Alsatian dogs to hunt down Jews.

'You know the St Bernard that belongs to the man up the road, the white one with very thick fur?' mother asked rhetorically not long after the war had ended. I don't recall how the subject of uncle Vladimir's dog arose. 'Well, they are often used in the Swiss Alps to carry a miniature barrel of brandy to help injured skiers or people caught in avalanches.' I had to have explained what an avalanche was.

'Why?' one of us asked.

'Well, they can get into places people can't and much faster.'

'Uncle Volodya and his Alsatian did a similar job, only this time on the battlefield in Russia. He was a first-aid officer and used the dog to carry emergency medical supplies when giving first-aid to wounded soldiers.' By referring to Vladimir as a first-aid officer (*Sanitäter*, in German) she set off a misperception which would take me years to correct.

The winter of 1942–43 was bitterly cold. It played a crucial part in the defeat of the Germans at Stalingrad and helped to turn the tide of war in favour of the Soviets. Along the entire Russian front, fighting was brought to a near standstill as snow covered the country so deeply, as one villager in Nivki (where I eventually found Volodya's grave) described it to me, that trucks were driving through tunnels, totally enveloped by ice and snow. The German Army was not equipped to fight in the winter, as Hitler had planned a Russian defeat before the cold set in. Nor did he anticipate the success of Stalin's 'scorched earth' policy, whereby anything which might support the advancing German troops was destroyed: stores of food, whole villages which might provide shelter were burnt down, and bridges, roads and railways were blown up. Vladimir's Company was moved south of Novgorod towards Kholm. He was stationed in Nivki, well behind the front line, where his task was to interrogate local villagers suspected of assisting partisans. By establishing their innocence, he saved many from being executed. Partisans were so effective because they were desperate and ruthless, not bound by rules of conventional warfare, and they used locals who either volunteered or were forced to give them information and provide food and shelter. They did not hesitate to shoot their countrymen if they refused.

In early 1943, Vladimir was with his Company in Nivki, a village of about one hundred people. It is surrounded by dense forest and boggy marshes stretching for kilometres in all directions. Once the village had been occupied, the villagers agreed to work for the Germans as they offered to feed them. The Nivki villagers were hostile to the partisans. Partisans had alienated them when they burnt down their church with one of the villagers – an alleged Nazi collaborator – trapped inside. Stalin, needing to gain the loyalty of the people, had ordered the churches to be reopened at the beginning of the war. For this act and despite the atrocities he had committed against the church, the Orthodox hierarchy designated him 'Defender of the Faith', a title previously held by the Tsar (not unlike the British monarch). The responsibility of life and death decisions over the villagers must have added to Vladimir's stress. Conditions deteriorated as the weather became colder. Partisan attacks increased and German soldiers were driven to shoot on sight.

At the end of January 1943, the unimaginable news reached them that General von Paulus's Sixth Army had surrendered at Stalingrad in indescribable conditions and with horrendous casualties. The Soviets took 90,000 prisoners. Paul, on hearing the news in Frankfurt, believed that this was the beginning of the end for Hitler, as indeed it proved to be. He said so to his ten-year-old son, William, who remembers it clearly. German defeat was now the worst thing that could happen for Paul. Defeat at Stalingrad sealed Europe's fate. It emboldened Stalin and cowed the Western Allies so that the fate of Central and Eastern Europe was left in Stalin's hands. Not only did it consolidate Stalin's tyranny in Russia, but it paved the way for the further spread of that tyranny, at the same time as the Western Allies were forced to compromise on – some would say 'betray' – Poland. In the remote Russian hamlet of Nivki, the dispiriting news and the difficult conditions put a great strain on everyone. On the evening of 1 March, Vladimir was walking from his quarters to the mess when his heart gave way and he collapsed into the snow where he died. Today, the area around Nivki is dotted with war graves – ten, twenty, sometimes fifty of them in single or double rows. Surprising then that Vladimir was not buried in one of these. Instead, I found his grave in the Orthodox cemetery just outside the village. A riddle remains why a 'German' soldier was buried in the village cemetery. Does it show a respect for this man? Had the villagers acknowledged his efforts to save lives? When I spoke with some of the villagers who had memories of those times, I was told that there had been a mutual respect between the villagers and the German troops, perhaps sufficient to earn Vladimir his Orthodox burial in the cemetery. A journalist from the nearby town of Kholm wrote an article about my visit and my search for my uncle's grave and he asked any reader who may have had contact with Vladimir or his Company to contact him. No one came forward. Then, some years later, I chanced across a website which included the report of a columnist in Kholm who recorded that following that same article, a woman had made contact. She recalled an occasion in early 1943 when a German soldier – and she identified him as Dr Schlüsser – had helped her to dress a wound that she had sustained. (Since he assisted her medically, she may have assumed he was a doctor.) However, it also reopened the question about Vladimir's responsibilities in the war. I now believe that he may have combined the roles of interpreter and medical officer. That seems to fit the facts. It had been a persistent story in the family, but with all the disinformation there was a doubt about his role and I thought perhaps that it was being repeated to distract attention from less honourable acts.

One reason given for General von Paulus's defeat at Stalingrad in the winter of 1942–43 was the failure to adequately supply the troops with rations. Göring as chief of the *Luftwaffe* (Air Force) had assured Hitler that his planes would do the job. That was never realistic, and with the depth of winter setting in it became impossible. After von Paulus went against the orders of Hitler and surrendered, the hunt for scapegoats began. One man in Hitler's sights was Paul's close friend Rudolf Heiss. Dr Heiss had been in charge of the Food Technology Institute in Munich which was developing ways of preserving food for military personnel. He devised ways of extending the longevity of rations for troops in remote locations – canned, dried, condensed and concentrated foods which required only water to make a meal. His Institute developed techniques for using waxed cardboard and other treated materials. He had travelled to Argentina before the war to study the operation of a refrigerator ship taking animal carcasses to Europe. He also had some responsibility for distributing the rations in the quantities needed and to the right places. When William and I visited him in his later years, he ascribed his success to his ability as a good manager. He hadn't been the brightest person at his Institute, but he considered himself a good manager. Even as a student, he said, he hadn't the capacity to innovate that his friend Paul had. His effectiveness in the war was due to his hands-on approach to the task as manager, he explained. He flew extensively from one battleground to the other, following the paths of planes, trucks and goods trains to determine where any bottlenecks occurred or where additional resources were needed to expedite the delivery of supplies. I was now able to answer the question that I had been unwilling to ask Dr Heiss directly: whether he had been a member of the *SS*. The answer was 'yes'. But the explanation why made him less sinister. He needed clearance to fly on aeroplanes and commandeer railway goods wagons, trucks and the like. To make his job possible, he was given a senior rank in the *SS* and a uniform to match. Natalie, already wary of the Germans, was alarmed to have a friend who wore the intimidating uniform of the *SS*. She remained wary of him for many years, even though he proved to be a loyal friend even after her husband's death and as confirmed by my brother and my visit. With the defeat at Stalingrad, Heiss was given some of the blame. But was he to blame? In an enquiry that was subsequently held, he made the case to a tribunal that his conduct in supplying the troops at Stalingrad had been responsible and effective within the means at his disposal and the bounds of possibilities. He was exonerated. At the end of the war, the Americans thoroughly investigated his role. He was cleared and remained head of the Institute, which he ran effectively for many years.

At the Nuremberg rally of the Nazi Party on 15 September 1935, Hitler announced laws that classified all Jews as second-class citizens. The 'Nuremberg laws' defined who was a Jew, closed professions to Jews, prohibited them from marrying non-Jews, and declared sexual relations between Jews and non-Jews illegal. Anyone claiming to be 'Aryan' had to prove that there was Aryan blood in the family for three generations. Four grandparents had to be demonstrably Aryan. A spate of letters was sent to establish that relatives living or dead were Aryan. Paul used his 'Continental' typewriter to type questionnaires requesting dates, place and religious affiliation at birth, marriage and death, with documentary proof to confirm Aryan descent. The questions seem innocuous enough. Who were your parents, who were your parents' parents, where was each born, where were they married and buried, and what religion did they practise. Paul collected the answers and they form a convenient record of births, marriages and deaths over three generations. Everyone wanted to prove their racial purity. Was merely participating in the exercise a kind of collaboration, I wondered? Perhaps. Among the letters Paul received was one dated January 1939 and signed '*Oberstfeldmeister* Schlüsser'. No Christian name was given. From the details in the letter, it was clear that he was a relative, a direct descendant from Justus Friedrich Schlüsser. His great-grandfather, he explained in the letter, had gone to St Petersburg to set up an import-export trading company. The letter ended with the ominous salutation 'Heil Hitler'. This alarmed Paul. Even though the sender's rank, *Oberstfeldmeister*, was a modest one in the German labour corps, Paul felt that to have contact with this man could be dangerous, despite the fact that it could potentially help him to confirm his 'Aryan' ancestry. Paul kept the letter without replying. In the 1990s I searched for details of this man through the Red Cross, the German War Graves Commission and the town authorities of Parchim, from where the letter had been sent. I found no trace of him.

In occupied Paris, in the middle of the war, Paul's nephew Oleg Schlüsser completed his secondary schooling. Paul felt obliged to advise the youth on a career he might choose and did so in a letter. I was delighted to receive a copy of the letter from cousin Oleg, written by father in mid-1943. Despite his fear for what might happen in Germany after the defeat at Stalingrad, he wrote that he remained optimistic for the future of the country. In truth, no one could have anticipated that Hitler would choose to see Germany utterly destroyed rather than either to negotiate reasonable terms for peace or perhaps surrender. In his letter to Oleg, in carefully chosen words mindful that the censor would read every one of them, Paul praised tertiary education in Germany and the German manufacturing industry. He urged Oleg to think seriously about relocating to Frankfurt. Paul was aware of the tensions in Oleg's home, with the ambitious mother Olga playing somewhat fancy-free with German officers. This influenced the advice he was giving. Otherwise it is hard to explain why he should suggest that Oleg come to Germany at this critical time, especially as Oleg might have been conscripted into the German Army. On rereading the letter, it struck me that Paul mentions his brother three times and asks Oleg to convey his regards while never mentioning Oleg's mother. It appears that Oleg did not follow his uncle's advice but instead continued his ballet training in Paris, fulfilling his mother's ambitions for him.

Paul received the news of his brother Vladimir's death from Zinaida. She had received a telegram and wrote to her brother-in-law. Presumably for security reasons, the information given to her was incorrect. So as not to identify troop movements, the place of his death was changed, as was the cause of death. In cryptic terms they informed Zinaida that her husband had been shot while securing the Ice Road on Lake Ladoga, east of Leningrad. (The news was published in Russian newspapers in Berlin and Paris, presumably supplied by Zinaida.) Hitler had ordered the encirclement of Leningrad and starving out of the inhabitants. The Ice Road was the only route for the Russians to escape from Leningrad and for the city to be supplied with food and other essentials. Lake Ladoga is one of the biggest lakes in the world. In 2010, I was fortunate to retrace the journey that the evacuees took across the lake and along canals to the Volga River. In winter, the ice on the lake is so strong that it can carry heavy lorries. It was an escape route for many Leningraders while also a supply line for those remaining in the city. Despite heavy aerial bombardment and attacks by ground troops, the size of the lake made it impossible for the Germans to seal the escape route fully and supplies were able to reach the city, saving many Leningraders from starvation. Yuri Artsutanov, the inventor and a family friend, recalls that as a thirteen-year-old he escaped the siege in a truck in that winter of 1942–43. He saw a truck travelling in front of them break through the ice and disappear in minutes. The occupants were able to jump to safety. His own truck veered onto stronger ice and thus completed the journey successfully. Tragically, 600,000 Leningraders starved or froze to death. Natalie feared that her family was among the dead.

After learning of Vladimir's death, Paul invited Zinaida to come to Frankfurt. When she arrived, she was in great distress and unable to stop crying. My sister Tatjana remembers her slumped on a bed, sobbing. Despite everything, Vladimir had been the still point in her life and she was bereft without him. Paul judged that her best chance was to remain in Germany and exercise her rights as a German citizen. As a widow of a serving soldier, she would be eligible for a war widow's pension. Otherwise she might have returned to Paris where she still had relatives and friends. It was a total reversal of fortune from when they lived it up in Paris, without concern for the future.

Paul continued to see the Soviet Union as a failing state. His view was strengthened when he learned of the large number of Soviet soldiers who were defecting to the Germans. General Vlasov, one of Stalin's most brilliant officers had defended Moscow and had had initial success in relieving the siege in the south of Leningrad. But because of poor leadership, other army units could not capitalise on it and the Germans encircled his army and captured it. Learning what he did in captivity, he became disillusioned with Stalin's conduct of the war and his whole army went over to the Germans. In 1944, with Hitler's help, he created the Russian Liberation Army with over 100,000 former Soviet soldiers with which to liberate Russia from the Soviets.

Paul naturally welcomed these events. There were many Russians – captured Soviet soldiers, deserters from the Soviet Army and forced labourers – in camps around Frankfurt. They were transported to work in factories in the city during the day and returned to the camp at night. Once Vlasov's Liberation Army was formed, concerted efforts were made to persuade some of the *Fremdarbeiter* (forced labourers) to join. Few spoke German, so interpreters were used to help them understand the conditions. The interpreters assessed whether their desire to join Vlasov was genuine and had to establish that they were neither spies nor fifth-columnists. The threat of imprisonment in Russia persuaded many to change sides. General Vlasov endorsed a pamphlet, widely distributed on the Eastern front, warning Soviet troops that Stalin would execute all who had been prisoners of war or who had merely lived in territories under German occupation. Either Zinaida discussed these developments with her brother-in-law, or perhaps it was Paul's suggestion that she should become an interpreter in the camps. As I now know, she not only persuaded soldiers to change sides but also reported her interviews to the Gestapo, providing valuable logistical information. But most heinous of all, in the eyes of the Soviets, she persuaded a number of prisoners to spy for the Nazis. She would be harshly judged for these actions.

Whatever success she had, it was all in vain. Germany was inexorably heading for defeat. However, while acknowledging this, Paul could not anticipate that Hitler would see Germany destroyed rather than surrender. In fact, the time for surrender had passed. Hitler did not contemplate it and, anyway, the Western Allies had decided at Casablanca in January 1943 not to accept a negotiated peace; nothing less than the unconditional surrender of Germany and of the other Axis powers, Italy and Japan, was demanded.

Signs of German desperation had been growing. Soon after the Casablanca declaration and the defeat at Stalingrad, on 18 February 1943, Göbbels in a speech to a hand-picked audience in Berlin's *Sportpalast* (stadium) put the question to the people in the arena and the people listening on radio: 'I ask you, do you want total war? If necessary, do you want a war more total and radical than anything that we can even imagine today?' Göbbels was trying to turn the rout at Stalingrad into a rally for greater commitment to victory. The partisan audience shouted 'yes' and with that declaration by the Nazi Propaganda Minister, every man, woman and child became a combatant, making civilians legitimate targets for Allied attacks. (Although the Allies had already been bombing civilian targets – Cologne, for example, in May 1942.) In other words, a condition of total insanity existed from now on. 'Madness' can be defined as taking action without reference to the real world, or experience. Paul and Natalie, together with millions, heard the speech on the radio. They were dismayed at the escalation. Perhaps it was now merely wishful thinking, but they still hoped for the collapse of Soviet Russia. Paul in all likelihood was unaware of the worst German atrocities in the east, but the propaganda about the Katyn Massacres was widespread and it seemed believable that up to 20,000 Polish officers and members of the Polish intellectual and artistic elite had been executed on Stalin's orders. But, what did Paul know of the Wannsee agreement, where the extermination of the Jews was decided, the 'final solution', and of the scale and barbarity of the network of concentration camps in Germany and throughout Central Europe? Was his response the same as that of Joachim Fest's father, a convinced socialist and opponent of Hitler, who, when he heard reports of German massacres in the east, on the BBC, took the reports to be propaganda by the British? As ruthless as Hitler's regime was, this reached new levels of barbarity not credible to men like Joachim Fest, or Paul, I believe. Cousin Marina Makarova, when speaking to me in Heidelberg, said that her family, living in Berlin, had many intelligent, well-informed friends who in no way agreed with Hitler's racist policies. She defined it as an idea belonging to the 'Nazis', thus implying that people who did not belong to the National Socialist movement did not agree with these policies. People in Berlin knew of the atrocities, she asserted. People like her father had access to foreign newspapers and magazines, but she also believed that most people outside Berlin would not have had the same access to information and may have remained largely ignorant of the scale and vehemence of Nazi atrocities. A controversial assertion.

Immediate concerns loomed large. Paul's cousin Alexander Makarov and his family were still living and working in Berlin. Their home in Bielefeld bordered on Charlottenburg, where Paul's stepmother Theresa Vasilievna was also still living, together with her son Raymond. Her daughter Olga had married a musician, a Mr Sternat, and moved away from Berlin. The Makarovs were in the habit of visiting Theresa Vasilievna, as photos attest. On the night of 18 November 1944, some 440 Avro Lancaster bombers attacked Berlin. As it was an overcast night, little damage was done. But the Makarovs, afraid of things to come, wisely fled Berlin the following day. Marina was recalling these events as we lunched in a pleasant Heidelberg restaurant.

'We were lucky', she said in her impeccable English, 'father saw the danger and took us away the next day. Lucky because three days later there was another attack and that time our home was destroyed.' Bielefeld, I later learned, was the location of the headquarters of the *SS* in Berlin. Perhaps that had been the reason for the Allies' targeting this area.

She recounted those events with surprising enthusiasm. Despite her family's dislocation from Russia and experiences of war, she considered that she had had a good life. I reflected, not for the first time, whether we might have had a more fulfilled life had we remained in Germany.

'It did a huge amount of damage', she continued, 'large areas of nearby neighbourhoods were destroyed. That raid almost totally destroyed the Kaiser Wilhelm Memorial Church.' This church is now a well-known Berlin icon that has been retained in its ruined state in the middle of western Berlin as a reminder of the destruction. I was so engrossed in her story that I forgot to ask a vital question about whether she knew what had happened to Paul's stepmother, either in these raids or later.

I had earlier written to the Berlin archives for any records of my step-grandmother in the Berlin telephone directories between the years 1927 and 1945. What I learned surprised me. I believed that there were no other Schlüssers except our immediate family. Apart from the letter signed 'Heil Hitler' by *Oberstfeldmeister* Schlüsser, the name had not appeared in any other records that I had come across. My surprise then was understandable when, in their reply, the archives listed no fewer than eight entries with telephone numbers for 'Schlüsser'. One of those entries was my mother, Natalie Schlüsser, listed as 'Dr Schlüsser'. The title confirmed that her qualifications as a medical practitioner were recognised in Germany. Another entry was that of Theresa Schlüsser. She was listed as a *Rentner*. At first glance, that surprised me as well. I checked my understanding of the word in several dictionaries and found two meanings which could apply. The most common meaning is 'pensioner'. Could it be that Theresa Vasilievna had lost all her money and wealth in the Great Depression? But according to the directory, she remained living in the same apartment as before, which Fred Sevier had described as 'sumptuous'. A second meaning was a 'retiree' who is in receipt of some kind of income, either a state pension or from investments. I chose to take that as describing her circumstances at this time. When I looked at the 1944 entries, I was shocked that all previous Schlüsser entries had vanished. Natalie Schlüsser, of course, lived in Frankfurt by then, but what had happened to the other seven? My first thought was they had all been killed in the bombing raids. Yet it seemed unlikely that all would have met the same fate. Some would certainly have died, but others would surely have been evacuated, I reasoned. What would father have known about the fate of his stepmother and stepbrother? Why were they never mentioned? I did have an envelope with an address in Rudolstadt, Thuringia. It gave me a start and eventually I was able to establish that Theresa Vasilievna had lived there. It had been in East Germany and perhaps that was why she was not mentioned in the family. After the fall of the Berlin Wall and the end of the Cold War, the German Government was determined to honour legitimate claims for properties in Berlin and the former East Germany. I was expecting to identify some investment properties that my step-grandmother may have had. Not for the first time, I embarrassed myself. While laying claim to where she had lived in Berlin, I was promptly informed that the address had been in West Berlin all along! But also that Theresa Vasilievna had not owned the apartment. I was a little more accurate with the Rudolstadt address. Indeed she had lived there but she had not owned the property, something that was confirmed when I applied for the 'restoration of East German property'. It did, however, lead me to discover what had happened to her at the end of her life. I obtained her will. It showed that she had died in Rudolstadt in 1948, having survived the war, but that she was now virtually penniless. There is mention of an unknown man as a beneficiary of what little there was. She may have been in her eighties and in need of assistance. I presumed that this man had been of some help to her.

In 1943, we were caught in the first bombing raid on Frankfurt. 'Bomber' Harris and British Bomber Command had extended their bombing and were targeting civilians. Frankfurt was raided several times that year, the first time on 11 April, causing widespread damage and casualties. From the middle of the year, the bombing was intensified with the British attacking by night and the Americans emboldened to do so by day, unafraid because of the decreasing effectiveness of the German anti-aircraft guns. Besides the bomb shelters in every apartment building, Hitler had had public bomb shelters built at strategic locations throughout Frankfurt. It was law that on the sounding of an air-raid siren, everyone had to seek safety in a bomb shelter. If you were away from home, you were to find the nearest public one. Volunteer wardens fined anyone caught in the streets. Our upstairs neighbour, Herr Waggeg, was such an air-raid warden. We had all taken part in practice drills in anticipation of air raids, but now we were to experience the reality. On that first occasion, the sirens started to wail at about 9.30 in the evening, Natalie woke us up and hurriedly took us, still in our nightdresses, down into the cellar, a part of which was fortified as a bomb shelter. Father had not yet returned from work. There she put a rubber gas mask on each of us, instructing us to breathe through the snout-like metal filter. It was both uncomfortable and frightening. You felt that you could suffocate, and you sweated profusely. The tight fit around the cheeks soon began to hurt as we sat side by side on a wooden bench, waiting. Apart from the Waggeg family, the other occupants were our neighbours in the first-floor apartment, Herr Korselt and his wife, who feared for their florist shop in the centre of the city. When everyone had reached the cellar, the blast proof-door – similar to the door of a bank vault – was pushed shut and secured with two iron bars. Father was not with us, so Natalie had tried to delay this moment, as she was convinced that father was riding his bicycle back from work and would reach the house at any moment. The drone of a massive number of airplanes came closer, while the air-raid sirens continued to wail. As the first bombs began to fall and explode, Natalie tried not to panic at the thought of where her husband might be. His firm was located among industrial plants and factories in the west, where the bombs were now falling. It became stifling in our tightly sealed bunker. No one spoke. So massive was the bombardment that, despite the sealed door, the noise of the exploding bombs could be clearly heard. As they hit their targets, they seemed to come closer. The noise became more intense as the anti-aircraft guns targeted the bombers caught in their searchlights. Then the tension in the bunker eased a little as it appeared that the raiders were targeting other parts of Frankfurt, the industrial areas of Bockenheim and the satellite city of Hoechst. The gas masks were becoming increasingly uncomfortable and, as the adults removed theirs, mother felt that it was safe to remove ours, while the sound of planes receded. Now that the immediate danger had passed, mother became anxious again. Where was father? Had he returned and not been able to get into the shelter? She wanted to leave the cellar urgently to look for him. Sensing our fear, she persuaded Herr Waggeg to remove the levers and open the door. The raid had lasted less than half an hour. We made our way past the laundry, the store of potatoes, the bicycle rack and up the concrete steps to the front door. Glass windows and doors were intact, but the result of the bombing was visible through the glass door.

A bright yellow and red light lit the frosted glass. When mother opened the door, it seemed like the door to hell had been opened: the whole horizon was ablaze as searchlights were vainly seeking to pinpoint the planes disappearing in the darkness. It was at once an awe-inspiring spectacle, like watching giant fireworks, and an inferno seemingly capable of engulfing us all. We gasped at the sight. It seemed surreal. It couldn't be happening. Breaking regulations, as the all-clear hadn't yet sounded, mother went out into the street and looked up and down for signs of father. The gas streetlights had all been turned off, so only the fires and searchlights illuminated the scene. There was no sign of father. The drone of planes had gone, to be replaced by an eerie silence while the horizon continued to blaze. Would there be a second wave of attack? At last, the all-clear siren was sounded. Mother put us back to bed. She kept reassuring us that father would be all right. My cot – I was just four then – was in my parents' bedroom, while the other three shared the second bedroom. Physically and emotionally exhausted, we fell asleep quickly.

What really happened to father on that night has often been recalled. Twenty minutes after the all-clear had been sounded, father rode up on his bicycle. He was deathly pale. He had had a premonition, he told Natalie, not to seek refuge in the nearest public shelter but to ride on to the next one, further from his work. It was a life-saving decision. The shelter he had avoided received a direct hit that night, resulting in many casualties. Paul may not have been counting, but I believe he lost the fourth of his nine lives that night.

The bombing of Frankfurt continued, by October totally destroying the medieval centre of the city. On each occasion when the sirens sounded at night (the first daylight bombing occurred on 25 July), we would go down into the bomb shelter, and after a while it became almost routine. But when over that summer the bombing became more intense, the local *Gauleiter* (Nazi district governor), Jakob Sprenger, ordered the evacuation of all women and children. In August, every family was given instructions as to where they would be evacuated. Once at the destination, it was up to the family to negotiate with villagers – who were obliged by law to accept evacuees – the terms and conditions for board.

With my cot strung on the rear pack rack of his Mercedes, our neighbour Herr Korselt took the family to the central railway station. Archival photos show the railway station building decorated with swastikas and the banner, '*Ein Volk, ein Reich, ein Führer*'. I have no memory of this. The large glass and steel structure became the target for bombing raids when every pane of glass would be shattered. (I was astonished when I saw the restored station, its roof exactly as it had been before the bombings, on a visit years later.) Inside the station, the steam and smoke from numerous engines arriving and departing turned the air into a cauldron, the noise of the locomotives was deafening, and chaotic, apparently random activity was taking place everywhere. People had to shout above the din to make themselves heard. It was a relief when we found a compartment with seats for us all. The shriek of whistles seemed to be continuous, as were the slamming of closing compartment doors. Eventually, our conductor waved his red flag from the rear of the train to the engine driver and we slowly moved off. It was a relief to escape the inferno of people and machines. The experience I had then as a four-year-old has never left me. The overcrowded train headed towards the city of Giessen, sixty kilometres northeast of Frankfurt and an important railway junction. Progress was interrupted several times while the train was shunted onto a spur line, to give trains carrying military equipment priority. From Giessen, the train travelled along a branch line due east in the direction of Fulda. After a while and quite suddenly, without warning, it stopped in the middle of a field. No station in sight anywhere. We were told that this was our destination. Beyond yellow wheat fields we could see the village of Harbach, its church tower rising from the centre. It was a village of only a few hundred people, mostly small landholders, peasant farmers. We scrambled for our rucksacks, cases, bags, and bed sheets tied together to carry bedding, and we trudged across the field to the village. With four children in the family, it was difficult to find anyone who could accommodate us. Father knocked at a number of doors and explained our circumstances. Nothing suitable could be arranged. So father settled for temporary accommodation until something permanent could be found. The family was separated and put up in two homes, at either end of the main street. The next day, father left to go in search of an alternative host family. Three days later, we were on a train again, going down the Lumda Valley to the village of Allendorf. The name 'Allendorf' loosely translates as 'Everyman's Village'. It was certainly typical, and our experience was similar to that of many in all parts of Germany. Despite the threatening circumstances that had brought us to Allendorf and the continuing war, in many ways it turned out to be an idyllic time.

There was no one to meet us at Allendorf Station. Harvesting had begun. Father went to the address where he had negotiated for us to stay. But the owner, the local doctor, had for some reason changed his mind, though he had not abandoned us. He had arranged for us to be accommodated with a nearby farmer at an address I clearly remember: 18 *Bahnhofstrasse*. Father returned to the station, seated on the front of a wooden wagon drawn by two cows, next to the youngest son of our host family, Heinrich, holding the reins. The Damm family had agreed to host us and they became lifelong friends. Herr Damm, the head of the household, had sent his son Heini (short for Heinrich, or Henry) to collect us with our luggage, including my white baby cot, the short distance from the station. Harvesting could not be interrupted and the other family members – two daughters, father and mother – were working in the fields.

We were settled in two upstairs rooms with windows opening to the street. The other two upstairs bedrooms were those of Heini and his older sister Gretel (short for Margarete). Mother, William and I occupied one room, and Svetlana and Tatjana the other. Gretel later recalled with delight that when she returned from the fields that day, she saw me standing in the gateway asking her: 'Have you come to live here too?' She burst out laughing and said, 'Yes'. The day was sunny, the countryside peaceful, there were no signs of war. And yet it was on everyone's mind. The Damm family's eldest son, Friedrich, had recently gone missing, presumed killed. He had been conscripted into the army and sent to the Russian front. (Conscription for males aged nineteen years and over had been mandatory since 1935.) Only after the war did they learn that he had been shot and buried near the Budapest airfield, in Hungary, though the location of his grave has never been established. Perhaps it was the loss of the son and worker on the farm that influenced Herr Damm to agree to host us.

Mother, Svetlana and William were of an age where they could be very useful on the farm. Young as we were, Tatjana and I also did our bit.

Father bade us farewell and returned to his work at Schanzenbach the next day.

An Idyll in the Sun

The next two years were mostly bliss. 'We had a good war', brother William often observed, although that was only partly true. On such occasions he forgot about the aerial strafing of his train to school, the bombing of Allendorf, the drunken Russian prisoners of war (at least one of whom died following an alcohol-driven binge), the political ebb and flow in the village. Mother carefully navigated our stay for the next two years with her willingness to work hard and cooperatively, with her skills, her charm and her intelligence.

Despite the war being ever present, life in the country remained measured and calm because rural life had its established rhythm determined by the seasons, providing meaningful work for young and old, and a community with a long-established culture of mutual assistance and cooperation. Stalin ripped the heart out of the Russian rural population when he took away their land and collectivised agriculture. The workers on these farms became alienated, often had little local knowledge of the land or farming practices. In Allendorf, conservative farming methods had been refined over generations and productivity increased even with minimal mechanisation. Animal power and steam engines were the norm, although electricity had been brought to the village.

The winters were dark and cold with ample snow; the summers were sunny, warm and often balmy. Each change of season was dramatic and picturesque, marked by special events in nature and by changing routines in the village and on the land. In spring, as soon as the frosts were over, the ploughing commenced. The two cows that the Damms owned, Bella and Pfanni, were harnessed to the *Leiterwagen* (wooden wagon), loaded with a plough and taken to the hectare-sized strip on one side or the other of the village. (Some years later, I learned of the 'three-field system' of medieval English agriculture and recognised the similarities.) The cows were then harnessed to the plough. With great patience and periodic rest, during which they chewed the cud, the two cows went up and down, turning over the soil. Herr Damm knew his animals and had extraordinary skill and experience to work the plough accurately and efficiently. At the end of each furrow, he turned the animals around and then lifted the plough by its two handles to turn the blade over. In this way, he could go back and forth with the soil being broken on the same side. The cows then hauled a cartload of fertiliser – cow dung that had been maturing in the farmyard. Every day I helped with mucking out the stables, carting the straw heavy with cow dung to the dung heap. I helped to turn the dung heap to assist fermentation and, by the middle of spring, the manure was cured. It was spread over the field and allowed to lie fallow for a short period. Then the manure was worked into the soil and sowing could begin. Like a Breughel painting, Herr Damm strapped a hessian bag across his chest and scattered handfuls of wheat, oats or rye seeds. I learned that oats were the earliest crop, then wheat and last of all barley and rye. Another pass with the hoe and then it was left to nature. Cereal crops were sown first, potatoes were planted later and also beet for stock fodder and a small area of sugar beet. As the crops grew, cornflowers and poppies dotted them, beautifully captured by so many painters. Crop yields were average in this area and blights, pests and strong winds were always a threat to a good harvest. Herr Damm used every opportunity to teach me and pointed out that a flattened crop was difficult to harvest. Wind could flatten any cereal crop, but especially oats and wheat. Valuable labour would then be needed to scythe the crop by hand, sometimes with a sickle if the crop was bent to the ground. Working the fields engendered respect for the farmer and his work and to this day I will not walk on even the smallest part of a crop.

In late summer, harvesting began. Herr Damm, one of the more prosperous farmers in the village, owned his own harvester. It was a simple device consisting of two horizontal blades, one above the other, moving back and forth as the wheels turned, cutting the plant at the base, a large metal comb with movable teeth. As Herr Damm cut the crop, the women followed and scooped up bundles heavy with grain. My task was to hand out a length of string for them to tie their armful into a bundle. Next, we stacked the bundles into tent-like shapes known as 'stooks'. After drying for a period, they were pitchforked onto a cart and taken to the farmyard. Herr Damm was a progressive farmer. He had installed electrically driven belts and pulleys in the large three-storey barn. They powered hoists, cutters, saws and other tools. He did his own repairs, shoed the cows and butchered the pigs. The threshing machine belonged to the village. The village council, with Herr Damm as its rotating chair, drew up a timetable allocating the threshing machine to each farmer for the number of days required. When his turn came, the machine was brought into Herr Damm's barn and his crop was threshed over several days. Sacks of cereals were filled at one end, while straw emerged at the other. The straw was bundled up again and hoisted up a level using the electric pulley. From there, it was pitched manually several more levels to be stored on the top level of the barn until needed as bedding for the animals. Everything had more than one use and nothing was wasted. Herr Damm, like the other village farmers, practised largely organic farming while not eschewing artificial fertilisers. Autumn was the time to slaughter a pig, make jam and harvest the honeycombs, prepare silage for winter feed and pick apples and pears. The village orchard was on the northern, sunnier slope of the valley. The village council allocated each household an apple tree and half a pear tree, the fruit of which was to be picked by the family. Winter meant time to repair equipment, re-shoe the cows, and turn the hay in the barn to prevent mould. Butchering was done on site and the sausage and meat stored in the permanently cool cellar. The blood was used to make 'blood sausage'. The chickens needed tending, a calf would be born and myriad other jobs undertaken the year round.

Every two months, it was the family's turn to use the baking ovens. The grain was milled at the nearby water mill on the Lumda River, mixed and kneaded into dough and shaped into round loaves. They were placed on wooden planks, each plank with a dozen loaves of rye, barley or wheat bread, and skilfully balanced on the head to be taken a kilometre to the communal bakery. The bread was wholemeal, with milling kept to a minimum. Mushrooms were picked in spring and autumn and beechnuts collected in the forest to be pressed into cooking oil. Chicken feathers filled pillows and eiderdowns, and cowhides were sewn into work aprons.

My sisters and brother went to school six half-days a week, with the school day finishing at around 2 p.m. Much of the rest of the time they helped on the farm. The Damms had to supply a daily quota of milk and produced quantities of grain, potatoes and beet for sale. Farm and domestic activities slowed as winter approached. When the river froze over, we children could go skating, although it could be dangerous if you misjudged the thickness of the ice and broke through into the water. Fatalities occurred when someone – often a child – drowned in the icy water. The snow-covered hill slopes were perfect for tobogganing, either solo or as a group with a plank strapped between two toboggans. It could fit six or more people and come down the hill at speed, unless it tipped over before reaching the bottom, with much laughter. Christmas was celebrated in the traditional German way with a Christmas tree, carol singing and the ceremony of opening presents. The Damms regularly attended Sunday service at the Lutheran church. Spring arrived when the cherry trees began to flower and the annual cycle began again. The predictability produced a calm purposefulness in the life of the villager. Awareness that your wellbeing was directly related to the work and effort you exerted was both a spur and cause for satisfaction. It was a life lived largely in harmony with nature and strengthened thereby.

Eclipsed

I lived through the eight seasons I spent in Allendorf in a dreamlike state interrupted by the occasional nightmare. Country life and sharing dangers created bonds between people. Even the fiercest war in history could not for long disrupt the work, or the bonds of the village community. Despite some significant differences of opinion among villagers about Hitler and the Nazi regime, little changed in the village during those years. Nature continued to dictate the pace of life and the decisions taken.

But there was no escaping the folly of humans in the larger world. Natalie was under the greatest pressure. She and Herr Damm listened regularly to the midday radio news reports with details of enemy attacks, lists of casualties and damage inflicted. She knew that the reports were censored and selective, but she relaxed a little when Frankfurt or Leningrad was not mentioned. Inevitably, as German defeat loomed, the war came closer to Allendorf. There was the forced landing of a damaged German Junker fighter plane – the *Stuka*, as it was known – when Natalie was called to help the pilot who had sustained severe head injuries during the crash landing. Apparently, Allied planes targeting it from above had forced the fighter plane down. With regular Allied air attacks against trains, each train now had an anti-aircraft gun carriage coupled to its head and tail. For protection against aerial attack, all the villagers dug trenches in the oak forest up the slope beyond the railway line. Every time there was a threat, we ran to hide in these trenches. On some occasions we were caught out in the fields when we heard a plane approaching and we all ran for our lives without waiting to identify the plane as friend or foe. One night, the night sky in the west lit up as so-called 'Christmas trees' – flares to light up potential targets – appeared. It was an ominous light show targeting the railway junction at Giessen. Heavy bombers soon followed. From twenty kilometres away, we watched the conflagration in silence as another bomb exploded. On that still night we heard no sound because of the direction the wind was blowing from the distant action, but the severity of the bombing was clear. Just as the sky was lit at its brightest, mother became aware of a bicyclist coming up behind the watching crowd. Who might it be? To her horror, she realised that it was her husband. He was deathly pale, having exerted himself riding his bicycle to escape the bombing. The road from Frankfurt passed near Giessen and he hadn't heard the warning. He reached the group and as much in relief as in exhaustion let his bicycle fall to the ground, and himself into the supporting arms of his wife. She half-carried, half-led Paul into the house and into bed. That night, in escaping the bombing of Giessen, he had lost the fifth of his nine lives.

Father told mother about the worsening conditions in Frankfurt. Our apartment building at 29 *Fallerslebenstrasse* had been hit and the roof blown off, and the attic and top floor severely damaged. A bomb had struck a few metres from the building, creating a ten-metre crater, five metres deep. Every window and glass door had been shattered. The pilot had dropped his load aiming for the apartments, and a series of craters in line every fifty metres was evidence of his intention. Down the road, the U-shaped apartment building known as the *Glaspalast* (glass palace) had been hit, with a large section destroyed and not a pane of glass remaining intact in the entire building. Deep *Bombentrichter* (bomb craters) pockmarked the district.

Paul, as a condition of not being interned, reported to the Dornbusch police station, *Polizei Revier* 13, twice a week, thus he was kept under constant surveillance. Officially, he was prohibited from leaving the city. He eased Natalie's concern by assuring her that his employers, Schanzenbach, needed his skills and considered him essential to the war effort.

The war was coming closer. Gretel Damm, the 19-year-old daughter, was called up as a nurse to join the German troops who were now defending

Budapest, a long retreat from the front in Russia a year earlier. Meanwhile her sister Kathie was nursing in a hospital in Wurzburg, north of Allendorf. Decades later, she told me of that February day in 1945 when swarms of planes passed overhead. She later learned that they were Allied planes on their mission to bomb Dresden, where the city was enveloped in a fireball in which over 20,000 people died.

Allendorf itself became the target for a direct aerial attack. The villagers had dealt with a pilot who had bailed out of a crashing fighter plane, suspected spies who parachuted into the area and suspected agents who came to the village. They had dealt with the crash of an American Liberty bomber on the northern ridge of the valley. On that occasion the whole village, adults and children alike, walked silently up the hill into the forest, stared in horror at the body parts hanging from the fir trees, and then equally as silently moved back through the orchard down the valley, which was, as if to mock everything, in its full spring splendour: fruit trees flowering, meadows bright green, the clean spring sunshine creating deep shadows.

Mother and Herr Damm listening to the midday radio report heard Hitler announce on 16 October 1944 that all able-bodied men between the ages of sixteen and sixty were to register to join the Home Guard. Paul was forty-three. He had escaped serving in the Red Army during the Civil War, but Hitler was now desperate for manpower. Would they force him to join? In the event, he wasn't called up. Why? Probably because of his work at Schanzenbach.

On several occasions, the village was showered with aluminium strips by high-flying airplanes, which floated to earth long after the sound of the plane had disappeared. They were a pretty sight as they glinted in the sun on the way down. We were strictly forbidden to touch these, having been told that they were poisoned. We didn't have to be told twice. But the truth was that the British had discovered they could jam German radar by dropping these aluminium strips, making it impossible for the Germans to locate enemy aircraft with any precision. Allied aircraft now had more accurate targets while being able to calculate their own position more precisely as well.

Mother once saved us from a personal attack. The villagers had learned to deal with the Russian *Zwangsarbeiter* (forced labourers, of whom there were about three million in Germany) who were camped several kilometres east of the village and, at intervals, became drunk and unruly. On one occasion, a group burst in on us during our evening meal in the basement kitchen. They were drunk and demanded something. Only the women and children were at home. Mother kept her nerve and addressed them in Russian. Immediately the tension eased. She told Frau Damm what they were after and she gladly ladled milk from the large pail into the metal canister they had brought. After a few more minutes of Russian conversation, they left. Mother had recognised them as illiterate villagers and had put them at ease.

The prisoners were marched daily from their camp to and from the one factory in the village, a short distance from the Damm farmstead, east of the railway station. A spur rail track led to it. It was generally believed that the factory manufactured rope and twine. Near the end of the war, while the men in the family were working in the fields and my sisters and brother were at school, Frau Damm, mother and I heard the drone of an approaching bomber in the distance. We had become familiar with planes passing overhead and expected that it would also pass. But the sound grew louder and we became apprehensive as the plane seemed to head for the village. The noise increased moment by moment as the aircraft swooped low over the village. Then we heard exploding bombs coming nearer. First one explosion, then a second one, and a third one – each one closer. Frau Damm shouted 'Get down!' and we dropped to the stone floor, face down. It all happened in an instant as the plane passed so low that it felt like it would take the roof with it. The noise of the plane was deafening, followed by another bomb blast, quickly followed by yet another one. The blast felt so near that it could have hit our house. Was it a lone, rogue bomber or were there others? Lying on the floor, we listened for other planes before anyone dared to move. Frau Damm got up and opened the door to the yard but could see no damage there. Then when she looked up into the sky, she saw a huge plume of black smoke. Mother looked through the basement window. Momentarily stunned, we didn't know what had happened or what to do next. The plume of black smoke was quickly getting bigger, filling my vision of the sky. Then an acrid smell reached us. Rubber, rope, synthetics – all were in flames, creating the stench. There was no chance to put the flames out. The factory quickly burnt to the ground. Decades later, I learned that the factory had indeed been the target. The plane had been guided there by a ham radio operator in the village, assisted by two French forced labourers! The partisans remained undiscovered until after the war.

Frau Damm ran out into the street and up the *Bahnhofstrasse*, driven by a fear that something awful had happened to her parents and cousin living up the road. She reached their house to see her father dead in the middle of the cobblestone farmyard, a dead cow beside him. A direct hit on the double-storey barn had killed them instantly and left a crater metres deep. Her father had become curious about the approaching plane and left the basement kitchen, where he would have been safe, to see what was happening. Then the bomb had exploded on impact, the blast killing him.

Some good came from the bombing. When it was safe to do so, everyone in the village descended on the debris scouring the burnt-out factory for remnants of canvas and string – valuable items when such things had become unavailable. They were put to good use, lasting until well after the end of the war. Mother sewed some of the canvas into a rucksack for Svetlana. She would carry it on her return to Frankfurt and it stayed in the family for many years.

As father and mother saw that the defeat of Nazi Germany was inevitable, their hope of returning to Russia changed to a fear of being captured by Soviet Forces advancing into Germany. By early spring 1945, it was clear to most that Germany's defeat was imminent. There was talk of Hitler's 'secret weapon' but this was merely bravado. Somewhere in my own jumbled memory and understanding of what war was about, I can remember Herr Damm forcefully exclaiming:

'Our *Führer* has his secret weapon. Just wait!'

This statement made me believe that Herr Damm had been a keen supporter of Hitler at that time, but I was corrected later by his son who asserted that he had been a Socialist all his life. Herr Damm's comment may well have been intended as ironic, which my young mind couldn't understand. William recalls being told about the V1 and V2 – the *Vergeltungswaffe* (vengeance weapon) – by his teacher. He and his friends accepted their teacher's attitudes to the war and brought them home. The teacher was under pressure to follow Party instructions and lift morale by passing on only good news. I also saw what I believe were V2 rockets. Someone must have pointed them out to me, though we were used to scanning the sky for aircraft. They were travelling high across the sky from east to west and, at this late stage of the war, were possibly aimed at Allied troops near Remagen. They were eerie as there was no sound and they were visible only by the vapour trail they created.

Attitudes and perceptions were contradictory, and understandably so at this time when every family had lost someone in the fighting, and when most people had compromised themselves to some extent by accepting and supporting Hitler's promises. Yet, I believe that most people in the village at the time did not know of the genocide which had been perpetrated in their name.

The low point of the war for us wasn't a bombing attack or occupation by the Allied Forces. It came on a spring day in mid-March 1945, a few weeks before Germany's surrender. We were working in the fields when an unfamiliar sound came from up the valley to the east of the village. At first faint, it steadily grew in volume. It was coming from the highway that ran through Allendorf from Fulda to Giessen. I knew nothing of what was happening but Herr Damm and mother may have heard something on the radio. They put down their tools, left their animals tethered in the field and went down to the side of the road, as did the rest of us. What we saw was the sorriest sight. As far as we could see men, women and children were not walking but dragging themselves along the road. They were shabbily dressed. Some were helping the injured or exhausted, while others were pulling handcarts carrying an old or frail person. Some were pushing bicycles, their metal wheels without tyres, loaded with their meagre belongings. The only sound came from the shuffling of feet, the crunching of cartwheels on bitumen and the metal rims of the bicycles. We looked at them but they did not look at us. No one spoke. No one cried. Utter despondency written on the faces of those fleeing and those looking on. The exhausted refugees, many of them German settlers persecuted by the Soviets, were heading West desperate to reach behind American line before the Russians captured them. They appeared leaderless and yet they seemed to know where they were going. When we returned to the fields, dusk was approaching, remnants, stragglers of refugees continued trudging through Allendorf.

How do you prepare for the coming of an invader, perhaps a vengeful one? In Allendorf, they hid their food supply and their valuables. Despite wall posters threatening that deserters would be shot and urging resistance, there was no appetite left for war. Days before the US troops took over, Herr Damm loaded the wagon with bags of potatoes, tinned food and smoked meat wrapped in hessian, and took his team of cows to the edge of the forest where the makeshift bomb shelter trenches were. He buried the supplies and returned to the farmhouse. Frau Damm and mother looked for a place to bury their few valuables – rings, pearls, silver- and gold-plated cutlery and serving dishes. They chose the small orchard at the back of the high barn. Naively, they thought that because it could only be accessed through an obscure wooden side gate, the soldiers might not discover it. Mother kept a few personal valuables – her rings, earrings and a few precious trinkets – in her purse, also naively thinking that she would not be searched.

'How silly can you be!' she exclaimed when telling me about it in her video interview.

Something close to panic now set in. With defeat inevitable, the instinct for self-preservation became paramount.

'*Frau Doktor*', said Herr Damm as he addressed my mother, as always by her title, 'time to clear things out'. He had agreed with her that it was dangerous to keep anything which might suggest support for Hitler. First they turned bedsheets into white flags of surrender and hung them out of upstairs windows. Soon one was hanging from every house. All swastikas disappeared from the flagpoles in the village square and along the streets. They removed all Nazi insignia and any references to Hitler in books and pictures. Photos of Hitler were destroyed. Books were purged of any pages referring to Nazism, newspapers burnt.

Work in the fields could not wait and, despite the apprehension of what might happen, farm work continued. Two days later, the spring sounds of insects and birdsong were replaced by a jarring noise coming from the southern hills. Even I had learned to identify the sound of tank tracks, which were now coming from the *Autobahn* (motorway) just over the horizon. The rattle of chains on concrete came from beyond the village of Windeck and was rapidly coming nearer. Mother addressed all us children.

'The Americans are coming', she said. There was a note of relief in her voice as she said 'Americans'.

A history of Allendorf published after the war pinpoints the date as being the morning of 29 March 1945. The US Army was advancing and the clatter of men and machines seemed endless. How many tanks could there be? General Patton's Army after occupying Frankfurt was moving northeast, meeting only light resistance. From there they would link up with the Russian troops on the Elbe River. Would they attack Allendorf or bypass it? We didn't have long to wait for the answer. Another column of tanks could already be heard coming up the valley from the direction of Giessen. This is what it is like to experience defeat. Everyone hurried home, fearing for their life and property. Several tanks fired shots from around the slopes of the valley, aiming to cow the population, not to inflict casualties or damage. It was their way of warning the villagers not to resist. And they didn't.

Mother was frightened but relieved that the approaching tanks bore white stars, not red stars, on a khaki green background, identifiably American. But these were young men in a war, and she had a daughter of sixteen to protect. As they drew nearer, she could see black soldiers manning tanks. Mother was not a racist but Nazi propaganda had been relentless. It had described in graphic detail what would happen if a foreign army invaded and what black soldiers might do. The propaganda referred to them as 'Moroccans', I recall in my jumbled memory, with the implication that they were somehow worse than black US troops. We had gone back to the farmyard. It was now around midday. Heini wanted to protect me and kept me close by his side as he and I tried to look unperturbed, turning the dung heap in the farmyard. Then the farmyard gates opened and an enormous, towering Sherman tank rolled into the yard, the huge barrel of its gun pointing directly at us. We were literally like rabbits caught in a headlight, totally petrified, unable to move. The tank kept rolling and if it maintained its path was sure to crush us. Then it stopped. That seemed to release us from our paralysis and we ducked around the side of the tank into the basement kitchen of the house. The tank crew climbed out of the turret and one asked whether anyone spoke English. When Svetlana said that she had learned some at school, he negotiated with her. Herr Damm and the other men of the village had been ordered to assemble on the village square to be interrogated and given instructions. There they would have answered questions about weapons, valuables, stores of food and attitudes to the Nazi Party.

Back at the house, as mother recalled it, she was ordered to lead the lieutenant in charge through each room to establish that no one was in hiding and that there were no weapons, booby traps, or even a desperate ambush.

'I was so silly', mother recalled, astonishingly light-hearted about her memories after all this time. 'When we got to our room, there was my handbag lying on the bed. And of course the lieutenant immediately emptied it out. There were my rings and other valuables ready for the taking.'

Mother never saw her jewellery again. It was fair war booty, but the incident dogged her for the rest of her life. In her mind, as she grew older, she couldn't accept that she had made such an obvious mistake. The memory played tricks with her and months before her death she had the delusion that it was the Damm daughter Kathie who had taken the jewellery, not the American lieutenant. When I visited Kathie in Giessen, to talk to her about these times and particularly this incident, she said:

'Your mother was so upset! There were things from her mother and things sentimentally so valuable she wasn't concerned with what they cost. I felt so upset for her. I could really understand your mother's pain', she repeated several times.

Mother, when in hospital for a check-up in the last year of her life, suffered from paranoia provoked by this episode. At four in the morning, I got a phone call from the hospital:

'Mr Schlusser, can you please have a word with your mother? She is walking up and down the ward disturbing other patients claiming that she is being poisoned.' I agreed to speak to her and they brought her to the phone.

'Mother, Kathie is in Giessen, in Germany. Why would she want to come all that way to poison you?' I tried to reason with her.

'I have a letter where she threatens to poison me. You know she is the one who stole my valuables!'

'No, mother, she didn't. That's all nonsense.' I was becoming short with her because of her irrationality. I managed to calm her down and she agreed to go back to bed. But an hour later, I was wakened by another phone call.

'You are going to have to take her away. She is becoming totally unmanageable.'

On returning home, she scoured her house for the letter she believed she had received in which Kathie threatened to poison her. I kept challenging her delusion and in exasperation even accused her of not listening to me because I was her youngest son. I hadn't had much sleep and was exhausted. After several hours of searching, she came and sat next to me and said:

'What is happening to me, Kooka [my childhood name]? Of course there is no such letter.'

We continued to talk about it and eventually she agreed to return to the hospital.

In Allendorf at war's end, after the house had been declared secure for US personnel, we were ordered to leave everything behind. Tatjana and I found a bed with the neighbouring farmer while the others found accommodation elsewhere. The tank crew stayed in the farmhouse for three nights, took what they needed by way of food and drink, and moved on. There was no violence on either side. The villagers were too traumatised to offer resistance and the troops were well disciplined; no one came to any harm. A month later, on 30

April, Hitler committed suicide in Berlin and the unconditional surrender of Germany followed nine days later.

What would happen now? What could follow in the wake of perhaps the fiercest war in human history? How would mother and father survive post-war Germany? Father was in occupied Frankfurt and mother with the four children a hundred kilometres away. What would their status be in an Occupied Germany, as defectors from Soviet Russia, without German citizenship? What had happened to mother's family in Leningrad? How would any of the family be treated whether in Germany, Russia or France? What agreements had been made among the Allies about what to do with them and the estimated sixteen million homeless and displaced persons? Where could they go? Where might they be taken?

Left

Natalie and Paul, checking their location on one of their many hikes through Germany, 1927

Below

Jour fixe at the home of Paul's stepmother, Theresa Vasilievna, left on the couch with Mrs Makarova senior, Paul's step-brother Raimund (left) and step-sister Olga (bottom right), Mr Makarov (right), and Mrs Makarova (bottom left), c.1927

Paul photographs 1 May 1933 parade, Karlsruhe. Hitler is creating his *Volksgemeinde* and *Volksgenossen* (national community and comrades) to eradicate class and regional identities

Zinaida's mother (extreme right) and brother (extreme left) are with her. How did that happen? Nadya (seated left), Vladimir (on floor) with Zinaida behind him, Olga and Nicolai (rear), Anna Bruni seated behind husband Konstantin on floor

An attentive crowd at a graduation at the Karlsruhe Institute of Technology

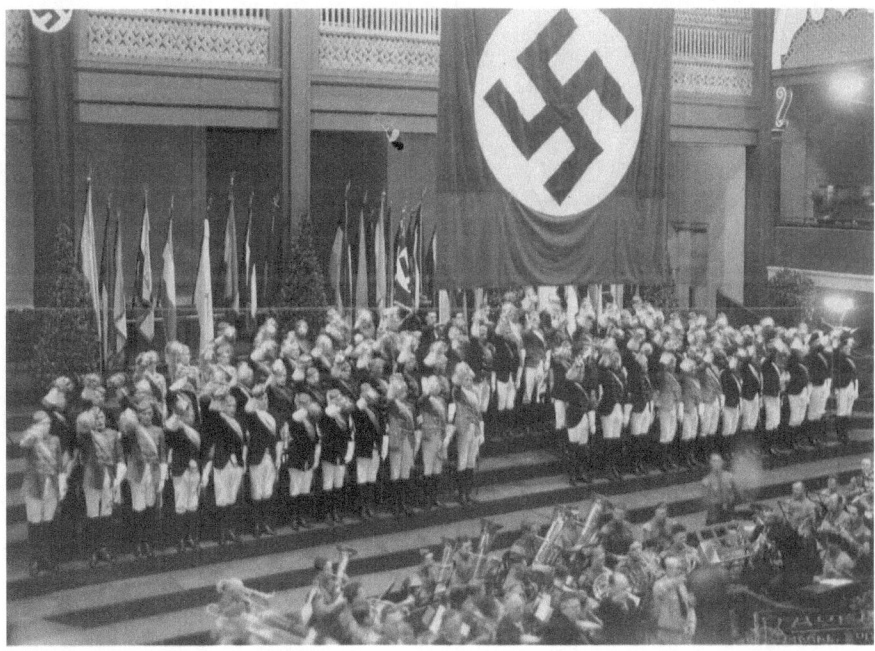

Graduation ceremony at Paul's Institute. All give the Hitler salute though it is not yet compulsory, c.1934

С.С.С.Р.
Всесоюзное Акц.О-во
"ИНТУРИСТ"

гор.Москва, ул.Горького, II
гостин."Националь"
телегр.адрес: МОСКВА-ИНТУ-РИСТ

"15" февраля 1935 г.

Гр-ну _Schlüsser_

В ответ на Ваш запрос относительно условий выезда заграницу сообщаем следующее:

Интурист принимает к оформлению дела по выезду заграницу только на постоянное жительство и на следующих условиях: у Вас должно иметься разрешение на въезд в ту страну, куда Вы предполагаете ехать. Должны быть оплачены за Вас Вашими родными заграницей в одном из наших заграничных представительств:

Стоимость советского заграничного
паспорта /для трудящихся и их
иждивенцев/ . . . . 550 р.зол.

и л и
для нетрудящихся . . . . 1100 р.зол.

Стоимость проезда от места жительства до места назначения, от Ленинграда до Кайрстеди примерно зол. р/ч
и 10% с общей суммы - комиссия Интуриста, при проезде в страны восточн.и европейские страны
или 5%   "   "   - комис.Интуриста при проезде в заокеанские страны и Палестину.

Уплата производится только инвалютой по курсу дня.

Платить можно в наших представительствах заграницей, имеющихся в столицах всех европейских стран, а также в Нью-Йорке и в Палестине - фирма И.ГОЗ и К-о, Тель-Авив. Там Вашим родным укажут полную сумму по курсу дня, а также дадут другие нужные сведения. По получении извещения об уплате денег Интурист начнет Ваше дело и даст Вам все дальнейшие указания.

В случае отказа Вам в выезде деньги вернут Вашим родным, за вычетом половины комиссии.

Дети до 16 лет вписываются в паспорт родителей.

ВАО ИНТУРИСТ
ЭМИГРАЦИОННЫЙ СЕКТОР

ВСЕСОЮЗНОЕ АКЦИОНЕРНОЕ ОБЩЕСТВО
"ИНТУРИСТ"
ЭМИГРАЦИОННЫЙ СЕКТОР

№ 261/50
Сп./ам/5/XI

Conditions for emigrating from USSR. Hundreds of gold roubles are too much for Paul

Schulabteilung   Rüppurr.

Vorrtragsfolge

zur

feieflichen Einführung der Schulanfänger

15. April 1936 nachm. 3 Uhr.

Fahneneinmarsch.

1. Winter ade.
2. Ansprache.
3. Den lieben kleinen Jungen u. Mädelchen.
4. Singspiele: a. Es zog ein Bäuerlein.
   b. Die fleissigen Handwerker.
   c. Das Rädchen am Uhrwerk.
   d. Das Käsperlein.
5. Freund Frosch.
6. Sonst war ich klein.
7. Häschenspiel.
8. Der kleine Gernegross.
9. Fahnenspruch (alle Kinder).
10. Aufhebt unsre Fahnen.
11. Bittgebet für den Führer.
12. Deutschland- und Horst-Wessellied.

Fahnenausmarsch.

Anschliessend Klassenverteilung.

Svetlana's first day at school proceedings, includes oath of allegiance and prayer to Hitler, 1936

Left

29 *Fallerslebenstrasse*, with Natalie at the kitchen window, 1937. The attic and top floor will be destroyed in the war

Below

Natalie's mother in Leningrad pines for her

Natalie (centre) at Paris World Fair, 1937. Posing between the pavilions of Nazi Germany and the USSR

View from London Stock Exchange, 1937. Paul in London tries to secure his money in the British Merchant Bank, J.H. Schroder & Son, in which his great-great-uncle Alexander had been a partner, to become *'riche comme un prince'*, as Schliemann recorded after meeting him

Paul's photo of Victoria Station, London, when he returns to Germany, 1937

Oberstfeldmeister Schlüsser
Alexandrastr. 21

Parchim, d.23.1.1939

Sehr geehrter Herr Schlüsser!

    Zunächst entschuldigen Sie bitte, dass ich Sie nicht mit Rang und Titel anrede, doch habe ich von einem Kameraden lediglich Ihren Namen und Ihren Wohnort erfahren können.
    Da wir beide gleichen Namens sind, hoffe ich nach jahrelanger, vergeblicher Forschung, in Ihnen einen Verwandten begrüssen zu können.
    Mein Urgrossvater hiess Friedrich Justus Schlüsser. Er wurde in Berlin am 17.7.1760 geboren, wanderte nach Petersburg aus und gründete dort die Firma Schlüsser & Co. Seine Frau war Dorothea Elisabeth Bode.
    Ich würde mich sehr freuen, von Ihnen zu hören, ob meine Vermutung zutrifft, und wir derselben Sippe angehören.

                      Mit freundlichem Gruss

                            Heil Hitler!

A letter from a distant relative signed 'Heil Hitler', 1939. Paul does not reply, even though it could assist in 'proving Aryan roots'

Left

L to r: William, Tatjana, Svetlana. Kneipp cure in Bad Worishofen, 1940, camouflage for Paul taking his family south, evading a feared invasion

Below

Close, loyal neighbour and friend, Dr Heiss, with his three daughters, 1943

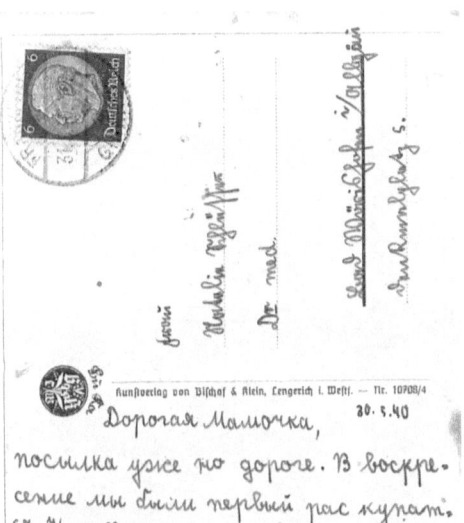

Left

Svetlana writes home: German, Russian, Latin cursive and Sueterlin script. The complexities of communication across languages

Below

Paul captioned this "Only mothers know what it is to love and to be happy" A. Von Chamisso. Eugene and Christa, blue-eyed and blonde, 1943

Paul's niece, Beatrice, marries a German, 1944. They flee France when the Allies invade, on D-Day

Above

Springtime in Allendorf, 1944

Left

Allendorf panorama. Herr Damm with his two work-cows, Bella and Pfanni

Pitching hay; William, Eugene, Frau Damm. Everyone works

Natalie harvesting wheat, 1944. She keeps the family safe in evacuation but the forest on the right gives protection during aerial attacks

Eugene and Tatjana bring lunch, 1944

Lunch break in the field. Herr and Frau Damm, Gretel (extreme left), Natalie, William, Svetlana (standing) and Eugene

G. SCHANZENBACH & CO. G.M.B.H.
ELEKTROTECHNISCHE UND LICHTTECHNISCHE SPEZIALFABRIK
FRANKFURT AM MAIN-WEST 13

FERNRUF AMT MAINGAU
SAMMELNUMMER 70077
TELEGRAMM-ADRESSE:
SCHANZENBACHCO
FRANKFURTMAIN ●

FRANKFURT A. M.-WEST 13, 29. Februar 1948
ADALBERTSTRASSE 15

DIREKTION

Z E U G N I S

Herr Dipl.Ing. P a u l   S c h l ü s s e r, geboren am
29.März 1900 in St.Petersburg, war vom 15.Juli 1937 bis
29.Februar 1948 ununterbrochen in unserem Hause beschäftigt.
Während dieser Zeit haben wir Herrn Schlüsser mit der Leitung unseres lichttechnischen Laboratoriums beauftragt und
in dieser Eigenschaft war er aufgrund seiner umfassenden
elektrotechnischen und lichttechnischen Kenntnisse mit der
Neuentwicklung, Ausprobe und Auswertung unserer elektrotechnischen Spezialerzeugnisse beschäftigt.

Herr Schlüsser befasste sich zuerst mit der Entwicklung der
modernen Quecksilberdampfleuchten für Innen- und Aussenbeleuchtung, später widmete er seine Tätigkeit der Entwicklung
der Leuchten für Transportwesen und den Scheinwerfern für
Verkehrswege und den Eisenbahnbetrieb. Die explosions- und
schlagwettergeschützten elektrotechnischen Geräte, einer der
Hauptartikel unseres Fabrikationsprogramms, waren dauernd Gegenstand seiner Ueberwachung, Untersuchung und Verbesserung.
Als das Problem der Trocknung und Entkeimung der Lebensmittel
und des Verpackungsmaterials mittels elektrischer Bestrahlungsquellen aktuell wurde, hat Herr Schlüsser diese Arbeiten in
unserem Hause ebenfalls mit Erfolg durchgeführt.

Diese Tätigkeit brachte Herrn Schlüsser in nächste Berührung
mit der Konstruktion und Produktion der entwickelten Geräte,
sodass er mit den Konstruktionsmethoden und der
serienmässigen Produktion der Erzeugnisse vollkommen vertraut
ist. Im Zusammenhang mit diesen Arbeiten hat auch die Planung
der elektrischen Anlagen gestanden, welche Herrn Schlüsser Gelegenheit geboten hat, neben seinen ausgezeichneten theoretischen Kenntnissen auch grosse praktische Erfahrungen auf diesem
Gebiet zu sammeln.

Herr Schlüsser besitzt eine gründliche allgemeine elektrotechnische und lichttechnische Hochschulbildung und dank seinem
ständigen Interesse für die Fragen des Fachs konnte er in
allen einschlägigen Fragen unserem Hause nur die besten Dienste
leisten.

Herr Schlüsser scheidet auf eignen Wunsch aus unserer Firma aus.
Wir bedauern dies umsomehr, als wir mit ihm einen zuverlässigen
und stets zuvorkommenden Mitarbeiter verlieren, mit dessen Leistungen wir jederzeit überaus zufrieden waren.
Für seine weitere Tätigkeit wünschen wir ihm den besten Erfolg.

G. Schanzenbach & Co.
(Gesellschaft mit beschränkter Haftung)

Outstanding reference after Paul's 'dismissal'

Paul's ID card, 1946. Valid for only a twelve-month stay in Germany

Paul and Natalie 'de-Nazified', May 1947. 'In the documents to hand regarding former members of the NSDAP [Nazi Party] or its affiliates, Schlüsser is not listed'

Name (bei Frauen auch Geburtsname): Schlüsser, geb. Kungurtzeff	Ort der Festnahme: Berlin-Pankow	Aktenzeichen: 4/1977/50
Vornamen: Sinaida	Letzte Wohnung: Berlin-Pankow, Bamberger Str. 8	Tag der Festnahme: 6.10.1947
Geburtstag und -ort: 21.9.1900 in Irkutsk	Jetzige Anschrift der Familienangehörigen: Maria Hentrich, Bamberg, Kunigundendamm 39	wo: Hoheneck Karteikarte ausgestellt am: 16.2.50
Beruf früher: Krankenschwester jetzt: Dolmetscherin	Größe: 152 cm	wo: Hoheneck
Zuletzt bei: Kontrollrat Berlin beschäftigt als: Dolmetscherin	Gestalt: schmächtig	Fingerabdruck genommen am: 7.5.50
Familienstand: verw.	Gesicht: längl. oval	wo: Sachsenhausen
Kinder: keine	Bart: ohne	Übernahme durch d. Dtsch. V.-Pol. am: 11.2.50
Staatsangehörigkeit: Deutsch	Augenfarbe: graubr.	vom:
	Haarfarbe: dunkelbl.	
Deck- Name: keinen Adresse: "	Besondere Kennzeichen: keine	Parteizugehörigkeit nach d. 8.5.45 bis:

Eintritt	NSDAP	SS	SA	SD	Gestapo	NSKK NSFK	HJ	BDM
Austritt	-	-	-	-	-	-	-	-

Sonstige Organisationen u. Verbände: keine	Vorstrafen: keine	Öffentliche Ämter: keine	Milit. Verbände und Ausbildung: keine

Innegehabte Funktionen (z. B. Kreisleiter, SA-Sturmführer usw.): keine

Wenden!

Zinaida's prison record, front. German citizen arrested in Berlin on 6 October 1947

Straftat: Agentin des ausländischen Aufklärungsdienstes	Verurteilendes Gericht: SMT Berlin Verurteilt am: 7.10.1947 Aktenzeichen: 63300	Strafdauer lt. Urteil: 25 Jahre Strafarbeitslager
Beginn der Strafhaft: 7.10.1947	Beendigung der Strafe: 6.10.1972	Entlassung am 19.1. 1954 Ul nach Berlin

Datum der Eintragung	Grundsätzliche Bemerkungen für die Beurteilung des Gefangenen z. B. Fluchte und -versuche, Ausbruch und -versuche, Gewalttätigkeiten, aber auch außergewöhnliche Leistungen	Verlegungen in andere Anstalten Auszufüllen nach Eintreffen in der neuen Anstalt	
		Von	Nach
11.2.50		Sachsenhsn.	Hoheneck

Zinaida's prison record, reverse. Spying for a foreign power, sentenced to twenty-five years in a penal labour camp

Eugene (4th left, 2nd row, standing with scarf) in class photo. Diesterweg School, 1948. A large class and, despite postwar hardships, seemingly happy

Keeping Russian culture alive. Svetlana, in the lead role, Tatjana, on Father Frost's left, perform in the Russian Fairy Tale 'The Snowmaiden'

Left

The three John sisters and Mr Ivanov. Lydia (centre) and Mr Ivanov (right) perjure themselves to help Paul and Natalie establish a false marriage date. Mr Ivanov is also a willing chauffeur

Below

'Cousins' Mr and Mrs Shoopinsky offer help, 1949. Why did the US Administration refuse entry visas?

EXECUTIVE COUNCIL
A. GOLOOBEFF
V. MARTINOVITCH
DIMITRY OLHOVSKY
A. THOMSON

BORIS V. SERGIEVSKY, Commander

A. W. MEYERSON, Adjutant
PAUL SCHOGOLEFF, Paymaster
MIRON SILBERSTEIN, M.D., Surgeon

HEADQUARTERS
Brigadier-General John V. Turchinoff
Garrison No. 297

1845 BROADWAY (60TH ST.), NEW YORK 23, N. Y. · TEL. COLUMBUS 5-8783

Army and Navy Union, U. S. A.

ORGANIZED 1886 — INCORPORATED 1888

OFFICE OF Sr. Vice Commander

Late Brigadier-General
JOHN V. TURCHINOFF
(1812-1901)

December 21, 1947

EUGENE GOLIKOFF,
Senior Vice-Commander

ALEXANDER FAIR,
Junior Vice-Commander

PAUL SCHOGOLEFF,
Junior Vice-Commander

EUGENE STADNIKOFF,
Chief Master of Arms

V. REV. A. KRASS,
Chaplain

J. J. BOLOTOVSKY,
Judge Advocate

LIBORIO TIGNETTI,
Quartermaster
& Officer of the Guard

SERGE SEKERIN,
Patriotic Instructor

EUGENIE RUCH,
Liaison Officer

VLADIMIR F. GNIESSIN,
Liaison Officer

MICHAEL YANENKO,
Historian

JOHN ZAVADSKY,
Officer-of-the-Day

MILTON W. KREJCI,
Color Sergeant

DMITRY TERESHTCHENKO,
Officer of the Watch

PETER KARAGANOFF,
Service Officer

EPHRAIM P. ENOVENKO,
Chairman
Auditing Committee

B. I. BUTLEROFF,
President
Trial Committee

DIMITRY OLHOVSKY,
Chairman
Welfare Committee

BORIS A. VON KUPFER,
Chairman
Resolution Committee

A. W. MEYERSON,
Publicity Officer

Honorable Consul General
Consulate United States of America
Frankfurt Am/Main
Germany

Excellency:

    This Garrison is taking the liberty of writing this letter on behalf of one of our oldes members in good standing, Mr. Andrew Shoopinsky, of 55 Tiemann Place, New York 27, New York.

    Mr. Shoopinsky, a naturalized citizen of this country, is very desirous to bring to the United States of America —

    (a) His first cousin, Natalie Schlusser
    (b) Her husband, Paul Schlusser with
    (c) their four children: Tatiana, Swetlana, Boris and Eugene,

who, as stateless persons, are located in the United States zone at 29 Fallerleben Strasse, Frankfurt Am/Main, Germany.

    Mr. Shoopinsky is a well-to-do business man of the City of New York, a reliable, strustworhty person of excellent reputation and we are certain that any obligation he undertakes will be faithfully discharged.

    Thanking you for any assistance you will kindly find it possible to help the family of Mr. & Mrs. Paul Schlusser with four children to leave Germany for this country as soon as possible and thus accomplish a real good deed for humanity, I remain

                                 Respectfully yours,

                                   Eugene Golikoff

One of a number of letters of support for the family, part of Paul's efforts to reach America

Passport photos. Natalie's own rueful captions 'Off to America'

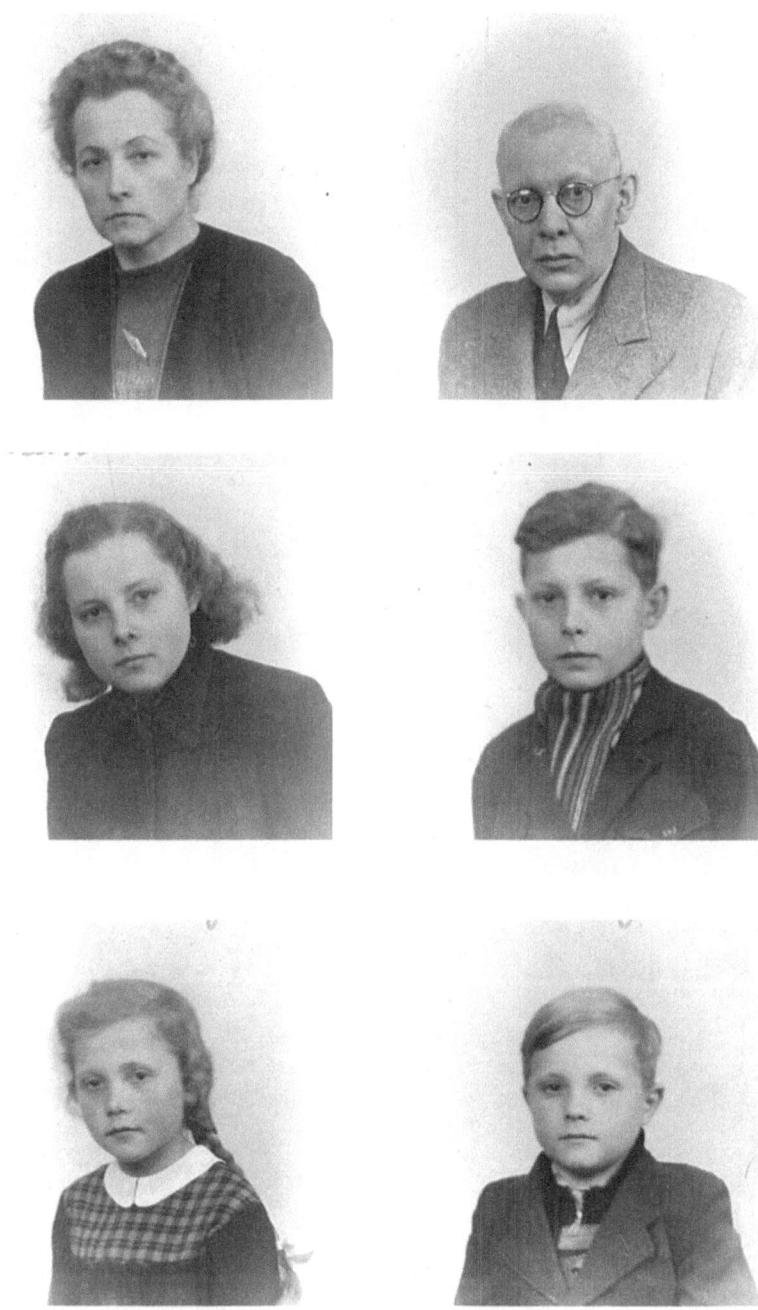

'Off to Argentina'

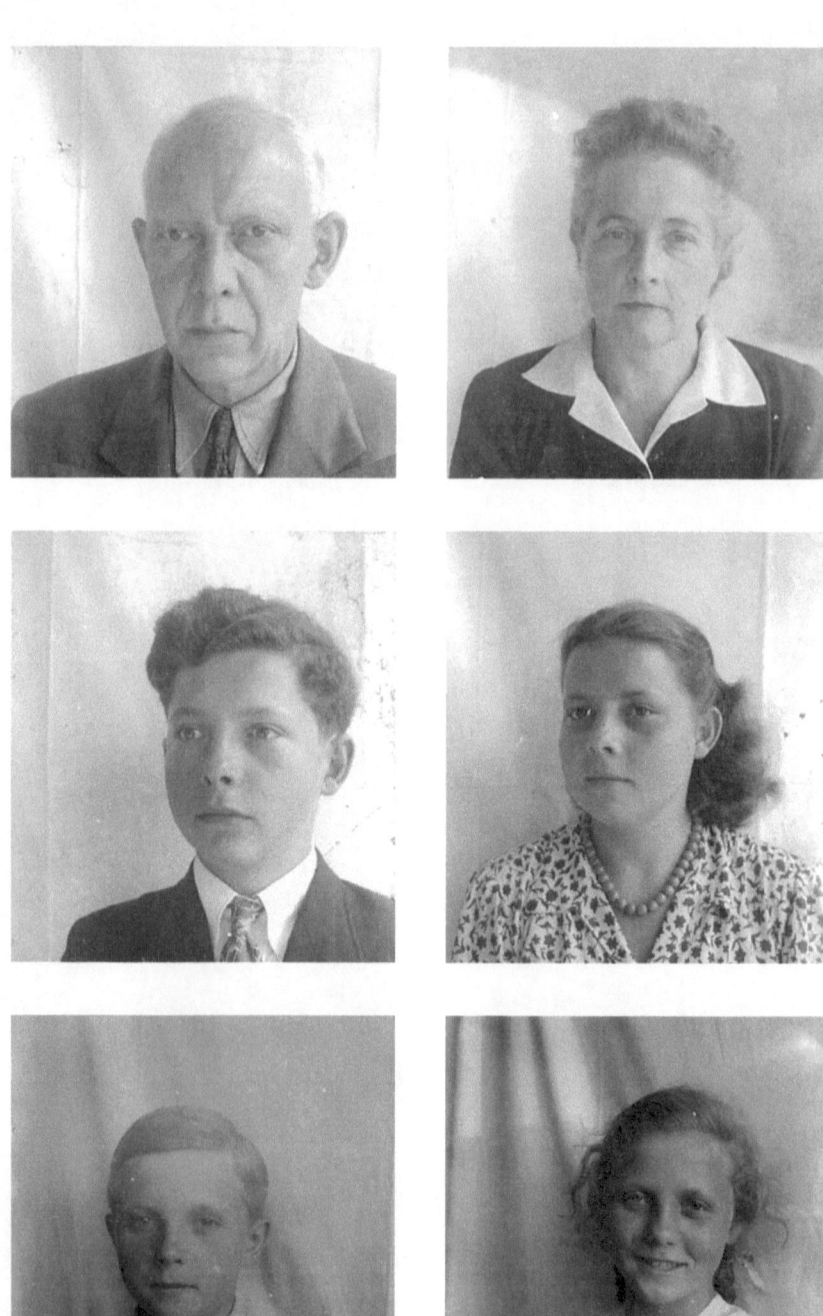

'Off to Australia'

Left

Oleg Schlüsser-Sabline on tour in Latin America, 1950. His stage name is taken from the location of the Schlüsser country property

Below

Kira (second from left) and sister Marina Makarova (right) visit their cousins in Frankfurt, Svetlana (left) Tatjana (second from right), 1949

ветских граждан и военнослужащих и получении от них информации разведывательного характера. Не отрицала Шлюссер и факта своего незаконного нахождения в советской оккупационной зоне, где была задержана.

Помимо этого, вина осужденной в преступлениях нашла подтверждение показаниями свидетелей Корепанова Н.А. и Негоды С.И. о задержании Шлюссер в советской зоне гор. Берлина, а также фактом изъятия у нее при обыске документов, подтверждающих ее сотрудничество с американской разведкой.

Таким образом, Шлюссер обоснованно привлечена к уголовной ответственности и осуждена на основании п. «с» параграфа 1 ст. 2 Закона Контрольного Совета в Германии от 20 декабря 1945 года № 10 «О наказании лиц, виновных в военных преступлениях, преступлениях против мира и против человечности» за преступление против человечности в форме враждебных действий против гражданского населения, преследования лиц на политической и расовой почве, а также на основании ч.1 ст. 58-6 УК РСФСР - за шпионаж.

Назначенное Шлюссер наказание по своему виду и размеру является справедливым и осужденная реабилитации не подлежит.

На основании изложенного, руководствуясь ст. ст. 407 и 408 УПК РФ, ст. ст. 4, 8 и 9 Закона РФ «О реабилитации жертв политических репрессий» от 18 октября 1991 года, президиум

ПОСТАНОВИЛ:

Заключение Военного прокурора Ракетных войск стратегического назначения удовлетворить.

Приговор военного трибунала гарнизона советского сектора города Берлин от 5 апреля 1948 года в отношении Шлюссер Зинаиды Ивановны оставить без изменения.

Признать Шлюссер Зинаиду Ивановну не подлежащим реабилитации по данному делу.

Постановление может быть обжаловано в Военную коллегию Верховного Суда Российской Федерации.

Подлинное за надлежащей подписью.
С подлинным верно:
Член президиума полковник юстиции   Б.А. Кожевников

Above

Paul's headstone consecrated, 1950. Why was the grave later moved and wrongly identified?

Left

The Russian Military Court rejects my appeal on behalf of Zinaida, 2010

PART 4
STALIN REDUXED

Chaos Threatens – Fear Rising – Educating for Democracy – Surviving on Ersatz – The Circling Sun – Marshalling the Economy – Win Some, Lose Some – Life Goes On – Paul's Final Escape – Mystery Solved

Chaos Threatens

Paul covered the distance on his bicycle from Allendorf to Frankfurt in less than a day, with me, his youngest, aged six, on the crossbar. Normally I rode on the rear pack rack, but it and the handlebars were loaded with provisions that the Damm family had given us to tide us over in Frankfurt, where little food was available. Paul had recently turned forty-five years old and, though he had periodic bouts of poor health, to me he remained omnipotent. In those chaotic weeks while the Americans established their authority and began organising the civilian population, it was everyone for themselves, with food and supplies obtained by any means.

The *Autobahn* (motorway) was heavy with military traffic in both directions, so father kept to country roads. He was reluctant to make stops, anxious to reach Frankfurt before nightfall not least because there was a curfew in place. My seat was made a little more comfortable with a cushion under my backside. When periodically I complained about a sore butt, he lifted me off the crossbar and we walked for a few minutes. I don't recall talking; Father's mind was on riding the bicycle, and on possible dangers. There was the threat of being robbed, the fear of striking remnant mines, unexploded hand grenades or other ordnances, and the risk of being detained by US military personnel.

From the crossbar I had a good view of the countryside, bathed as it was in summer colours, but my memories become more vivid as we reached the outskirts of Frankfurt. I thought I might have recognised some of the streets and buildings I had left almost two years earlier, but it was a foreign city to me.

As we came closer to our destination, closer to the city centre, the devastation was greater: *Trümmerhaufen* (mounds of rubble) were everywhere, the word itself since then seared into my brain. At nightfall we arrived in the district of Dornbusch. Father did not explain the reason for the high barbed wire fence that we encountered running along our left, but I soon learned what it was. Beyond it was the American Occupation Zone – an area which the US military had confiscated to house their personnel. It remains a paradox for me that from that first sight and for as long as it existed, the area behind the wire represented freedom, unlimited food supplies and opportunity, a fence dividing the 'haves' from the 'have nots', the punishment and prize of the victors over the vanquished. I had long grasped that 'we' were the losers. The image of that two-metre-high barbed wire fence epitomises powerlessness and an unbridgeable divide. My feelings are coloured by events that followed and, had they turned out less fraught, that vision might not have remained so indelible. What might father's feelings and thoughts have been? Outwardly he could not afford to be negative, as there were pressing problems of survival to solve. Inwardly he must have despaired that his world lay shattered around him, and yet I believe he viewed the perpetrators – the Americans – as liberators, representing some hope. Certainly, return to Russia had now become impossible and would remain so.

We passed a sentry box manned by an American soldier wearing an armband with the letters 'MP' (Military Police) on his sleeve. I recall the letters even though I had not yet learned to read. I registered that behind him on a wall was a blue lamp indicating a German police station, then not operating. I remember the district number – *Polizei, Revier* 13 – and it would become a place I instinctively avoided. It was the police station where father had had to report, under constant suspicion by the Nazis. Father bicycled on stoically, not wishing to attract the American's attention, so as not to have to present his *Ausweis* (identification papers) again. His papers were still those issued by the Nazi authorities. I must have complained about the long hours on the crossbar but he assured me that we were close to our goal. We continued along the bicycle path. We were the only ones on this side of the fence. I noticed tram tracks and overhead wires, but I saw no tram. I couldn't see any bomb-damaged buildings on the other side of the fence. It seems that the Americans had planned to use the eight-storey headquarters of the industrial conglomerate, I.G. Farben, as their headquarters, from which they would administer their zone of occupation, and so had avoided bombing that part of the city. I saw the tall yellow building in the distance but could not know that General Eisenhower, Supreme Commander of the Allied Forces and the future US President, was then in residence. The sense of being in occupied territory was intensified when we passed more guard posts with armed, steel-helmeted MPs. Jeeps were racing to and fro inside the perimeter, often one of the passenger-soldiers having his rifle casually placed between his legs. It had been only weeks since Germany capitulated, on 9 May, and the troops remained on alert for a possible resurgence of violence.

On my later visit to the I.G. Farben building, it was easy to see why it had been perfect for Eisenhower and why it had been chosen. It had been relatively easy to avoid bombing it, as it stands apart and surrounded by a green belt. I felt an antipathy towards it, though for me the name in 1945 merely suggested paint (*Farben* is German for 'paint') or coloured pencils. My antipathy towards it must have been gained from the people around me. As is well known now, the I.G. Farben concern was notorious for producing the *Zyklon B* gas, used in killing millions of people in the gas chambers of Auschwitz, Dachau and the other concentration camps in Germany and Central Europe. Was this fact known to the locals and hence the antipathy? And what does that suggest about the wider population's knowledge of the systematic killing of Jews, Roma and other minorities? On that visit to Frankfurt, I went inside the building for the first time and learned that, somewhat paradoxically, the building has more recently become part of the University of Frankfurt. Somehow it didn't seem right to me that an institute dedicated to free thought and learning should be housed in a building that had such a terrifying history. But perhaps I am wrong, and its use in teaching students to seek truth and wisdom may be appropriate – a constant reminder of the abuse of knowledge. Perhaps it is both a daily reminder and a way of purging the building. Environmental artists Christo and Jeanne Claude had purged the *Reichstag* in Berlin by wrapping the whole building; perhaps, I thought, this building needed similar treatment. I was a little reassured when I saw that each floor had exhibits documenting how the extermination of Jews, Roma and other minorities was carried out. The students cannot be oblivious of the building's history, and yet I felt it somewhat sacrilegious that they hurried past to their next lecture or cup of coffee without even glancing at the exhibits. Nor were there any students in the Holocaust Museum and Research Centre, which I discovered on the top floor.

The Museum, and every other floor, is reached by a unique elevator system known as a *Paternoster*. Wood-panelled cubicles move up and down continuously, and the visitor steps in and out while the conveyance continues at the same steady pace. It is an example of the building's modernity; the whole building forms the ultimate in *Jugendstil* design: clean lines, high ceilings with discreet Art Nouveau decorations, plain wood panels and doors, functional and inviting. The building houses numerous offices, large and small lecture halls, laboratories, stores, and cafés, a swimming pool and gymnasium. The entrance is spectacular in its size and the proportions of the stairs and corridors beautifully complement the dimensions of the building. The building retains a light and airy feel inside, while its curved construction reduces any sense of massiveness of the exterior. Nevertheless, it manages to dwarf the people and perhaps that was its purpose. It was built before the Hitler period and designed to be 'a symbol, in iron and steel, of German commercial and scientific manpower'. From here, the conglomerate was administered to make a profit for its owners and shareholders with little regard of the consequences in lives. The building expresses the contradiction of how a civilised and cultured people like the Germans could design and construct such a magnificent building and yet perpetrate such barbaric acts. It suggests that no single individual had to – or could – take responsibility for decisions made here. The whole was much larger than any of the parts. Still, the German people did abdicate their responsibilities and it remains beyond belief how the gas chambers came into being for the purpose of exterminating a whole race and classes of people. I visited the first concentration camp built, in Sachsenhausen, outside Berlin. The words on the metal arch over the entry – *Arbeit macht Frei* (Work is liberating) – are chilling in their cynicism. The parade ground, barracks and showers form part of a museum today. It was a surreal experience to walk through the spaces where thousands had died. Executions, maltreatment and medical experimentation killed some 30,000 men, women and children in this camp alone. How could this have been allowed to happen?

Our street, *Fallerslebenstrasse*, led to an oval at one end. It became the favourite playground for the neighbourhood children. Mother gave me permission to play there provided that I returned home at the designated hour. Apart from teaching me the virtues of punctuality, it was a way of keeping track of me in what remained a dangerous environment. The streets, backyards, parks and playing fields were still not safe but it was unrealistic to expect us to remain confined to our apartments. We had no balls or other play equipment; they had disappeared during the war. The attraction on the oval was a collection of burnt-out machinery: fire engines, tip trucks, steamrollers. We sat behind the rusting steering wheels, 'driving' in every direction, or played hide and seek around them. I believed at first that these burnt-out wrecks had been destroyed in the war and cleared from the streets. However, on discussing this with my friends, I learned from one whose parents knew about the matter that the Occupation Forces had deliberately torched the vehicles. This was hardly credible to us children and we concluded that it had been stupidity on the part of the Occupying Forces, who were already losing status in our eyes for their profligate and wasteful lifestyle while we were barely surviving. It was perhaps also a way for our young brains to accept military occupation and diminish the occupiers' power.

I thought that this version of events was true but what I have since learned, while wholly different, is no less bizarre. While it may have been common knowledge to others, it had escaped me. I am referring to the 'Morgenthau Plan' agreed on by the Allies in 1944*. It stipulated that Germany be punished for instigating two world wars and reduced to an agrarian country

---

* Morgenthau's chief advisor on the plan was later revealed as one of a number of Soviet sympathisers close to Roosevelt.

stripped of all industrial capacity, even down to preventing the education of Germans for any technical careers. Germany was to be divided into several states and converted 'into a country primarily agricultural and pastoral in its character'. All industry was to be dismantled, the coalmines destroyed and the industrial workforce dispersed. Importing food was banned until December 1945. CARE packets – relief donations from the American relief organisation – were not allowed until June 1946, and US military personnel were forbidden to give food to Germans. Surplus food was destroyed rather than being distributed to the needy population. I had believed the years 1945–47 had brought us near to starvation because of the chaos of the aftermath of war. It never occurred to me that the hunger we suffered had been deliberately created. We were subject to a plan to starve us into submission, as father and I returned to Frankfurt.

Father turned into *Raimundstrasse*, leaving the barbed wire behind. Totally and partially bombed-out houses now marked our path. Some had collapsed roofs, some had their front wall blown out leaving slabs of masonry hanging in the air, others were merely heaps of rubble. What shops remained intact were closed with their metal shutters. Father skirted the bomb craters and mounds of rubble and came to a stop outside 29 *Fallerslebenstrasse*. I saw that the broken windows of the basement and first floor apartment had been secured against the weather with pieces of cardboard and wood and, in the centre, a small piece of translucent perspex to allow some light in. The severest damage was to the top apartment, which had its kitchen and two of its four rooms destroyed. It gaped at you, obscenely revealing its innards. At that moment I had a strong feeling of violation of the people who still lived there. That feeling of empathy and sorrow for the suffering of bombing victims has never left me.

Our ground floor apartment was intact but desolate. Father had not yet brought the furniture up from the cellar, where it was stored securely – we hoped – from bomb damage and looters. The apartment felt hostile and abandoned, as if no one had lived there for some time. Father demonstrated by trying switches and taps that there was no electricity, water or gas. There was one water tap near the front drive though, which operated for two hours a day; during this time, we and the neighbours would fill up all available containers, buckets, pots and pans.

Conditions had become so bad that nothing and no one was safe from desperate people who had lost everything. Only secure locks and barbed wire provided some protection against thieves. There were burglaries and break-ins almost daily and virtually no one was spared. The population was traumatised by the bombings; the loss of relatives, friends and neighbours; the loss of property. Now came the revelations of the death camps and other atrocities, particularly those on the Eastern front. There had been rumours and information clandestinely obtained from foreign radio broadcasts, but now they were confirmed and families and neighbours had to deal with the facts – confirming, I feel, what in many cases they must have suspected.

New people appeared in the area. Some I knew and they were also returnees from evacuation, but most were strangers hopeful of finding a place to live. Anything even barely habitable was soon occupied. If you found an attic to live in, you were lucky. Others occupied the basement laundry, while the least fortunate found some corner of a bombed-out building that gave protection from the elements. With more than four million German soldiers killed in the fighting and many more civilian casualties of the bombing, there were streams of women and widowed mothers searching for a way to survive. Many were forced to steal and loot for food. It was some time before ration cards were issued and the beginnings of an orderly food supply, however meagre, became possible.

Going out at night was unthinkable, even had there been street lighting. Previously, street lighting had been gas lit but now, there was no gas. Stealing was anathema to father but the times were desperate. In a minor act of vandalism, he told my brother William to shin up the nearest lamp pole and unscrew the timer. It was a mechanical clock, wound by hand every eight days. Now it no longer timed the lighting of the gas lamp, but it became the family's only working clock.

Returned prisoners of war added to the problems of daily life. Many were traumatised by their experiences, disoriented and despondent, seeking charity. Others tried to make themselves useful. They would come to the front door and offer to do small repairs and other menial tasks. Others again came to beg, often amputees or blinded soldiers.

Another returning family from evacuation was the Webers, and Herr Weber found it difficult to reintegrate into civilian life. Their daughter Christa and I were close friends. Only a short while after the rest of the family had returned from evacuation, Christa's father returned from a prisoner of war camp. I recall him as a quiet, withdrawn man. Visiting Christa years later, she told me how her father, a qualified engineer, refused to return to his profession and instead set himself up to provide a radio repair service from his home. Christa believed that he had chosen this to avoid speaking with people about his wartime experiences on the Russian front. He never spoke to her about the war.

My sixteen-year-old sister Svetlana found work almost immediately in a fruit and vegetable nursery, 'Sinai' on the *Eschersheimer Landstrasse*, which had been operating there since before the war. More important than money was the pay she received in vegetables. They were a godsend, though not sufficient to feed a family of six. Mother went to forage for food and, on one occasion, she took me with her. It was dangerous to leave me at home alone, but perhaps also she was taking a child who might gain her sympathy for getting a lift with a truck driver. It was in October 1945, soon after harvest time, and the farmers had new stores of produce. We left home while it was still dark and, as there were no trams, we walked the three kilometres from our home to the truck stop at the *Opernplatz*, almost in the centre of the city. Our walk was longer as we had to go around the fenced-off Occupation Zone. In the dawn I could see rows of trucks filling the square in front of the bombed-out shell of the Frankfurt Opera House. They had arrived with produce to sell on the black market and were returning to the country. Mother successfully negotiated a ride on the rear tray of a lorry bound for Fulda.

The truck was full beyond capacity with people desperate to get into the country to barter valuables for food. There was no petrol, so the truck ran on wood gas. I had become familiar with their operation as our upstairs neighbour, Herr Korselt, had fitted one on his Mercedes car. On passenger cars, a middle-sized stove was installed at the rear; on the truck, it sat on the tray near the engine. The driver stoked the fire with wood chips and the gas thus generated powered the engine. We set off as dawn made the city ruins that we passed look even eerier than they were in full daylight. The truck drove along the *Autobahn* and after about three hours stopped to set us down near the village of Climbach. From there, we walked 2.2 kilometres to Allendorf and what had been our home until recently. The Damm family welcomed us and were anxious to help. They were generous, giving us as much food as mother and I could carry in our improvised hessian bags and rucksacks, in exchange for valuables including a silk scarf, then particularly prized. Our rucksacks were those sewn together from the canvas which had been scavenged from the bombed Allendorf factory. We stayed the night before, next morning, returning to Frankfurt.

We became marauders as food shortages worsened in the summer of 1946. Some trams were running again, so Paul and Natalie took us once to the *Stadtwald* (urban forest) and at other times into the foothills of the Taunus Range. With many others, we combed the forest floor for the three-cornered beechnuts, and collected mushrooms. The six of us were able to collect a sizeable quantity. Mother took our haul of beechnuts to the nearest grocer, who exchanged it for a bottle of vegetable oil.

'Millions of people are slowly starving', reported William S. Clayton, advisor to President Truman. And we were. We needed urgently to grow our own fruit and vegetables. Our backyard was too dangerous to dig in because of the unexploded grenades and mines. But we could pick fruit from the loganberry and gooseberry shrubs along the fence. I was envious of my sister, who had her birthday in June when the currants and raspberries were ripe; she could have them on her birthday cake. We were allocated a small plot of land on a demolished anti-aircraft site, three kilometres from our home. It was a barren, clay area on top of a hill which, until a few months previously, had been an ack-ack installation (an anti aircraft gun installation, also known as Ack-Ack). I imagine that these had been the guns in action when I had looked out over the scene from our front door during the 1943 aerial attack. Spent anti-aircraft shells almost a metre long were scattered everywhere. They were a valuable building material, as we stood them up on end to form a low fence. It couldn't stop thieves but at least it delineated our plot. The remnants of a bunker provided the bricks for paths along the length of our seedbeds. Other scavenged materials were used to build a shed where a few garden tools were kept, a strong padlock securing the door. That didn't always stop thieves. When a crop came to maturity or ripened, we harvested it as soon as possible before it could be stolen. It is a hard truth that desperate people will steal from other desperate people. And they stole from us. We took our handcart to our plot every few days and each time we feared that the crop might have been stolen or the shed broken into. We were relieved when everything was in place, though on several occasions we had break-ins – always confronting, but an accepted part of life. William also recalls (while I had forgotten) that father rented a cherry tree in the satellite town of Oberursel in 1946, and that he and father harvested one crop in early summer.

Fear Rising

The archives that I inherited document father's increasing fear that the Soviets would come further west, while mother's love–hate relationship with the Germans was now tested further. The part she was asked to play in the de-Nazification did not endear them any more to her. To establish who had collaborated with the Nazis, every adult in Germany came under investigation. If found guilty of collaborating, they could be gaoled; if found not guilty, they were given a clearance and considered 'de-Nazified'. About 900,000 people in the US Occupation Zone alone were brought before a court. With such large numbers, it became necessary to simplify the process and soon even acquaintances could vouch for another person.

'There are some *falsche* people in this world', mother explained, using the German word with which she meant 'devious' or 'two-faced'. As so often, she did not elaborate. From snippets of other conversations, I gather that she and father were approached to vouch for neighbours who had not been above reproach and had made difficulties for our family. I suspect that she was, among others, referring to the secondary school teacher who lived opposite our apartment. We were always urged to steer clear of *Herr Professor*. I imagine he had been an ardent Nazi and proud of it. He was elderly and perhaps thought harmless because of this after the war. Whether he had a 'history' or not, he and his wife mourned for their son missing on the Russian front but they never lost hope he would return. The wife kept his room immaculate and even washed his bed linen once a month. He did not come back, and she died broken-hearted. Mother may have been approached to vouch for them.

She refused to confide in me on this subject, but I have a strong sense that she was approached by a number of her neighbours to vouch for them and felt compromised whatever action she took. As a doctor and not being German may have given her added credibility, in the circumstances. Mother would have been very aware of the irony that she, classed as a 'sub-human' only a short period earlier, being asked to vouch for the integrity of her detractors, further alienating her from them.

It took until August 1946 for Paul and Natalie to be *Entnazifiziert* (de-Nazified). A letter from his employer, Schanzenbach, detailing Gestapo surveillance of Paul, must have been invaluable.

Paul was issued with a twelve-month visa for himself and his family to remain in the US Zone. That would take him to August 1947. What then?

I learned to read the headlines and short items of the American-sponsored *Die Neue Zeitung* newspaper, but not early enough to read about the first Nuremberg Trial held in 1945–46, which tried the Nazi elite and found them guilty. Many were sentenced to death, while some committed suicide before they could be executed. I don't know what father felt about these criminals, but he would have been perturbed by the growing influence of the Soviets. They had insisted on the public trials and determined much of the procedures. Churchill made his 'Iron Curtain' speech in 1946, dividing Europe, and with the decisions at Yalta in mind Paul feared increasingly that we would face forced repatriation to Russia. But, I now know, it was the actions of his sister-in-law Zinaida that presented the greatest threat. She had been living in Frankfurt since the death of her husband, uncle Volodya, until war's end when she moved to Bonn. Her activities and movements were always a secret and mother refused to speak of her. What did father know at the time? Even if initially he knew little of her activities, he would soon have found out. The fear this aroused made him desperate to take his family out of Germany. There had been the chance to get entry visas into Great Britain, which was botched when his cousin Fedya Sevier entrusted the visas to the postal service. A second set of visas was apparently not possible. Where could he now take his family so that we all might be safe from the Soviet threat? He made repeated efforts to gain visas for the United States. He contacted the Tolstoy Foundation, headquartered in New York, to register the details of his family. Alexandra Tolstoy, the youngest daughter (and secretary) to the author of *War and Peace*, Lev Tolstoy, had created the Foundation to assist Russian refugees after she herself had left the Soviet Union in 1929 to settle in the USA. Father applied to the Foundation for US entry visas. The United States had a quota system for various nationalities to migrate there. Mother made the obvious point that the quota for Russians was very small, perhaps 2,000 people annually as compared to about 50,000 for Poles and comparatively large numbers for Latvians, Lithuanians and Estonians. The numbers were arrived at for political reasons. The Baltic States had been particularly opposed to the Soviets and were thus favoured, while Russians, although allies in the war, had now become combatants in the struggle for control over Europe.

What nationality were we? Soviet? Or since we were born in Germany, were we German citizens? Paul moved to distance himself further from any connection either with the Germans or the Soviets. The family name was obviously of German origin. It had stood him in good stead as long as he needed to emphasise his German-ness, but now it was an impediment. He decided that it would appear less so if he dropped the umlaut in the name – the double dots above the 'u' – changing the name from Schlüsser to Schlusser. Once, Tatjana and I were required to sign a document. 'SchlOOser, Schlosser' she hissed at me several times as I wrote the name, fearing I would use the umlaut. I didn't. After several failures, father decided that his best chance to receive US visas was to have the family classified as 'displaced persons' (DPs). DPs were people other than German nationals who were displaced during the Nazi period up to the end of World War II. Our family did not legally qualify, however, because Paul and Natalie had come to Germany before the Nazi period. But he did succeed in persuading the authorities to classify our family as 'stateless'. There was a small quota of visas to the USA for stateless passport holders. But this approach also proved unsuccessful, as the waiting list was so long that it would take years before our turn came. Paul persisted. He learned of another option. The Norwegian Friedjoef Nansen was a scientist, polar explorer, diplomat, statesman and humanist, with a deep compassion for his fellow human beings. Through the League of Nations he created a nationality called 'Nansen'. This could be issued to people displaced by the Russian Revolution and Civil War, considered to have begun in 1917 and ended in 1924. Holders of such passports were also allocated a quota for the USA. Paul used every contact to obtain Nansen passports. He even told us in anticipation that we were holders of such passports. In reality, there was an insurmountable legal and bureaucratic obstacle. To become eligible, a person must have left the Soviet Union by 1924. This was the cut-off point after which people were no longer considered as escaping Soviet persecution following the 1917 Revolution. Paul and Natalie had married in March 1927 and come to Berlin in May 1927 – too long after the Revolution but not early enough to fall within the Nazi period. Since he had exhausted all legal options, he tried an illegal one. He had seen others do so, and even helped some individuals to 'doctor' documents, as already noted. He made the false claim that he and Natalie had 'escaped' Russia in 1924. But their marriage certificate was issued in 1927! To 'prove' that the marriage had taken place in 1924, he sought the help of Russian friends, Pavel Fyodorovich Ivanov and Lydia John, and asked them to swear to a statutory declaration in German that they could testify that Natalie and Paul had married in 1924, and then fled Leningrad. Whether the authorities believed this or not, Paul's Nansen passport application was rejected. He was running out of options, but it is a sign of his persistence or perhaps desperation that he refused to give up. Could perhaps an American sponsor be found?

Cousin Oleg wrote to me saying that when he had met his uncle Paul after the war, Paul had been determined to locate a branch of the Schlüsser family which had emigrated to the USA in the early 1700s. Presumably he hoped to find family, however distant, who might sponsor a 'reunion'. Sadly he failed. The heart aches, however, when I think that with the aid of the Internet, I have recently located dozens of Schlusser families and even a small township of that name near Carlyle, in Pennsylvania. Surely one of them would have offered assistance had Paul been able to make contact.

Seemingly miraculously, a distant cousin of Natalie's, of whom I had had no knowledge, in New York, was prepared to help. When in later years the name of Shoopinsky did not appear anywhere on Natalie's family tree, and I asked her why. She replied with a 'how naive can you get' look:

'Of course, he wasn't a real cousin!'

Paul had become familiar with 'adjusting' the truth to achieve a necessary outcome. He had been elected founding chairman of the Frankfurt Russian Immigrant Committee. In this role he helped many people, mainly with their documentation. Through these contacts, Paul got to know a middle-aged Russian couple in New York, so-called 'Old Migrants' who had left the Soviet Union at the time of the Revolution. The Shoopinskys held US citizenship and owned a dry-cleaning business on Manhattan's 55th Street. The Shoopinskys generously agreed to sponsor our family, prepared all the legal documents, got their Buffalo Lodge to vouch for their income, confirming they were fit and proper to sponsor the Schlusser family to migrate to the USA. They also agreed to maintain the family financially until it could establish itself. Everything looked hopeful and even I, though not privy to any details, was made to believe that it was only a matter of time before we left for the USA. To strengthen Paul's case, the Shoopinskys arranged for a friend of theirs, a Catholic army chaplain who was serving in Germany for the Catholic Relief Service, to visit us in Frankfurt. The chaplain wrote a glowing report about the suitability of our family to migrate.

Asked in his application the reason why he wished to emigrate, father wrote:

> Fled with my family from the communist tyranny, which existed and still exists in Soviet Russia. Looking forward to citizenship in US for my family, away from the menace of communism, an opportunity to live as human beings under Bill of Rights and Constitution, which we believe in and as potential, good and useful citizens will always uphold.

The application continues under 'Why did you leave your homeland?':

> Having been set free from a concentration camp I was forced to leave my homeland by reason of political and religious persecution caused by my democratic convictions as well as by birth in a family of a proprietor.

These were truthful declarations. Fudging some other details in the application, Paul simply did not answer the question of how long he had lived at the Frankfurt address and for 'Religion' he entered 'Catholic-Orthodox'. Both answers were designed to make the family appear better qualified as migrants. Sadly, despite the strength of the application and support, this application was also rejected. This was father's last attempt to get to the USA. Was there something in Paul's biography that brought this repeated negative response? Was it merely bureaucratic intransigence or was there more to it?

Apart from the then usual childhood diseases and periods of under-nourishment, neither my siblings nor I had any serious ill-health. Our parents had taken good care of us, even in the most difficult circumstances. I never saw mother ill either, though there was always some concern about father's health. This question of health now became crucial, though it concerned mother not father. Would-be immigrants had to have a clean bill of health from American immigration officials. Some medical conditions disqualified you instantly – chief among them venereal diseases, tuberculosis and a heart condition. This is where the story takes a bizarre twist. Natalie was never ill, yet mysteriously, her health records, compiled as part of the process of migrating, showed that she had a venereal disease! There was no explanation except the most sinister one: either her blood tests had been switched or her records had been falsified. On another occasion, it was claimed that mother's X-ray had shown traces of tuberculosis on her lungs. I can believe that Paul suspected Soviet agents had infiltrated the system and that they were determined to foil his attempts to leave Germany. It was a common ploy by Soviet intelligence not to attack the victim directly but to target his family, especially his wife. Final reasons for rejections were never given, but the information of imputed ill-health was passed on to Paul and Natalie.

Dejected but not beaten, he canvassed possibilities of migrating to other countries: Canada, Venezuela, even Morocco.

Paul, now close to desperation, made a drastic and in many ways an inexplicable decision. He resigned from Schanzenbach & Co. to take work with the US Occupation Forces. Did he hope that this could give him contacts to help with an escape from Europe? Family lore, often repeated, was that he had been dismissed because he was a foreigner. This was a fabrication, designed to dis-inform everyone as Paul tried to hide his increasingly desperate state.

The strain was telling on his health. His blood pressure was high and he seemed to be tired all the time. As medication was not available, he tried water and steam baths to assist with his breathing, cleanse the skin and above all reduce his blood pressure. He improvised a sauna in our living room and tried to replicate the Russian *banya*. After a period in the sauna, I would see him exhausted, on the living room sofa trying to get his strength back with an afternoon sleep. We would be sternly instructed to remain quiet, speak in whispers and above all not slam any doors.

It is unclear what information father kept from mother, but she also felt the increasing stress. We all felt it. Loud voices of frustration came from the kitchen more frequently. Their tone of voice revealed their state of mind. I imagine that when the disputes were not about finances, they were disagreements about Paul's reasoning, and his plans to get the family out of Europe. Naturally, Natalie worried about his health and the many things he was involved in: his job, his family, the Russian Welfare Society. He had also recently undertaken to help build an Orthodox church in Frankfurt. All this took time, in addition to the long irregular hours he worked. His income had dropped considerably, as his teaching earned him much less than his salary as an engineer. He still had money deposited at Schroders in London but he could not access it. Natalie needed to find work. She found it as a medical orderly in the refugee-processing centre in Hanau, a satellite town of Frankfurt. My sister Tatjana and I, aged eleven and eight respectively, needed supervising after school. School finished at 12 o'clock for me and at 2 o'clock for Tatjana. Natalie employed a woman who had become a family friend, one of those people who had moved into the neighbourhood desperately needing somewhere to live, and father had helped by finding a basement laundry in a nearby apartment block. Mother employed Frau Aderkas for several hours a day at a modest wage. Frau Aderkas was a Russian in her sixties. She had escaped the Soviets with her daughter, who had lost her husband in the war. Frau Aderkas had a younger sister also in her sixties, and was a surrogate father to her grandson, Georgi. Frau Aderkas, speaking in broken German more pronounced by the lack of teeth, was always kind to me.

To work as a medical orderly, Natalie needed her qualifications verified by the United Nations Health Organisation. They determined that her Russian accreditation, her occasional work in a medical facility in Karlsruhe and her record at the Robert Koch Institute qualified her to practise in Germany. On receiving this clearance, Natalie was allowed to work with the immigration authorities. She may have hoped to make some contact there or to get information that might allow the family out of Germany. Even the faintest possibility had to be followed through.

As of 1 January 1947, father was employed to teach Russian at night classes to members of the US Forces. He was still concurrently employed at Schanzenbach, until 29 February 1948. A timetable of his classes shows that, from the beginning of April, he gave classes in 'Russian 1' on Tuesdays and Thursdays at 6.45 p.m., and 'Advanced Russian 1' on Tuesdays and Thursdays at 8.20 p.m. Classes lasted an hour and a half, with a five-minute break in-between. The US Army Administration had created the Frankfurt Army Education Center, where by teaching a range of skills they aimed to 'make the American soldier a better representative of the American Democracy', which would somehow 'lead to a more successful rehabilitation of a Democratic Germany'. They taught men and women whose education had been interrupted by the war. What use would any of them make of the Russian language? Given the Cold War scenario that was unfolding, such instruction would have been useful for broadcasters and journalists, those employed in propaganda and actual or potential intelligence work. Did that make father a more important target for Stalin, or by gaining the confidence and protection of the American authorities did that make him safer? Outside classes, he met with individual students to give them conversation lessons. Was it significant that he rarely met a student in the same place twice? On at least one occasion, the lesson took place in the open at a public swimming pool. Father had taken me with him on his bicycle. The American student had his two young sons with him. US military personnel had requisitioned the swimming pool for their own use, in an exclusive part of Frankfurt. Father's student – I believe his name was Mr Pencost – held the rank of captain and he bought me my first ever bottle of Coca-Cola. His children asked for some and Mr Pencost, true to the reputation of American generosity, did not leave me out. Even at my age, I was fully aware of how affluent their lives were compared to mine. Was the conversation perhaps all it seemed? I had an answer to my question about father's possible involvement twenty-five years later, when it seemed safe to speak of these matters. As already mentioned, when I met father's cousin Fedya Sevier in London, I knew from mother that he had been working for Britain's MI6. Fedya recalled speaking to his cousin, Paul. In answer to my question about father's possible involvement with the American Secret Service, he replied, in English:

'In the way those things could be spoken of, both in my position and his, I formed the strong impression that he was working for one of the American Intelligence Agencies.'

This is the only evidence I have of a link between father and the US Secret Service. Fedya died about a year later and I attended his funeral, where I met several of his colleagues. When I raised the issue with them, they strongly advised me not to pursue the matter. Such involvements were better to die with the person, they said. What was I to believe? Wouldn't it throw light on father's behaviour if his fear of capture by the Soviets were connected with work for the Americans? It could help to explain why he was desperate while other Russian *émigrés* were content to remain in their professions in Germany. But if father had worked for an American agency, why did the US authorities not accept his application to migrate to the USA? In that circumstance, would they not have had some obligation towards him? Did they have other reasons, unknown to me, to reject him? These questions and that of how closely he worked with the Americans remain unclear and may never be answered.

Through his teaching of American service personnel, Paul was improving his own command of the English language. On occasions, I saw father pacing the living room practising his 'th' sound – a sound unknown in German or Russian. His command of English was sufficient that by 5 October 1948, according to a document, he was recommended 'for the position as English teacher'. This seems to me to be a contradiction. Why employ a Russian to teach Americans their language? Or was he teaching someone else, or something else?

He occasionally invited some of his American students from the Russian language classes to our home. Paul was not paid for these sessions and since food was more valuable than money anyway, they paid with food: smoked bacon, spam and tinned butter were eagerly received presents. On one occasion, he invited a student to share Christmas Eve with us – our most important family celebration. He was a tall soldier, dressed in full army uniform. Having friends among the US military gained us status in the neighbourhood, although by then I had been thoroughly trained not to say anything to anyone outside the family. We rehearsed Christmas carols every year, but this year – 1948 – as father had invited his American student to join us, he taught us the English words to 'Silent Night', which we would perform. I knew little English but had somehow picked up the English word for 'peas'. Our guest arrived on the night, bringing generous gifts, with bacon and oranges among them. It was the first time that I ever saw an orange, and bacon was a rare treat. We duly sang our carol in the presence of our guest. The evening was a great success. Father, as always, was an exemplary host. But one thing puzzled me for a long time: why was baby Jesus urged to sleep in 'heavenly peas'?

Occasionally, mysterious visitors came and went. I never asked who they were but knew that they had come to seek father's help. They came several times, father typed some documents for them and they left satisfied. On one occasion, I entered the living room and saw a dark-haired, middle-aged woman sitting on the edge of the sofa. She was a stranger so I was a little embarrassed, excused myself and withdrew. When I bumped into my brother in the corridor, he whispered to me:

'Did you see that on her arm?' I hadn't had time to look. 'Go and have a look', he urged me. I returned to the room, excused myself again and went over to my cupboard and pretended to fetch something. She was sitting there in short sleeves and I had just enough time to see some numbers tattooed on her left arm.

'She's come out of a *KZ*!' whispered my brother back in the corridor.
I knew enough that he was referring to a *Konzentrationslager* (concentration camp), some kind of prison, but nothing beyond that. I am a little ashamed to admit and even today I am mystified why my young mind was repelled by the thought that here was a former prisoner in our living room.

Educating for Democracy

Many schools all over Frankfurt had been bombed. As soon as even temporary repairs had made a building secure, schools re-opened. The buildings had to be cleared of rubble and debris to make a few classrooms usable, even while the rest of the building was sealed off for fear that the building could collapse, and hand grenades or other explosives might still be buried in the rubble.

In spring 1946, I had my traditional first day at school. Like my sister Svetlana in 1936, I was given a *Schultüte* which our parents had managed to fill with some writing material, greeting cards and even a few sweets from somewhere. Unlike Svetlana, I did not have to swear allegiance to Hitler. With the shortage of classrooms, grades were combined. My friend Peter, who should have been a year ahead of me, was therefore in the same class. Classes were held in relay: primary school children in the morning, secondary school students in the afternoon. Tatjana and I walked two and a half kilometres to the same school, *Diesterwegschule*. A short time later, Svetlana's high school, *Ziehenschule*, was made safe and she went there in the nearby district of Eschersheim. William had slightly further to walk to the *Musterschule*. It was two years before the tram tracks were repaired on Route 17, along *Raimundstrasse* to Ginnheim, and travel to school by tram became possible again. We could not afford the few *Pfennigs* (pennies) it cost and, with most other children, we continued to walk to school.

The curriculum had been radically rewritten to excise all references to Nazism. Because of the shortage of paper, we used a slate and graphite pencil.

Classes of between fifty and sixty students were not uncommon, with boys and girls in separate classes. Many children had lost a parent or other relatives. Consequently there were many behavioural problems that required special skills from the teacher to resolve. However, the teachers were ill-equipped for this, particularly those who had been brought out of retirement to fill the gap in teacher shortages. A teacher's best tool was often a cane, which my teacher used frequently. One or another of the repeat offenders at some stage in the morning were commanded to come to the front of the class and told to drop their shorts. The bare buttocks were then caned with all the force that Fräulein Kopfstädt, our minuscule teacher, could muster.

Gradually, the crisis in rooms and teachers eased and the quality of schooling improved. I was separated from my friend Peter as he was promoted to his age group in Year Two. Father kept a close watch on our progress and was a harsh critic if the marks we brought home were below his expectations. He had been a good student and expected his children to be so as well.

The view among the Allies grew that if Germany was to become a functioning democracy, then the advantages of a democratic, open society must be demonstrable. None too soon, in March 1947 the Morgenthau Plan was abandoned and the American authorities started organising food supplies. Army personnel brought containers of food to our school. We brought our own aluminium containers, many of them former army issue. The food was wholesome though not very appetising, but it was food alien to us. Breakfast cereals with milk, prepared in large pots, seemed tasteless to us. Sugar was not available. To compensate for this, and as a bribe to combat absenteeism, once a month we received a small bar of Hershey chocolate, the name and colour of the wrapping still clear in my mind.

We made new friends in the neighbourhood and renewed friendships from before our evacuation. Christa Weber was one of them. She lived in the ground floor flat in the rear of our apartment block. There was something special about Christa. She was fair-haired with plaits and blue eyes. Unwittingly, according to Hitler's racist ideology, she was the perfect Aryan child. An itinerant photographer, who took photos of children and then offered them to the parents, took a photograph of her in the street, in the early summer of 1943. It was so admired that he managed to sell it to Kodak, the photographic suppliers. They chose to use it to advertise their products. It appeared in many of their publications and so Christa's image became equated with the quintessential blue-eyed, blonde Aryan girl. Kodak continued to use the photo even after the war and I recall seeing a copy in a photography magazine in the early 1950s.

In a country where Hitler had boasted about 'racial purity', the evidence to the contrary could be seen all around, with my own family offering the nearest example. I also formed a friendship with a new girl in the district, Ursula, who was living on the top floor opposite our apartment building. Ursula's father was a handsome, swarthy man with black hair, more Italian than German. He had come from the Tyrol Mountains close to Italy. My closest friend, Peter Piroth, only a few months older than I, was descended from the French religious 'heretics', the Huguenots. (The family name may originally have been Pierrot or a variation of it.) Another family with a very un-German name, with two girls, was called Bourquine, also of Huguenot descent. Their father was a sports journalist who had made his reputation reporting the 1936 Berlin Olympics. I befriended a second boy called Peter, and his parents were Spanish. It was a very mixed neighbourhood, reflecting the liberal nature of the city of Frankfurt.

The street was our playground and father reminded us repeatedly that when playing with others we were to remain silent about our family. We were not unique. There was little trust among neighbours and many rumours circulated of what people had done in the war and what they might be involved in now in the struggle to survive during the difficult times. We were discouraged from bringing friends home as the apartment was too small, but it also avoided any awkward questions being asked.

Father insisted on teaching us Russian, taking us to the Russian church and trying to maintain the Russian culture. But it came at a cost. Father was often stressed and my relationship with him was always tense. It seemed that every time we were together, he needed to teach me a lesson or correct me in some way. Perhaps this was his way of maintaining some control in his otherwise chaotic world. Working irregular hours, he could be at home in the afternoon. We were at school in the morning and free to play in the afternoon. He would choose these times to call me in and sit me down for a Russian lesson. My discomfort was intensified by father's teaching methods. I sat on the couch and he gave me a Russian phrase to repeat. They were easy, but his tendency to become censorial as soon as I made a mistake raised my anxiety. I understand that he wanted to teach us Russian because he hoped to return to Russia or at least become involved in the Russian community. His impatience cancelled out his efforts. I lost any confidence in speaking Russian. When father took me to church and wanted me to speak with Russian friends, I became catatonic. I began to resent my time with father. His wish to discipline me in other areas was just as strong. Behaviour and manners had to be impeccable. Whenever father took me to church, he would take the opportunity to comment on my clothes: 'pull up your socks' was a frequent reprimand, as was 'take your hands out of your pockets'. He made no allowance for the fact that the elastic in the socks had worn out, so keeping up socks was difficult. The strictest standards of honesty and integrity had to be maintained. On one occasion, one of my more unruly friends and I walked past a neighbour's garage and found the door open. We looked around inside and there on a shelf was a box of nuts and bolts. Having seen my brother forage in rubbish heaps for usable discards, nuts and bolts appeared valuable. Perhaps my brother could put them to use, I thought. My friend urged me to take several and so did he. At this moment, the owner came into the garage. My friend bolted but I was caught, literally taken by the scruff of my neck and marched home. Father was not there but mother reported the incident to him on his return. I was summoned to the living room, sat down and lectured on the need for honesty and the sin of stealing. He regretted doing this, he said, but theft was so heinous that I was to be given three days' house arrest. Being isolated was itself lonely and interminable, but what was worse was that the whole neighbourhood learned of my 'crime'.

Learning to swim was a frightening experience. The banks of the River

Nida had concrete steps allowing for easy entry into the water, which was flowing at a pace, and cold. Father took us on his bicycle, Tatjana on the pack rack at the rear and me on the crossbar. As we cycled to the river, down the main street of Ginnheim, a middle-aged man stepped into our path, causing father to swerve violently, throwing the two of us to the ground. Father was furious. He rounded on the man with a string of abuses and got into an arm wrestle with him. I was petrified. Thankfully the man withdrew. We walked the rest of the way, with father pushing the bike, too shaken to ride. His method of teaching was to stand on the concrete steps, hold me in the deep water with his arms under my chest and legs, and instruct me on my arm and leg movements. The less success I had, the more insistent were his instructions. I never learned to swim from him but recall the fear I had of drowning. When I did learn to swim, it was because I learned how to hold my breath to achieve buoyancy; arm and leg movements were secondary; father could be wrong.

Surviving on *Ersatz*

The winter of 1946–47 was extreme. The central heating in our apartment had not been repaired and the small pot-bellied wood stoves in two of the rooms generated barely enough heat. The apartment was always cold. Paul and Natalie were concerned for the health and welfare of the children. Our clothes were threadbare and there was little to buy. I was the luckiest, as I could wear hand-me-downs from my three siblings, though not so for underwear or shoes, which could not be fixed beyond a certain point. Our shoes had a metal plate at the front and on the heel to prolong their life. These plates frequently came loose or off, and then mother would nail them on again, while reprimanding me and cautioning me not to play football in them. Natalie found some ingenious solutions to the shortages. She sewed torn pieces of bed linen together to make underpants and singlets. She obtained some parachute nylon and knitted the strands into underpants and singlets. It seemed like a good idea, but the garments were impossible to wear. The synthetic fibre had no stretch at all and did not take on the body shape. Without elastic – also unobtainable – the 'underpants' constantly slipped. I kept them up by grasping them with my hands in my pockets. I then got into trouble for having my hands in my pockets! It could have been solved with a safety pin, but they too were impossible to obtain. While the nylon singlets lasted for a little while, shoes were a greater challenge. All kinds of substitutes were tried, even maize leaves woven into makeshift shoes, but no one told us that, unlike parachute silk, the material would stretch when first worn. I was playing football in the street when I saw my 'new' maize leaf shoe follow the ball into the air. At another time, aluminium sandals came on the market and we hurried to the *Kaufhaus*, a rebuilt department store in the centre of the city. But no one, it seems, had tested them or they would have discovered that a rigid sole made the sandals unwearable. I could not take two steps without falling; thankfully they were soon abandoned.

While the family's poverty stressed father, it made me feel ashamed. In our middle-class suburb, many of my friends were better dressed. If they had adequate clothing, why didn't we? Admittedly, there were four of us and other families had fewer children. My friends Ursula and Peter came from one-child families and Christa had just one brother. Tatjana's friend Almut was a single child, as was William's best friend Stefan. The Bourquines had two girls, and the Kramers a boy and a girl. (Did the small families point to a lack of faith, almost a protest against Hitler's One Thousand Year Reich? After all, Hitler had urged women to bear children for the Reich.) There was envy of those who had more, but at the same time there was suspicion as to how they had acquired what they had.

Life remained precarious as robberies continued. Anything not locked away, disappeared. Father had built a cage of six rabbit hutches. Rabbits were easy to rear, quick to mature and become edible, and their fur made gloves, hats, vests and even overcoats. The rabbits were fed with household scraps and the grass we collected from the verges of paths and fields. The hutches were in an enclosed corridor alongside the garage, which normally housed bicycles, but those were now kept in the locked cellar for greater security. The rabbits were almost mature when, one morning, Natalie went out to feed them and found all six padlocked hutches broken open and every rabbit stolen. The thieves were never found. Suspicion again fell on our upstairs neighbours. The Waggeg family had been staunch Nazis and that made them easy suspects, perhaps unfairly.

The word *Ersatz* (substitute) was about to be introduced into common parlance, even beyond Germany. While the real articles were not available, substitutes were introduced. Instead of eggs, a yellow powder in small packets was sold with the suggestive name of SowEi, implying that it was an egg product (*Ei* being German for 'egg'). In fact it was dried, ground-up soybeans. Mixed with water and lightly fried in a pan, it could at least take on the colour of a fried egg. In the absence of coffee or tea, mother used potato peels lightly roasted and with water added the resulting liquid looked like coffee.

I was still wetting my bed almost every night, as was my brother. With the cold and a shortage of bed linen, this was a further demand on mother. Drying pyjamas and bedding was difficult in the confined, cold spaces. Linen was normally washed only once a month. On these occasions, the sheets were merely allowed to dry as best as they could. A string over the pot-bellied stove became a washing line. The smell of urine pervaded our room. I was often aware that I smelled, and feared that others would notice. Natalie would frequently express her frustration over my incontinence, adding to my sense of shame. Regular baths were impractical, but on Sundays a large saucepan of heated water was poured into the sink and with soap and a facecloth served as a bath. What was the cause of my bed-wetting? Psychologists ascribe it variously to anxiety, silent protest or rebellion, or merely late development of bladder muscle control.

The Frankfurt City administration provided some help in that winter of 1946–47. To prevent long-term consequences of malnourishment, particularly of children, closely monitored ration cards were introduced for access to cod liver oil, syrup supplement and honey. Conditions started to improve for us when we received food aid from America. Who put us on a list to receive such parcels is unclear, but we were extremely grateful. We received six CARE packages over the next two years, large parcels assembled by a relief organisation in the USA. Each time one arrived, there was immense joy. That someone, somewhere, would share our plight was in itself very touching let alone the goods that we received. Each parcel contained items of clothing, tinned beans, a welcome tin of Spam, tinned potatoes and a treat of a one-pound bar of chocolate. Certain items – such as coffee, ham and sugar – were more valuable to barter with than to consume.

The donor in America paid US$10 and the parcel was addressed by name to needy families. Perhaps the mysterious 'relatives', Mr Shoopinsky and his wife, were our benefactors. Or did our family come to be recipients through one of Paul's students, perhaps Mr Pencost and his wife? No other family in our neighbourhood received CARE packets, to my knowledge. By chance some of the clothing had the nametag 'Eugene Brown'. It felt as if I knew him because of that shared first name, even if it did have an 'e' at the end, making me somewhat uncertain about whether the previous owner had been a boy. Mother was delighted to receive a black fur coat and hat, made from North American beaver pelts. She wore them for many years, one of the few luxuries she possessed.

With the cold winter came seasonal, childhood diseases: mumps, measles and chickenpox. Penicillin was not yet widely in use, so every epidemic had to run its course. Bouts of colds and influenza were inevitable in the crowded, inadequately heated rooms. Personal hygiene was very important and strictly enforced when the public places were so crowded with people from different regions, with varying attitudes towards cleanliness. Polio was a widely feared disease – there was a severe outbreak in 1942 – but tuberculosis was more likely in these conditions. Mother, often following father's advice – even though it was she who was the qualified doctor – treated the children's illnesses with a combination of patent medicines, sweat baths, hot compresses and sugar drinks. Usually the illness would respond in a week or so, in the meantime severely disrupting family routine. For us children, the chance to miss a week of school was attractive once the pain had subsided.

A Russian Orthodox church was built in a classroom of a school building and father took one of us to church in relay every Sunday. The building was half in ruins, but the remaining rooms housed the church and Russian and East European refugees. Paul had believed that a purpose-built Russian Orthodox church was essential, so he persuaded the Russian Frankfurt Immigration Committee to sponsor the project. He devoted what spare time he had to raising funds. It was an extraordinary undertaking and Paul would not have committed himself to it but for his strong religious belief. The Soviet threat was that of an atheistic ideology, based on an arbitrary morality. Right and wrong were decided by one man, Stalin, backed by the use of violence. The church, Paul believed, for all its imperfections, offered a superior process to that of the Communist regime, which had already led to so many deaths. Paul raised funds, obtained building permits, organised a design and helped to supervise the construction of the church. The design was based on churches in rural Russia. Natalie was less enthusiastic about the project. Much less of a believer than father, she was fearful when she saw how much he was tiring himself out.

During my initial research trip to Frankfurt, I visited father's grave and then tried to find the church. I had vague memories of where it had been, but though I scoured the district I could find no trace of it. A friend assured me that there was a Russian Orthodox church in the suburb of Ginnheim. I found it tucked away in the bend of a road some distance away, but it was nothing like the church that father had helped to build! It was a different church altogether. I was told that there were no records of father's church ever having existed. This is contradicted in his obituary, published on the front page of the Russian language weekly, *Posev*, which mentions his role in establishing the church. It also contradicts an article in a Russian language newspaper in the USA, describing the church in glowing and nostalgic terms. But there is no evidence of it either on the site or in the memory of the current clergy, who are largely recent immigrant arrivals from Russia. Since my visit, however, and a detailed letter that I wrote to the church authorities, a brief mention has been made on the church's website, so Paul's efforts seem not to have been totally in vain. But I believe that he deserved more acknowledgement for what was a substantial sacrifice on the part of himself and his family.

The Circling Sun

Paul understood the plight of people in similar circumstances and he helped many to remain out of Stalin's reach. The *émigrés* who came to seek his help often had no documents and no references. If they did have papers, they were in Russian or some other language. Paul was able to translate these into German and, with the help of Svetlana, into English. He owned two typewriters, one fitted with a German keyboard and the other with a Cyrillic keyboard – rare at the time. Documents looked more authoritative when typed. Svetlana, like many other young women, had learned shorthand and typing skills, hoping to qualify for secretarial work. She had an aptitude for languages and edited father's English when typing his translations. Paul found it difficult to turn anyone away, even when he was stretched to the limit. This work brought strangers into our apartment. Some were in near hopeless difficulties, and not all could be helped. Sometimes, in particularly needy cases, he would offer the attic room, which had been furnished as Svetlana's bedroom, as temporary accommodation. One woman, Rima Vasilievna, and her twenty-year-old daughter, Varvara, stayed for months before receiving visas to immigrate to the USA.

Among those seeking help from father were ethnic Russians, Poles, Estonians, Ukrainians and Byelorussians. They had escaped from Eastern Europe by various means and were stranded in Germany. They told different chilling stories: some had escaped by clinging to the underside of railway carriages; others had walked the breadth of Europe to find an unguarded border crossing and then moved westwards to reach Frankfurt. They could be forcibly repatriated to the Soviet Union under a provision agreed to at the Yalta conference in 1945 by Roosevelt, Churchill and Stalin. It was suspected that those repatriated were sent straight to Siberia, as their contact with the West made them perceived security risks. To escape this fate, they tried everything to get out of Europe. In one instance, Paul became suspicious of a man's story, in which he detected some inconsistencies. Once his suspicions had been aroused, Paul put a few questions to him. The answers confirmed his fears that the man was connected to the Soviet Secret Service; he didn't ever return. Another instance was even more fraught. Ironically the Soviet Military Mission was located only a few streets from our apartment, at the far end of Grillparzer Street. Soviet Military Mission staff throughout Germany were targeting Russian *émigrés* and even kidnapping some across the border into the Soviet Occupation Zone, and on to Russia. Our family was visiting friends for a celebration when, at a particular moment, a plain-clothed American man came to the apartment wanting to speak to Paul. They spoke briefly in the hallway and without a word Paul gathered us and urged us to return to *Fallerslebenstrasse*. It seems that the Americans had information that Paul was in danger. Whether the warning was necessary and genuine, and how the man came to know where father was, remain unknown. However, for Paul, fearing for the safety of his family was never far away.

Did father share his fears with anyone? His cousin Alexander Makarov had been lecturing at Tübingen University for some years. He had survived the Nazi period teaching international and civic law. The topics he taught and researched included the controversial one, considering the Nazi context, of the 'responsibility of the state to its citizens'. How was he allowed to teach this topic during Hitler's time, when surely Hitler would have banned it unless it had confirmed his view of law and the state? Yet Makarov was unlikely to have compromised his integrity during the Nazi period, even when so much of the law, education and much else besides was subverted.

Could father speak frankly and seek Makarov's advice, as he had done when they were both living in Berlin? The Makarovs with their daughters Kira and Marina visited the family in Frankfurt in August 1949. Paul and Alexander Makarov must have spoken then. Marina said her father had strongly advised Paul against leaving the country. Makarov believed that by 1949 the Western Allies could counter any Soviet threat, and that Paul and his family were safe in West Germany. What made father ignore Makarov's advice?

Marina Makarova believed that our father had forbidden us to speak Russian during the war while she, her sister and the entire family living in Berlin had no fear of doing so. She thought perhaps that this was a difference between the large city of Berlin and the much smaller one of Frankfurt, the former cosmopolitan the other somewhat provincial. In the same vein, Marina was of the opinion that while the existence of extermination camps was widely known in Berlin, friends in Hamburg had no knowledge of them and, she assumed, neither did people in other regional cities, let alone those in rural areas. Perhaps, she added, her father had privileged information. Before taking up his position at Tübingen University, he had been working at Berlin's Kaiser Wilhelm Institute, renamed the Max Planck Institute in 1935. He had access to foreign journals where he read reports of the atrocities perpetrated by the Nazis. The foreign press had reported atrocities against Jews since at least November 1939; by June 1942 they were reporting the killing of a million Jews. Marina was aware that people disappeared from her neighbourhood and never returned, and she knew that they were Jews. On strict instructions from her father, she never spoke of these things outside the home.

Marshalling the Economy

On 20 June 1948, William, then fourteen years old, recalled how, unexpectedly, the currency, the *Reichsmark* (*RM*), was declared redundant and replaced by the *Deutschmark* (*DM*). Everyone received 40 *DM* of the new currency, with a further 20 *DM* later. The then recently formed Economic Council, forerunner to the soon to be German Federal Government – led by former mayor of Cologne, Konrad Adenauer, and spearheaded by Ludwig Erhardt – brought in the currency reform at the exchange rate of 10 *RM* to 1 *DM*. The reform was needed to make the Marshall Plan for European reconstruction work, to eliminate the black market and to bring about a better balance between available goods and the money in circulation. It marked the beginning of West Germany's improving financial fortunes. In a few years, they would talk about the German *Wirtschaftswunder* (economic miracle). The response from the Soviets, to Paul's alarm, was to cut access to West Berlin. West Berliners were to be starved out of existence in retaliation for the currency reform introduced by the Western powers, without consulting them. But the blockade led to one of the greatest victories of the Cold War. The *Luftbrücke* (airbridge) to Berlin was a heroic effort to break the Soviet blockade. Paul nevertheless feared that the Western powers would not have the resolve to confront the Soviets. I became aware of the crisis through my stamp collection. To finance the airlift, a levy was introduced of a 2 *Pfennig* surcharge on every letter sent. A small blue and white stamp with the words *Notopfer Berlin* (emergency fund) was issued and glued to each envelope. The money raised provided food for West Berliners, while the Americans met the transport costs. By May 1950, after months of diplomatic brinkmanship, it was clear that the blockade had failed and the Soviets were forced to lift it.

The Marshall Plan promised to be a magic wand with which all our problems would be solved. General Marshall was a pragmatist who, on President Truman's initiative, was the driving force behind the Plan. US President Truman decided that Europe, devastated by six years of war, needed rapid rebuilding to forestall political extremism of the left or the right. As reported in detail in the US sponsored *Neue Zeitung* newspaper and on Radio Frankfurt, he authorised the sum of US$20 billion in economic and technical assistance for this purpose. The Soviet Union and the Soviet sector of Germany were invited to participate, but they refused. This in spite of the benefits that the Soviets had gained from a previous Western economic support programme, Lend Lease, that had greatly assisted Russia's war effort, with America supplying vehicles and armaments. But Stalin feared that the Marshall Plan would undermine his authority. He manipulated the neighbouring countries – Poland, the Baltic states and Czechoslovakia – into also refusing to join the Plan. Had they rebuilt their economies as West Germany and France did, then perhaps Soviet power would not have become so strong and with the many human tragedies that this brought about. The effect on West Germany was electric. The large capital investment in such a short time galvanised the economy and the society. In a few years, Germany regained its muscle as an industrial and financial powerhouse, while Central and Eastern Europe developed so-called 'centrally planned economies', building-in their own eventual demise. Initially, Paul was alarmed as the Soviets seemed to achieve significant economic success, as this enhanced Stalin's power and ambitions. Paul also continued to fear a possible Soviet invasion of West Germany. It was not an unreasonable fear and was one shared by many in the US Administration and the West German Government.

I puzzled later, how did Stalin get away with these violent attacks on his own people, potentially including our family? It seems that the answer lay in part in the way the United Nations was compromised by Stalin. When the UN Charter was drawn up, it contained articles defining 'genocide' and what constituted 'criminal destruction' of political groups. Stalin had these articles struck from the Charter, which allowed him – legally under international law – to destroy his political opponents (a strategy followed by many since, in Indonesia, Chile and Argentina, for instance). Without these safeguards in international law, my family and all *émigré* communities continued to live with this threat to their lives.

Win Some, Lose Some

Endless applications, consultations, interviews, discussions and advice – appropriate and inappropriate – finally brought Paul some success. There was jubilation in the family though also disappointment that finally it was Australia and not the USA who might take us as migrants. On a fine spring day we were called to Butzbach, a town fifty kilometres north of Frankfurt. Butzbach was the processing centre, which handled all migration formalities from applicants in the state of Hesse. We were going for our final interview with an Australian Immigration Officer, who would decide whether the family would be issued with visas for Australia. Mother had dressed us in our Sunday best. We arrived on the third floor of the former German *Wehrmacht* barracks to wait to be interviewed. Father knew the conditions: a free passage on an International Refugee Organisation (IRO) ship, a two-year work contract for whatever work was offered. His qualifications as an engineer and Natalie's as a medical doctor would not be recognised. After a short wait in what seemed like an endlessly long corridor, we were led into a room. Like a vision splendid in a film, the afternoon sun was streaming through large windows falling on the Immigration official's wooden desk, which while large was dwarfed by the size of the room. We were asked to sit on the other side of his desk and the interview began. I had been told that this was a make-or-break occasion. The tension in the family had been escalating since the call to attend had come. I was too young to make any sense of what was being said. I don't even recall whether the interview was held in German or English. The official was polite and friendly and it seemed to go well. We were on our best behaviour and answered every question with a simple 'yes' or 'no', as we had been rehearsed by father. The consular official seemed to take to us, so we came out of that room floating on air, elated by the encouraging comments that he had made about our chances of going to Australia. But, as after an audition for a play, we were now caged in a state of uncertainty. It was agonising. No departure plans could be made and plans for remaining in Frankfurt were on hold. Father warned each of us repeatedly not to speak to anyone lest our departure be sabotaged or compromised, as had happened at least twice before. We tried conscientiously to follow our normal routine. I had entered the *Mittelschule* (the fifth year of schooling) the previous August and was eagerly participating in the two weekly English lessons we had. Svetlana had matriculated, and William and Tatjana continued at their school. Not a word passed my lips to anyone about our family's possible departure. Long, slow weeks went by without any news.

What did we know of where we might be going? Virtually nothing. Mother had a book into which she glued cards, which came with packets of cigarettes. (Both Natalie and Paul were smokers.) She pointed out the peculiar Australian animals featured: a kangaroo and an emu. Attractive as these animals were, I was more impressed when she told us that orange and lemon trees grew in Australia, and there were parrots. These defined this strange new world for me (and to an extent, they still do). Something else she said, now forgotten, triggered a vision of living in a white canvas tent on some vast plain. She believed that would be our home for the first while. Years later, on seeing paintings of the Australian gold diggings in the 1850s, I was surprised by the similarity of that picture and the vision I had then of our future in Australia. It was going to be a pioneering phase before we would enjoy a better life and – this was repeatedly stressed – better educational opportunities than in Germany.

Life Goes On

Life in Germany was improving steadily ever since the currency reform of 1948. Frankfurt had also become a safer place to live. For the population, the desperation following the collapse of the Third Reich and the end of the war had passed. Despite the crisis over Berlin and the Soviet threat, there was a sense of freedom and people took advantage of it. I was envious of my brother William going on hiking tours with his friend Stefan and their girlfriends, visiting the *Edersee Sperre* (Eder Dam) north of Frankfurt. After I saw the film, I realised that this was the dam featured in the famous *Dam Busters*, when British scientists devised a bouncing bomb to scoot across the water to explode against the dam wall, piercing it and releasing a torrent of water, with seventy lives lost in the resulting flood. Father took us on hikes across the Taunus, the low range of hills that form a backdrop to Frankfurt. I was apprehensive about whether I would have the stamina to keep up, and am not sure I enjoyed these outings. However, I will not forget one special occasion. Father led us to a Roman fort and explained that people living then had enjoyed a form of central heating. Indeed the remnants of the under-the-floor central heating system were clearly visible. I was impressed by the sophistication of Roman culture. At the same time, it taught me something of the richness of human culture and of the temporal nature of things, as many of the buildings lay in ruins. From the Roman fort, called Saalburg, father took us westwards, past the magically named Fuchstanz (Fox Dance), leading to the highest point in the range, at 1,000 metres. The peak, called the Grosser Feldberg, offers a panoramic view across Frankfurt and the River Main valley. To the west is the Rhine gorge. Svetlana and two friends rode their bicycles on a camping tour there, past the 'mouse' tower at Bingen, the place that gave rise to the cautionary tale of a greedy nobleman hoarding grain, then on to the Loreley, site of the folklore made famous in Heine's poem of golden-haired sirens luring sailors to their death on the rocks, and all the way to Hameln, the home of the Pied Piper, who spirited away the town's children with his flute. These stories learned from mother and school fed my imagination. Svetlana joined the Russian scouts in the town of Mönchehof, northeast of Frankfurt. Largely funded by the US Administration, this brought together Russian youth to learn Russian language and culture. On camps they sang Russian songs, recited poems, learned survival skills and undertook extended hikes through the countryside. One reason for training the scouts, I was surprised to learn from William's friend Alex von Füner, was to prepare them for guerrilla warfare if war came between the Soviet Union and the West. I had to learn to cope with this contradiction: if there were preparations for a Soviet invasion, why was the advice to Paul not to leave the country?

Father insisted that I also join the scouts, even though I was only ten. I was sent on a two-week camp in the Vogelsberg, a mountain range northeast of Frankfurt. The US Army supplied the tents, stretcher beds and sleeping bags, a mess tent and food. American personnel ran much of the programme and they taught us to sing 'She'll Be Coming Round the Mountain' in English, as well as several Latvian and Estonian songs. There were other nationalities in the camp, all from Eastern European *émigré* communities. But I was too young for this experience. The nights were cold and I wet my stretcher bed and sleeping bag every night, and only coped with William's help. He was one of two dozen others who shared my tent. I felt miserable, cold and homesick. Father and mother came to visit at the end of the first week, driven by our neighbour and friend Mr Ivanov in his US Army jeep station wagon – he was employed to chauffeur US personnel. Mother appreciated my distress and they took me home to Frankfurt.

How did father feel about these activities that were bordering on political activism? Among the *émigrés*, there were a range of views and attitudes on the political left and right. These found voice in an organisation called the National Alliance of Russian Solidarists (NTS) and their Russian language newspaper *Posev* (Russian for 'seed'). Their headquarters were in Frankfurt, where Paul no doubt knew of their activities. However, he avoided any direct involvement even though he sympathised with their strong anti-Communist stance. The NTS's aim was for a second Revolution, as opposed to the 'botched' first one of 1917. It would make the individual pre-eminent and create conditions where the individual could exercise their obligation to society. One extreme faction in the NTS even wanted to reinstate the Tsar as a constitutional monarch. Father referred to members of that organisation as *Naphtalinchiky* (from 'naphthalene', a pesticide). But despite this dubious aspiration, *Posev* aided the West's success in the Cold War by publishing articles exposing the Soviet regime and supporting Soviet *samizdat* (self-published) books. They were the first to publish Solzhenitsyn's exposé of Stalin's labour camps, *The Gulag Archipelago*, for instance. The KGB targeted reporters for *Posev* and notoriously, in 1956, its editor was assassinated.

By 1950, five years after the end of World War II, mother had not had any communication from her family in Russia. She remembered her sister-in-law's admonition in a postcard: 'Please, no letters or postcards until we write to you'. Father had written to the Tolstoy Foundation in New York with the details of our address in Frankfurt, in case the Kamenzevs tried to make contact via a third party. As the news from Russia worsened and it seemed that postwar Stalinism was even more repressive, there were two possible conclusions to be drawn. Either the family had died in the 872-day siege of Leningrad, or they had been sent to a *gulag*, not least because they had relatives in the West. Would a move to Australia make it more difficult to find out what had happened to them? That wasn't a consideration. For Paul, it added urgency to his determination to move his family further from the Soviet Union. For Natalie, life had for years been a struggle for survival and there was no time for introspection or despair. What helped her was the strong inner core she had gained while growing up in a secure, loving family in Russia. She also had ways of releasing tension, one of them with a popular Russian expression *plivats na nikh* (colloquially, 'let them go to hell' and more literally, 'spit on them'). When all ways forward were blocked by intransigent bureaucrats and other circumstances, she could walk away from them with 'Spit on them!'

It was a shock when the telegram finally arrived with the news that we had been issued visas to immigrate to Australia. It was good news, but only now did the enormity of the move become comprehensible. We were to travel 20,000 kilometres, halfway around the globe, leaving behind virtually everything and everyone we knew. There was a totally new challenge now. After so many years of scheming, planning, changing identities and adapting suddenly, our departure became urgent not for any political reasons but for bureaucratic reasons. We were given just six weeks to pack up and leave. We had to reduce our lifetime possessions to what would fit into two trunks, four wooden boxes and some hand luggage. Each of us was given an allowance (fifty kilos, if memory serves correctly) to be loaded into the ship's hold, and as much hand luggage as each could carry. Father and William assembled four wooden crates, and with the two trunks that Natalie and Paul had brought from Russia, a red US Army ammunition box which father had pilfered, and the crated bicycle, that was the extent of our belongings to be shipped to Australia. Father's bicycle, an 'Adler' (Eagle), was a valuable item, the next best thing to a car. We knew so little of conditions in Australia that we didn't even know whether we would be able to buy a bicycle there. We were ignorant of the climate and packed our warmest winter clothing, which would become largely unsuitable in the mild Australian climate, and the pair of ice skates that Natalie had bought for her brother Michael. I chose to take three books, which my friend Peter had given me, and almost nothing else. William, the future engineer, took the microscope which he had built according to instructions in the science magazine, *Kosmos*, to which mother had been subscribing to help with his education. The microscope and three issues of *Kosmos* – one of which, coincidentally, contains an article on Australian Aboriginal fishing methods – remain in my possession. William also took a physics and mathematics textbook, several novels and a collection of Nordic myths and legends. Tatjana took several books and her treasured porcelain doll, which she kept for years. Svetlana included a history of German literature, a textbook from her last year at school. Natalie took her favourite Russian books: the poems of Pushkin, a story of St Petersburg by Bely, a Russian cookbook and some medical texts – a reflection of her abiding interest. Father took a set of books on the history of architecture and philosophy, both in German, and Karamzin's four-volume *History of Russia*, also in German. Together they took the silver which came from both sides of the family, wine glasses, plates and cups, memorabilia, photo albums with photos even of great-great-grandparents through to 1949. In severing geographical links with our past, it seems that we need objects to stir our memory and prevent the past from being lost. Equally important were documents with proof of our past and present status: copies of birth and death certificates, qualifications (in three languages), statutory declarations of marriage, records of applications to emigrate, and letters of support from friends and kind strangers. We each had a folder of our own where important papers were kept, including birth certificate, immunisation records and school reports. It included also a lock of hair taken at each child's first haircut, and congratulatory telegrams on the birth of each child from relatives in Russia and France, and colleagues in Germany. Father kept the paperwork of his attempts to migrate to the United States. It has been suggested that he was planning to immigrate there once we had made it to Australia. The letter from Moscow in reply to his application to emigrate from the Soviet Union was also preserved. There was the will, from which so much of my enquiry sprang, and a rolled-up oil painting of the founder of the Schlüsser dynasty in Russia, Justus Friedrich Schlüsser. Remnants of the paperwork establishing the family's Aryan blood, mandatory in Nazi Germany, also came with us. Mother kept the records of her medical studies and work, and many letters from relatives in Russia and France and from her aunt in Switzerland.

Although 28 March was father's fiftieth birthday, there were no celebrations. The day of our departure, 25 April, was looming. Until the very last, only the closest family friends were told of our plans. I was not allowed to tell anyone and even left without saying goodbye to my friends. One of father's last tasks was to deregister his family with various Frankfurt authorities. The only evidence of our life in Frankfurt which I could find in the public records is a document in City Hall, a printed form with the sole entry against the name Schlusser: 'De-registered 1950'. No reason is given. It seems hard to believe that thirty-three years in Germany had virtually left no paper trail in Frankfurt of father or the family. I don't recall whether father informed the schools of our departure. Only William received a school reference; there was no opportunity to arrange any others or perhaps father feared to reveal our plans. He must have made some excuse to the director of the American School for the short notice of leaving, and I expect that the Frankfurt Russian Welfare Committee was used to people's sudden displacement.

Now fifty years old, Paul looked older. He was gaunt and what hair remained was white. His fraught history was written on his face, though he remained an attractive man. He was slightly stooped, as if he was carrying a heavy burden on his shoulders. With Natalie's help, he had taken care of his health as best he could, given the conditions. He was working irregular hours, sometimes late into the night. In these last weeks, he had been hurrying taking trams to all parts of Frankfurt to finalise the various documents, both originals and translations in multiple copies, which would satisfy bureaucracy, wary of postwar opportunists. He had to anticipate what might be needed in Australia and how he might support his family. Natalie had been working in the Displaced Persons Processing Centre in Hanau and similarly resigned at short notice. Svetlana had ambitions to become an interpreter at the United Nations, which had been formed in Geneva in 1947. She spoke Russian, French and German and had a good grasp of current affairs. She was an excellent stenographer, priding herself on her shorthand and typing. Would she be able to use these skills in Australia? It appeared so, but it was difficult to get reliable information about Australia as the publicity was designed to persuade migrants rather than inform them. Official government publications painted a very positive picture of life in Australia but gave few details.

Need it be said, moving continents and changing cultures is extraordinarily stressful. After reflecting on it, speaking to other immigrants and examining my own experience, I cannot say that it was worth putting my family through it. Half a century later, I was disturbed when mother's cousin Valentina Nicolaivna, speaking in Moscow, queried the wisdom of mother's having left Russia. Of course it was the right thing to do then, I felt. Now, as I piece together what had been broken up by circumstances, I shock myself by my view – which I can only describe as reactionary – that in some sense she may have been right. I don't mean to minimise the cruelty and danger to my family of the Stalin period. I mean to convey that I have learned to appreciate fully how long and how much experience it took to establish a secure material and cultural base for our family when we migrated.

Tension in the family grew daily, and I avoided both mother and father. As the day of departure approached, it still didn't seem real that we would soon be on a ship crossing the oceans. It was beyond me to imagine what might happen and what our life in Australia might be like.

The crated luggage was dispatched. We each had our own case and a rucksack, containing our clothes, a few necessities and some personal items. Among my treasured possessions were a comic book, in colour, and a ten-centimetre hunting knife in a leather sheath. I had been allowed to buy one item to take on the voyage. I fancied that it would become a necessity in the Australian bush. I practised carving my initials into tree trunks and learned how to flick the knife in many ways, taking a delight when I succeeded.

Father had planned for a six-week journey: a week in a holding camp, four weeks on the water and another week or so in a holding camp in Australia. In reality, it took seven months just to reach Australia, followed by another two years in migrant camps.

Paul's Final Escape

On the day we left our apartment, father invited the Russian Orthodox priest to come to bless our journey. With a sprinkle of holy water, he 'released our spirits' from each room, and with a sprinkle of water on each head, he invoked the Holy Spirit to bless our odyssey. My friend Christa Weber told me years later that she had looked out from behind her curtain, seen us departing and wondered, 'Where are the Russians going?' Not even my closest friends had shared our secret. Little wonder that it seemed unreal. We piled our luggage into Mr Ivanov's car and squeezed into the station wagon. He drove us to the reception camp in Butzbach, where we had been for our final interview. The sentry, a benign American MP unlike the hostile ones from my first experience when returning to Frankfurt, opened the boom gate to let Mr Ivanov drive in. Father went to check on a notice board which room we had been allocated. There was a room for the six of us on the ground floor of 'H' Block, one of eight multi-storey barracks which, while able to accommodate several thousand army personnel, was not designed to accommodate families. We took our hand luggage and went to find the room, which turned out to be large enough for about a dozen soldiers. There were two large windows, six stretcher beds and a table and chairs near the window, a sink and kitchen bench in one corner. The thick walls and door did not stop the sound of passing traffic in the corridor, for it led to the bathroom and toilets a few doors down. Frequent announcements could be heard over the loudspeakers in the corridor. They echoed through the building and into the quadrangles. They were in three languages, German, Polish and English:

Achtung, Achtung! – *Uwaga, uwaga!* – Attention, attention! Then would follow an instruction or a list of names of those who had been selected to board a train for Bremerhaven and a departing ship. We settled in and waited. Our journey had begun and nothing was in my control. We made ourselves as comfortable as we could. The forced slow-down in pace was welcome. Even father relaxed, a good omen. Our suitcases served as bedside tables. In the quiet afternoon, I started making plans for the future. They weren't grand plans but plans to build a series of tunnels. I was obsessed with building tunnels. Wherever we went from here on, I would survey the area and plan my tunnel. My desire to tunnel underground may have reflected a need to be by myself, or more dramatically, to escape from a situation where I was powerless. I always kept my plans to myself. After my eleven years, including brushes with death (though I never admitted that to myself), perhaps it was an expression of my survival instinct. On the other hand, and most likely, it was merely a boyish fancy.

I have often attempted to write about what follows. In my darkest days, I felt the need to write this down perhaps to keep it real, perhaps as a kind of prayer, strangely, always to calm me and focus me.

There were coffee-making facilities in our room. A canteen nearby sold milk. Otherwise the camp was organised on military lines. Main meals were served in shifts in the mess hall. Breakfast from 7.30 to 9.00 a.m., lunch from noon to 1.30 p.m. and dinner from 4.30 to 6.00 p.m. The schedule was pinned on notice boards around the camp, and reminders were given over the loudspeaker. No exceptions were permitted and if you missed a sitting, you remained hungry until the next scheduled meal. I wet my stretcher bed on the first night.

Everyone in the camp was a displaced person – DPs as they were known, mostly pejoratively. Most had come from other camps where they had been living since the end of the war, but for us it was a new experience – one from which father had so far protected us. But the temporary discomforts were offset by the knowledge that he was taking his family to safety at last.

On the next day, we had unexpected visitors. My friend Ursula and her parents, Herr and Frau Mangott, drove up from Frankfurt. They had learned we were leaving and, as Ursula and I were close friends, they came to say goodbye. She was an only child and her parents had found me a welcome friend to her. They had taken us on many outings in Herr Mangott's Mercedes Benz. Mother was suspicious of how he had earned the money to afford such a car in the difficult years after the war. All that was known about him was that he was in retail sales. He now demonstrated why he was successful. I had always wanted a watch. I mentioned this to Ursula as she wore a wristwatch, which was most unusual at that time. Her father overheard my comment and immediately asked whether I might like her watch. It was an attractive offer, both for itself and as a memento of my girlfriend. I said 'yes', but rather than make me a present, as I had expected, he mentioned a price. It was modest but even so, 15 *DM* was considerable. Father had given me a little money to buy something for myself and with it I bought Ursula's wristwatch. Watches were valuable in themselves but also to barter with. It was so precious that I did not dare wear it but kept it in the side pocket of my papier-mâché valise. A few weeks later when cleaning it, I shook it out of a window. I had forgotten that I had packed the watch away. It fell out of the side pocket on to the concrete below. The fall broke the spring balance and the watch was valueless. I had to throw it away.

By the second day, I was familiar with the routine. I began to explore other parts of the camp. At mid-morning the loudspeakers announced the list of names of those who would depart the next day. A silence descended on the camp while everybody listened. Several hundred names were read out, in alphabetical order – a trainload of people. We didn't expect our names to be among them so soon but still had hopes. The announcer came to surnames beginning with 'S', but our name was not among them. Once the names had been announced, they were posted on the notice board and we checked to see whether we had heard correctly or perhaps in the hope that though our name had not come up it was still listed.

I attended an English lesson that evening and was pleased that I could keep up with the others, mostly adults. I had delighted in my English lessons at school, though my knowledge of the language consisted of a few words and phrases.

The third day proceeded quietly. Father had befriended an Estonian woman and with his characteristic warmth he invited her to share a coffee in our room. Perhaps there was a specific reason for father wanting to talk to her, but we will never know. A photo shows Natalie rather sombre and tired, looking straight into the camera, Tatjana standing behind her holding a coffee pot about to pour, and the unknown Estonian guest. Tatjana always had a sunny, open personality and here she is also smiling. Father is not in the photograph; he took it. The afternoon wore on and we followed our own interests, moving in and out of the room. The sun set. Svetlana was elsewhere. At some stage, father was told to open the crates for inspection by customs and he and William went to where our 'big luggage', as we referred to it, was stored. Customs took some time to check each container. Tatjana and I were lying on our stretcher beds reading, and mother was tidying up. Father came in to announce that customs inspection had been completed and he excused himself, saying that he needed to go to the bathroom. Then chaos. Moments later there was a knock on the door and a man opened it, without waiting for an answer, and asked urgently, in German:

'Is there a man living in this room, yes?'

'Yes, my husband', replied Natalie.

'Something has happened.' I saw that mother was momentarily unable to move. She then rushed to the door. The man opened the door wide, as four men carrying Paul's unconscious body came into our room and laid him on the table. His face was deathly pale. Mother began to scream.

'Pavlusha, Pavlusha', she shouted as loud as she could. No tears, just screams. Tatjana and I had jumped up from our stretchers, impelled to go and help father, but we quickly moved back from the table letting mother and the men surround him. She continued to scream as if wanting to wake him or call him back from somewhere. Had we known about resuscitation someone might have applied it, but it was a procedure not used then. Mother screamed for what seemed an interminable time. Someone said, 'Heart attack'. Father had had a heart attack but was still breathing. After some minutes of frenzied activity around father, Tatjana was told to find William and Svetlana. They returned and were horror-struck to see their father lying helpless on the table. Svetlana burst into tears, sobbing with fear. Natalie continued to plead with her unconscious husband not to 'leave'. In vain. Before a doctor could arrive, he was dead. When the doctor did arrive, he certified the death, giving the cause as 'probably a heart infarct'. Mother went into a state of automatic actions. She tied a piece of linen around his jaw so that, as the body became rigid, his jaw would be closed, and she dressed him in his suit. Not a word was spoken. Time stood still. It was near midnight and I was cold and numb. No emotion was possible. People were milling around in the corridor, every now and again someone could be heard to ask, 'What happened?' Indeed, what had happened?

The shock of father's sudden death caused William's strong aversion to funerals – 'I've never forgiven him for dying so suddenly' – and his insistence that his children would have ample warning of his own demise. Aged in his eighties, he reported details of his condition to his family after every medical examination. Tatjana, for years in adult life, once she had established that any given phone call was from a family member, answered with a breathless 'What's happened?' or 'What's wrong?', anticipating the worst. We all became paranoid about possible heart attacks.

On that day of father's death, on 28 April 1950, in the Displaced Persons Camp of Butzbach, Lenin lay displayed in a glass case in Moscow, where he had been embalmed like a saint. Father never saw the grotesque sight but I did, on my first Moscow visit. A whole industry of people busy working on it claim it to be Lenin's preserved body. To me, it looked more like a wax dummy than anything else, in the underground section of the mausoleum built against the north wall of the Kremlin, on Red Square. Lenin had died aged fifty-two, in 1923, and in other circumstances his botched, misguided attempt to hold on to power based on 'inevitable historical forces' would have died with him. Certainly father's cousin Antonia, living in Sablino, hoped for a return to some rule of law, particularly as it applied to private property.

Why else would she have made her will bequeathing a property legally belonging to the state? The extended Schlüsser family also believed that change would come; why else would they have urged Paul to remain in Russia? I read of the attempts to foment socialist revolutions in Berlin and Munich, which had failed. Then a little-known Ossetian, a convicted criminal and possible double agent in the Tsar's service, saw his opportunity to grasp power. His rivals and enemies constantly underestimated this man, perhaps because of his lack of skill as an orator or writer. By the time Paul and Natalie married in 1927, Stalin had so neutralised all opposition to his power that he could abolish the New Economic Policy, destroying Paul's hope for liberalisation of the Soviet economy and social policy and dashing the hopes of the extended Schlüsser family that the rule of law might return. Natalie and Paul had judged the situation correctly.

It continued to prey on my mind that I knew so little of my family's fate in Russia. When I spoke of my concern to friends, they would urge me to research further. There were so many bizarre elements to the story. When I heard that the academic Orlando Figes, author of acclaimed studies on Russian history – *Natasha's Dance* and *A People's Tragedy* – was to attend the Melbourne Writers' Festival, I was determined to consult him. I felt that I could learn something from him on how I might use the information to understand Paul and Natalie's experiences. When I eventually had the chance to do so, I blurted out a naive question:

'What remains to be done?' I asked, hoping that it would lead to a conversation about my parents' history.

He merely asked,

'Was anyone in your family repressed?' 'Repressed' was a Soviet euphemism for the process that saw people exiled to a labour camp or executed.

'Not to my knowledge', I replied. The author visibly became less interested in me at that point, while kind enough to point me to some local contacts. The encounter bothered me. I felt – as so often – that my story was worth telling, but merely because I knew of no deaths when deaths were so commonplace, it warranted less attention. I have since discovered that there were family members who had been 'repressed', imprisoned and shot, increasing my need to write of Paul and Natalie's success in surviving Stalin's forces.

My next memory is of mother entering the attic room to which we had been moved, under the sloping roof of 'H' Block. Mother asked us to stand and observe a silence as a tribute to father. We stood next to our stretcher beds, lost in our own thoughts for what seemed a long time. Eventually I ventured to ask a question.

'Is father really dead? For certain?'

'In all probability, yes. There have been instances where a person has been revived. That's why we let the body lie for three days before burying it.'

We sank into another silence. I am almost ashamed to confess it, but father's stern presence had been such that I felt a relief that he had died. I had resented the constant tension he brought into our life. I accept, of course, it was the circumstances that had brought this about. Having examined his life, I understand his fear. But at that moment, I felt relief that the tension had gone.

Finally mother said to the four of us, speaking in German:

'*Wir müssen jetzt sehr stark sein*'. (We have to be very strong now.)

Three days later, we were on the tray of a covered truck heading along the *Autobahn*, which we had taken only days earlier on the start of our journey to Australia. The coffin was in the middle of the tray and we were variously squatting and sitting on the metal surface, on either side. The canvas cover obscured any view of the countryside, no one spoke – the engine noise made that impossible – and only the rush of cars overtaking the truck could be heard. It seemed like no time at all before we arrived at Frankfurt General Cemetery. I remembered seeing it from the tram along the *Eckenheimer Landstrasse* but had never been inside it. It seemed a sterile place. We delivered the coffin to the morgue, near the entrance. Generously, family friends, the Magnus family, who lived two blocks away from our *Fallerslebenstrasse* apartment, offered us beds for the night. Thankfully, I didn't wet my bed that night.

As this was the first funeral I had attended, I did not know what to expect. Would it be a family affair, or perhaps attended by a few close friends? To my surprise, the chapel became crowded with so many people that not all could fit.

Mother kept a copy of the Russian language weekly *Posev*, which published an obituary on its front page on father's death. The people attending must have included some who had reasons to be thankful for father's help.

> Vale P.F. Schlusser. On 21 April, this year in the transit camp at Butzbach, shortly before departing for Australia, engineer Paul F. Schlusser unexpectedly died of a heart attack. The deceased was the first Chairman of the Frankfurt City Immigrant Committee, and thereafter its honorary Chairman. Always responding to the most immediate problems, he left no request unaddressed when made by people seeking help from the Committee. P.F. was the inspiration for the construction of the Orthodox Church in Frankfurt and participated in the project most enthusiastically. We express our deepest sympathies to the Schlusser family. The Administration, Frankfurt Immigrant Committee

I recall nothing of the service, but I remember being unable to see the front as adults blocked my view. Curiously I don't remember being a member of the funeral party. But I must have been. Once the service was over, the coffin was carried by six men in a procession to the graveside, led by the priest. There it was lowered into the grave and we filed past, each scattering a handful of earth on the cask. Svetlana couldn't stop crying throughout, at times becoming near hysterical. Several young men friends around her held her by the arms to prevent her collapsing. When it was over, we were driven back to the Magnus family's apartment, which was already full of people who had come for the wake. Many of father's colleagues, friends and acquaintances came to pay their respects to mother. For me, it was just a blur of adults. I did hear mother's being asked continuously what she would do following her changed circumstances.

'What will happen to you now, what will you do?'

Natalie did not know, could not know. No one knew at this point. Would we want to continue to Australia or would we even be permitted to do so? Eligibility was the prime requirement. To qualify for immigration, there had to be the same number of 'independents' – that is, working-age people – as 'dependents' in the family. Persons between sixteen and sixty years were considered 'independents'. Mother and Svetlana qualified, but William's sixteenth birthday was four months away. Even if permission were granted, would mother want to immigrate? If it were true that father was desperate to escape Soviet persecution, his death would not alter that. Did the danger remain as imminent or was some threat removed with his death? Natalie never found the answer. Not until 2009, almost sixty years later and many years after Natalie's death, would I find a satisfactory explanation. Two questions kept disturbing me: why was Paul's fear greater than that of his friends and relatives in the face of the Soviet threat, and why did he choose to come to far-away Australia? Mother's comments about father's 'schizophrenic' paranoia and 'inability to take responsibility for his actions' continued to haunt me, as did her unwillingness to talk about Zinaida.

We still had no answer whether Natalie's family had escaped the siege of Leningrad by way of the Ice Road or whether they were among the 600,000 people killed, starved or frozen to death. Mother believed the latter to have been the case. Why else had she been unable to trace them? After grieving for the loss of her family for over thirty years, she received that fateful phone call from Sweden. All would be revealed following that contact. Fortuitously, she lived long enough to learn that her family had been among those evacuated from Leningrad: they had survived. The phone call mother received in her Sydney home in 1984, over forty-five years since last contact, purporting to refer to her Russian family, had not been a deception by the KGB but had been true. Natalie's family had survived the siege of Leningrad as they had been evacuated in time. Her brother Michael, who had visited his sister in Karlsruhe over fifty-four years earlier, had led an Institute, and his daughter was able to visit her aunt, my mother. They had been evacuated to Sverdlovsk – now Yekaterinburg – and, as it was far behind the front line, they lived through the war quite safely, in contrast to our experience. This seemed ironic, as father had tried so hard to save us from harm at the hands of the Soviets. What were the consequences for mother? How, I still wonder, could you retain your sanity through these experiences? But mother did. She was kindness itself. There are touching letters between mother and her niece, Natasha, where mother enquires after Natalie's mother, Olga, who had written the postcard urging mother not to write when war between Germany and Russia threatened. But the scar was so deep that mother could not bring herself to write to her sister-in-law. Whatever the reason, over forty-five years of living in different parts of the world, with different values, was a divide that neither of them even attempted to cross. The effort was beyond either of them to explain or even recount their decisions, motivations, actions. Mother wisely felt that there were too many wounds whose scabs should not be disturbed, as it would only lead to further pain. I believe that she was right.

Mystery Solved

With this almost miraculous resolution of the fate of the family in Russia, I was emboldened to solve the other riddle, of Vladimir and Zinaida and their part in father's distress. Cousin Natasha's former husband, Lev, played an important part in this. I visited him in Moscow to try to find my own Russian roots. Casually I asked him where I might turn to locate Volodya's grave.

'Try the German War Graves Commission. The Germans are superb at keeping records. They'll know.'

I had not known of such an organisation. Its purpose is to care for the war graves of fallen German soldiers, wherever they might be found. Would that include Russians in the German Army? When I returned to Australia, I wrote to the Commission. I enquired after Vladimir Schlüsser, Paul Schlüsser (to see whether they held any records of father), and the Schlüsser of Parchim who had signed his letter 'Heil Hitler'. Quite soon, I received a reply. They had no information on a Paul Schlüsser or of the Schlüsser from Parchim. But they did have an entry on Vladimir Schlüsser. This showed, contrary to what I had been told, that Vladimir had not been shot on Lake Ladoga. Instead, he had died on 1 March 1943 in the hamlet of Nivki. Parts of the letter read:

> VLADIMIR SCHLÜSSER, born 07.04.1897 in St Petersburg/Russia, Interpreter with the 3rd/ East Battalion 667 (volunteer), died on 01.03.1943 in Nivki as a result of heart failure. His final resting place is in the Nivki Cemetery, a single grave, 500 metres north of the northern exit of the village of Nivki, southeast of Dedonichi /Duo.

Where on earth might Nivki or Dedonichi be? Were they Italian names? Were they in the north of Russia? There was nowhere a recorded location by the name of 'Dedonichi'. Would I ever find it?

Confirming the facts became an epic task, but I just had to find uncle Volodya's grave or some other verifiable facts about him. Was he shot at Lake Ladoga or did he die in Nivki, wherever that might turn out to be? Where did the story originate that he had been shot? Was there proof of that? It took me years to find Sablino, and so did locating Nivki. No atlas, no index, no register anywhere mentioned the name. I scoured the index of every atlas that I came across. Eventually I found an entry in an index to an atlas in, of all places, the Sydney Public Library. But it gave no coordinates, merely listing the name. On visits to St Petersburg, I combed the bookshops and libraries without success. I consoled myself with the thought that the Soviets had been reluctant to produce maps accessible by the public, because of their paranoia. And then I had a stroke of luck. Ever on the lookout, on another visit to St Petersburg I was perusing the stalls on *Nevsky Prospekt*, ignoring the offerings of magazines and fake van Goghs and Cézannes, when I came across a stall selling maps. Flicking through them, I found one covering the Novgorod region. I had by then established that a town called Dedovici (not Dedonichi, as in the records) was in the Novgorod region. Could this be the right town? I searched the index and to my delight and amazement found an entry on Nivki some few kilometres from Dedovici! This had to be it, I thought. I bought the map for 15 roubles, and high as I was on this discovery, I resolved immediately to visit.

I assumed that Zinaida had received a telegram with the news of her husband's death, the circumstances and location. To reconcile the contradictory information, I postulated that for military security the place of his death may have been deliberately falsified. There were even reports in Berlin and Paris, in the Russian language newspapers, that he had been shot in Lake Ladoga. It may have been Zinaida who informed the papers. Paul advised Zinaida that she might be eligible for a war widow's pension. As the wife of a soldier in the *Wehrmacht*, she had become a German citizen by default. She relocated from

Paris to Frankfurt, hoping to find work. She spoke three languages – Russian, French and German – and was offered a job as interpreter to liaise with the Russian *Fremdarbeiter* (foreign workers): forced labourers, prisoners of war and civilians living in camps around Frankfurt and working for German firms. That summer of 1943 was when we were evacuated to Allendorf. Since there was room in our Frankfurt apartment, father may have offered Zinaida accommodation. As Zinaida dealt with the Russian prisoners of war and *Fremdarbeiter*, she found that many were disaffected with their Soviet motherland. It was only a small step for her to become an active interrogator and be asked, perhaps instructed, to report to the Gestapo what she learned from them. The Gestapo in turn suggested that she try to persuade the Russians to volunteer for the newly formed ROA, the Russian Liberation Army under General Vlasov. The Soviet General had been taken prisoner near Leningrad and when he saw the true nature of Stalin's rule, he defected to the Germans, taking thousands of his men with him. Zinaida had everything to lose from a Soviet victory and everything to gain from a German one, unlikely as that now seemed. Did Zinaida succeed in persuading any Russians to change sides and join the ROA? Had her involvement with the Gestapo been the major cause for father's fear? I felt that I was getting closer to the truth.

Natalie sent us back to Butzbach. She had received permission to stay in the camp while the Australian authorities decided our future. Natalie stayed in Frankfurt to canvass friends about what she should decide. Should she take the family to Australia if given permission? When I spoke to these families in later years, they told me to a person that they had strongly advised her against it. They reasoned that an unknown future in Australia was a risky alternative to her circumstances in Germany, where she at least had friends and a profession. But she was without work, without a home, and conditions in Germany were not as positive as they would soon become. These friends were anxious to know why she had not taken their advice. All this perplexed me. I had not suspected that leaving for Australia after all the crises was decided by the narrowest of margins. But for mother, we might never have ended up in Australia. This thought unsettled me. There were too many contradictions.

Mother's reasoning, I believe, was that she felt an obligation to complete what her husband had started. The state of the Cold War heightened her fear that the Soviet Union could yet overwhelm Western Germany, and Europe for that matter. Russia was using its veto to frustrate the work of the United Nations to prevent armed conflicts, and events in Korea were leading to a possible military conflict. Leaving Europe had been her husband's wish, and it had now literally cost him his life. She couldn't let the sacrifice go without a justification. She came back to Butzbach and told us of her decision:

'If we are given permission, we will do as your father wished and go to Australia.'

I felt relief. I could not contemplate, after all that emotional effort, returning to Frankfurt, to live in a different district away from my friends, to attend a different school.

Interviews with Natalie, Svetlana and William persuaded the authorities to give us permission to emigrate. It took five weeks and many false alarms, but eventually our names were announced over the loudspeakers – 'Schlusser Natalia, Schlusser Svetlana, Schlusser Vasily, Schlusser Tatjana, Schlusser Eugen' – booming through the quadrangle for all to hear. I was only too aware that father's name was missing. But there was a change of plan. Our names had been called not to take us to a departing ship, but to be transferred to another camp instead. Our delayed stay in the Butzbach camp had seen world events overtake our circumstances. Departures of ships to Australia had been suspended because of increased Soviet belligerence. Young as I was, I understood the main thrust of events. Rather than Germany, divided Korea in the Far East became the proxy battleground between the Western powers and the Soviet bloc. Fearing Soviet expansion in Europe, President Truman declared that Korea would be the line to hold against the expansion of Communism. Chinese Communists had defeated Chiang Kai Shek a year previously and declared China a Communist state. North Korea invaded the South by crossing the 38th parallel on 25 June 1950. On 27 June, the USA decided to send troops to Korea under the command of the United Nations. Despite our distance from the crisis, we were immediately affected. US troops stationed in Japan needed urgently to be shipped to Korea. As a consequence, the US Navy could not make shipping available to the International Refugee Organisation to take immigrants to Australia. We were put on hold in limbo. As a temporary expediency, we were sent by train to another former *Wehrmacht* camp, outside the village of Wildflecken. The former officer training camp had been adapted to house refugees. Wildflecken, however, we discovered, was uncomfortably close to the East German border. To mother's dismay, rather than escape the Soviets we were now closer than ever, in fact within hiking distance of Communist East Germany. Rumours began to circulate that several people had been abducted to East Germany, or had fled across the border. Whether fact or fiction, such stories unsettled everyone.

We had no information about how long our stay would be, as weeks turned into months and the military situation in Korea deteriorated. Paul's old friend Dr Rudolf Heiss came to see mother. She met him at the railway station and he expressed his concern for her and her family's future. Like other family friends, he urged her to abandon her plan to emigrate. But she would not be dissuaded, a failure he regretted greatly and spoke of when William and I visited him in Munich in his ninety-ninth year. He gave her some money and then caught the train back to Munich. She appreciated the visit but kept to her original decision. While I understood that there was logic to this, I was nevertheless unable to fully accept the reasons. For years afterwards, I suspected some additional reason for her decision. And I was right.

The most dramatic and persuasive explanation for father's fear came to light only after the Soviet archives were opened following the collapse of the Soviet Union in 1991. With the help of the Red Cross, I discovered that on 6 October 1947, Zinaida Demianovna Schlüsser – my aunt, widow of father's brother Vladimir Schlüsser – was arrested in Berlin by the Soviet authorities on charges of 'spying for an unknown foreign power'. It cannot be a coincidence that Paul's extreme paranoia became evident towards the end of 1947.

This is what I believe happened, based on scraps of information told to me over the years, some speculation, my suspicions when mother was unwilling to talk about certain things, searches by the Red Cross, archives at the Sachsenhausen Concentration Camp Museum, my own memory of events and, most importantly, the judgment of the Moscow Military Tribunal. Zinaida's path to prison started in Frankfurt. Soon after Germany's surrender on 9 May 1945, in anticipation of our family's return from evacuation in Allendorf, Zinaida left Frankfurt to find accommodation in Bonn, where rooms may have been more easily available. She asked for some furniture and household items stored at our Frankfurt apartment to be sent to her. They included a piano and a record player, a few records, and a supply of spare record needles. How had they ended up in our apartment? I believe that she lived in our apartment while we were living in Allendorf. But why all the secrecy and no explanation from mother? Zinaida's free lifestyle in Paris made me think that her relationship with father may have become intimate. Svetlana had said that mother had suspected father had had an affair with my wet-nurse, Liselotte. Might this have been only half-true and the affair have been with Zinaida? Does this help to explain mother's bitter comment in the video interview about Paul's being 'not a strong man but a weak man'? I do not judge him, as those were different times. Besides, father showed his affection to mother in many ways. In the difficult period of 1944, he lovingly prepared a twelve-month calendar with photographs of Natalie and for each month an appropriate quotation on love, womanhood, loyalty and parenthood. I believe that this is true to the man I knew: a warm and loving father and husband, capable of great empathy and affection.

Zinaida's case was tried on 7 October, though a Soviet Military Court sitting in Berlin didn't pass sentence until 5 April 1948. It was for twenty-five years' hard labour, incarcerated in the Berlin-Sachsenhausen Concentration Camp. Only two years earlier, the world had been revolted by the barbarities committed there, and now, incredibly, it housed prisoners of the Soviet Secret Service. How or when or even whether father received news of her arrest and sentencing is unknown. It is possible, even probable, that he learned it through one of his US Army contacts. Even if Zinaida hadn't already revealed the whereabouts of her nearest relatives, she would be broken by the torture to which she was surely being subjected. She would be forced to give names and addresses and even be coerced into making accusations of collaborating with the enemy. The six-month delay between arrest and sentencing was possibly the time it took to get a confession from Zinaida, as it was claimed by the prosecution that she did confess.

From that moment on, Paul became frantic with efforts to avert what he feared was otherwise inevitable: repatriation to Russia and exile to Siberia, if not instant death. He could take no one into his confidence. Any information held by a member of the family, or well-meaning friends, could be a threat to our lives. He kept it to himself and even spread deliberate disinformation. It was in February 1948 that he claimed he had been dismissed from Schanzenbach, when in fact the documents show that he had resigned and been given a very favourable reference.

I could not accept that Zinaida had been guilty of espionage. She may have had dealings with the German military and the American Administration after the war, but I could not believe that she had deserved the harsh sentence she received. However, if the information I received should prove correct, the situation for our family had been far worse than I could have imagined. Yet I also accept that in the chaos of war, many unimaginable things can happen and be done. Researchers at the Red Cross were the first to give me details of Zinaida's whereabouts after the war. They believed that the guilty verdict was likely to have been a miscarriage of justice and an appeal would establish that. They sent me a form to complete and address to the Russian Military Tribunal in Moscow, which I duly did. In surprisingly short time, I received a four-page finding via the Red Cross, the result of my appeal. It read like a James Bond thriller and, for once, the phrase 'it came to me like a bombshell' is an understatement.

I collected the envelope from my post box at the North Carlton Post Office. I had been alerted by the Red Cross, by phone, that a verdict had been reached and the findings were in the mail. They believed it contained a favourable verdict. As I handled the envelope I had tears come into my eyes feeling the satisfaction of having persisted with the work to clear my aunt's name. I opened the envelope and unfolded the several pages it contained written in Russian. I looked for the final paragraph expecting to read something like, 'For this reason we find Zinaida Schlusser innocent ...' Instead I read with shock registering just a few sentences: '... the finding ... is upheld ... the sentence shall be left unchanged ... Zinaida Schlusser is declared ineligible for rehabilitation.' I was stunned as I realised that all my efforts had failed. It took me several days before I had the strength and courage to read the full document.

What I read took me into a parallel universe in a way I had never experienced.

That universe was the one father had sealed off for us for our protection. There, in that universe was where the threat and the truth lay. I can now claim, with mother in mind, that I understand a great deal more, rather than 'you don't understand anything'.

According to the finding, the Soviets had extracted a confession from Zinaida. She admitted that under the codename 'Agent 13' she had encouraged Russian foreign labourers in Frankfurt to defect from the Soviet Union and join General Vlasov's Russian Liberation Army. She passed this information to the German secret service, the Gestapo, and admitted to persuading at least ten people to change sides. Further, in July 1947 she illegally crossed the inter-zone border and arrived in Berlin, where she had contact with an American Counter Intelligence Corps (CIC) agent code-named 'Joerg', who recruited her to work for the Americans under the code name 'Aida'. (Was it derived from her name?) She helped to recruit at least seven agents for the American secret service while illegally in the Soviet sector of Berlin, asserted the finding.

If father had only a modicum of an idea of this, it would have been enough to panic him like nothing had ever before. I believe that here is the explanation for mother's 'schizophrenic' statement, and even her statement that he was 'unable to take responsibility for his actions'. All pieces of the puzzle finally fell into place. And I believe that I understand father's anger, fear, attempts to control events and people, and the consequent actions he took. My only regret is that I did not learn of these facts earlier, so as to be able to share them with mother and perhaps relieve her of some of the anxiety that had blighted her life. But I also accept that keeping the truth from the children was a wise decision. With the ongoing tensions of the Cold War and my inadequate understanding of the danger that my family was exposed to, mother rightly judged that I might have responded inappropriately and perhaps even put the family at risk.

After two years at Sachsenhausen Concentration Camp, having extracted all useful information from her, the KGB in 1950 handed Zinaida over to the newly formed East German Stasi (*Staatssicherheitsdienst*, 'State Security Service'), of the German Democratic Republic. Meticulous about keeping records, the KGB files show that she was handed over to the Stasi on 11 February and locked up in Hoheneck Prison, the notorious women's prison in Karl Marx Stadt (now reverted to its original name, Chemnitz), East Germany. The Stasi had been formed three days earlier, on 8 February. Anna Funder, in her book *Stasiland*, quotes the experience of a former inmate, of her water torture and physical abuse by sadistic women guards. Another inmate, Erika Rieman (she may even have known Zinaida), was interviewed for Peter Molloy's BBC documentary series *The Lost World of Communism*, where she recalls her final months in Hoheneck. After Stalin died on 5 March 1953, the inmates learned of a general amnesty granted to prisoners of war in Russia. When their demands for a commission of enquiry were rejected, they went on a hunger strike. Zinaida most probably was among them. People from outside demonstrated in front of the prison on their behalf. The hunger strike was broken and Erika put into solitary confinement. She attempted to hang herself in December 1953 but was saved and put into a single cell. She was finally released on 18 January 1954. Zinaida may have had a similar experience. Her prison record index card shows that she was released from Hoheneck on 19 January 1954 and reportedly returned to Berlin. Each prisoner was made to wear a scarf of a particular colour, which restricted them to living in designated areas of Germany. Should they attempt to move elsewhere, the authorities would immediately recognise this. Zinaida would have been given a red scarf, confining her to Berlin. Before leaving Hoheneck, each woman had to sign a document stating that they had been treated well in prison and would not reveal the circumstances of their arrest.

Mother had received a mysterious postcard towards the middle of 1954. I remember seeing it. It seems that some time before being released, Zinaida wrote that postcard to Natalie, addressed to our former address in Frankfurt. It was forwarded by Frau Aderkas to mother in Perth, Western Australia, where she was living by then. Frau Aderkas was the wonderful soul who had helped us when we were children in Frankfurt and who continued to correspond with Natalie. In the postcard, Zinaida claimed that she was being kept in an insane asylum and begged for help. Mother was horrified to receive it and suspected that it was a KGB trap. She destroyed the postcard immediately and never referred to it again. According to Tatjana, mother was agitated for months afterwards. She still felt the fear of Soviet power, that fear that had killed her husband. But what was this about an insane asylum? A French colleague who is familiar with the East German prison system is in no doubt that the claim Zinaida was released in 1954 was false. He believes that this is a cover for her death in prison. I have investigated the addresses given on her prison record, but there was no trace of her. Had she settled in Berlin, there would surely have been applications for permits, perhaps a pension and so on. The Red Cross has been unable to find any trace of her after her alleged 'release' from Hoheneck Prison.

On 12 August 2012, I received a letter from the Russian Federal Security Service (which Putin once headed) and I learned of the fate of father's cousin, Artur Arturovich Schlüsser. I had requested details of the charges and his sentence. It transpires that he was arrested again (he had been arrested and imprisoned in 1924, precipitating Paul and Natalie's departure from Russia), on 15 June 1938, during the great Stalinist purges and was sentenced to death. The sentence was carried out on 28 June in Leningrad's Kresty Prison. I recalled my visit to the Anna Akhmatova memorial in St Petersburg and the soul-destroying sight on the other side of the Neva River, of the red brick walls of Kresty Prison. I now learned where he had been executed but I have yet to discover where he is buried – probably in an unidentified mass grave.

When I asked for further details, the FSB explained that there were so many executions then that details such as these were not recorded. This might prove to be incorrect. In his book *Moscow 1937*, Karl Schlögel documents executions and executioners in Moscow prisons that year. Perhaps similar information may yet come to light about executions at Kresty Prison.

Paul had survived Lenin, outlived Hitler and escaped Stalin. This was his victory. But for reasons that are unclear, father's body in the Frankfurt Central Cemetery was re-interred in 1958. He was taken to a different area of the cemetery, dedicated to 'victims of the Nazi regime'. This is a final irony. If anything, he could proudly claim that he had survived one of the most brutal regimes in history rather than become its victim. The new grave is a double grave. As if to inflict a further humiliation, father, proud to have been born in St Petersburg, now lies under a headstone inscribed with his birthplace as 'Denmark'. I searched among the photos to find one of father's original grave, to check what it said of his birthplace. To my surprise, the gravestone recorded neither his birthplace nor his place of death. Could it be that mother's fear was such that it literally reached beyond the grave and she didn't dare mention Leningrad (or St Petersburg) on his headstone? It seems hard to believe and yet ... I have sat by father's new grave a number of times and each time I reflect how his life consisted of misinformation and disinformation, from almost the beginning to the end. All in order to survive the chaos of the first half of the twentieth century. He was a victim not of National Socialism but of tyranny. Tyranny which did not value individual life, which knew no bounds to the evil it committed, which perverted all that is good in human beings. It was the fear of losing his freedom and his humanity, of coming too close to the sun, that drove him. Yet in another sense, all three tyrants killed father. It was fear that ate his soul.

An ultimate injustice remains: no one has been held accountable for his death or that of millions of others. Nor, on the other hand, has he received credit for remaining a man of integrity despite the circumstances, which defeated and compromised so many. By telling this story, I hope to have done him justice and paid him appropriate homage.

What would that wonderful woman who sat smoking by the window overlooking the sea in North Curl Curl have made of it all? 'You are silly' would have been her first comment, but then she would have come around to admit that she had saved all the documents, photos and correspondence in the hope that some day they could be ordered and reveal the pattern they form – a pattern of individuals like herself and father, surviving in the maelstrom of history, their integrity intact, conscious of their mistakes but with the satisfaction that they had escaped the tyrants alive, with their family able to enjoy the warmth of the sun in a far more benign part of the world.

Appendices

1: Eulogy for Justus Friedrich Schlüsser – presumably delivered at his funeral in St Petersburg, March 1840*

Born in Berlin on 6 July 1760, he died in St Petersburg on 16 March 1840, at the age of seventy-nine years, eight months and ten days.

After completing his education in Berlin, he went to Lübeck in the year 1778 to the office of the trading company there, J.W. Croll, where he stayed until the year 1783.

Following an offer made to him by Eckhoff in Le Havre, he left Lübeck in the year 1783 and moved to Le Havre, where in the meantime the owner had been declared bankrupt.

As a consequence he remained in Le Havre for only ten months and planned, as he had lost all his means, to travel on foot to Nantes and Bordeaux, armed with his letters of recommendation from Croll and Gaillard in Lübeck, to see how to move forward.

In the meantime, before he could put his decision into practice, he was offered a position in Le Havre to become the German agent for Albrecht Müller in St Petersburg, which he commenced on 14 May 1784, where he later became bookkeeper in the same firm.

While holding this position, he married Dorothea Elisabeth Bode on 15 May 1791 and entered into business in the year 1794 with Friedrich Wolff, a travelling agent from Thurneyssen in Bern and St Gallen, who had been recommended to him by his first employer, J.W. Croll in Lübeck, as the firm of Wolff-Schlüsser.

In the year 1810, Wolff left the business while the firm from then on operated as Schlüsser & Co.

His marriage produced five sons and four daughters, of the latter one died in 1802. Besides that in the year 1797, following the death of her father, he took Marie Nabholz into his home as his adoptive child, from where she went in the year 1814, marrying Robert Ritter.

[* Translated from German]

2: Antonia Schlüsser's Will – a Declaration under Oath, 1923*

Finding myself in good health with a strong memory, I bequeath my property, including the land and three buildings and everything in them, fixed and portable, to my nephews Nicolai Feodorovich Schlüsser and Pavel Feodorovich Schlüsser. And I ask them to allocate (1) *Desyiatina* [hectare] of the land to Artur Arturovich and Dagmara Arturovna Schlüsser for them to construct a *dacha*. The land and houses are located 3 *versts* from the Sablino Railway Station on the NRL [Nicolaivski Railway Line], in the region of Trotsk.

1923   [signed] Citizen Antonia Vasilievna Schlüsser

27 November

[* Translated freely from the Russian by E. Schlusser]

3: Marriage Certificate, 1927*

With this church seal it is certified that on 20 March 1927, in the Church of Kiev Court, in the city of Leningrad, were married, both for the first time:

Pavel Feodorovich Schlüsser, 26 years old and the maiden/ spinster Natalia Vassilievna Kamentseva, 26 years old, both Russian Orthodox.

In witness of this for the bridegroom:
Michael Nikolaevich Bruni and Vassili Ephimovich Kamentzeff.
For the bride:
Michael Vassilievich Kamentzeff and Sergei Afrikanovich Bytshenkov.

The act of the marriage is recorded in the register Part 2, No. 13 of the Krasnoselskoya Holy Trinity Cathedral. The sacrament of marriage was performed by the Most Reverend Protoyerei Feodor Znamenski.
[signed] Protoyerei F. Znamenski
[The Seal] Red Village (Krasnoe Selo)
21 March 1927

[* Translated from the Russian by Svetlana Schlusser-Risco]

4: Conditions for Emigrating, 1935*

Intourist accepts applications for emigration abroad only for permanent relocation and under the following conditions:

You must have permission to enter the country to which you propose to travel. You must pay for yourself and family abroad, to one of our foreign representatives:

Cost of a Soviet foreign passport/ for workers and
their dependents   550 gold roubles
OR
Not employed   1,100 gold roubles

Cost of travel from the home – to the indicated place, from Leningrad to Karlsruhe.

And 10% of the final sum – commission to Intourist if travelling to eastern and European countries.

Or 5% commission to Intourist for travel overseas or to Palestine.

To be paid at the exchange rate prevailing on the day.

Payment can be made to our representatives abroad, available in all European countries and also in New York, and in Palestine – the firm of I. GOSS & Co. Tel-Aviv. They will accept the full sum at the exchange rate of the day. They will also make any necessary arrangements. On receiving the required payment, Intourist will begin to address your case and send you further notice.

In case you are refused emigration, the money will be refunded minus half the commission.

Children under 16 years old are to be written into the parent's passport.

VAO INTOURIST EMIGRATION SECTION
[signed]
261/50   Sp./am/5/XI

[* Translated from the Russian]

5: Establishing Aryan origins, 1939*

Captain Schlüsser, Parchim, 23.1.1939
21 *Alexandrastrasse*

Highly Esteemed Herr Schlüsser
Firstly, forgive me that I don't address you by your rank and title, but I only managed to get your name and address from a comrade.

As we both have the same name, I hope that after years of fruitless searching I am able to greet a relative in you.

My great-grandfather was called Justus Friedrich Schlüsser. He was born in Berlin on 17.7.1760, emigrated to St Petersburg and founded the firm of Schlüsser & Co. there. His wife was Dorothea Elisabeth Bode.

I would be very happy to hear from you whether my assumption is correct that we belong to the same family.

With kind regards,
HEIL HITLER!
[signature unreadable]

[* Translated from the German]

6: Paul under Gestapo surveillance

Translation from German.

G. SCHANZENBACH & CO., LTD.
Electrical-& illumination-equipment works.
FRANKFURT(MAIN)-WEST 13

Frankfurt(Main)-West,
Adalbert Str.15

October 27th, 1949.

The engineer Paul S c h l ü s s e r was exposed to repeated persecutions on the part of the Nazi-organs and especially of the Gestapo. This took such shapes that the Gestapo summoned the manager of the works and drew his attention thereupon that the works will have to face with the fact of an early imprisonment of Mr Schlüsser.

In view of the critical position, the works made a last attempt to save Mr Schlüsser from the threatening danger, as they did not wish to lose him either as a workman or a human being. On the demand of the Gestapo, the manager of the works guaranteed for Mr Schlüsser and took upon himself the supervision of his activities, whereupon Mr Schlüsser was not confined to a camp, but lived under constant supervision.

G. Schanzenbach & Co, Ltd.,
/ Signature/   / Signature/

Certified true translation:

Hanau/M.,
November 3rd, 1949
Nr 5106

(K. Plaucitis)
Legal Counseller
IRO Area Nr 1

7: Reference from G. Schanzenbach & Co., 1948*

Paul Schlüsser (Graduated Engineer), born on 29 March 1900 in St Petersburg, was employed continuously in our firm from 15 July 1937 to 29 February 1948. In this period we gave him the responsibility of leading our light engineering laboratory and in this capacity, owing to his comprehensive knowledge of electric and light engineering, he was in charge of developing, testing and evaluating our specialty equipment in the electro-technical field.

Herr Schlüsser at first addressed the issue of developing contemporary neon lights for interior and exterior use, later he dedicated his work to developing lamps for transportation and headlights for trucks and for railways. Equipment which was secure where explosives might be used or where extreme weather conditions prevail – one of the foremost items in our production programme – was constantly supervised by him, examined and improved. When it became possible to dehydrate and sterilise foodstuffs and packaging by means of electric radiation, Herr Schlüsser carried this work successfully forward for our company.

This work allowed Herr Schlüsser to have intimate knowledge of the construction and manufacture of this equipment, so that he has extensive knowledge of the technical production and assembly line production of the equipment. In connection with this work, plans had to be drawn up for the installation of electrical equipment, which allowed Herr Schlüsser to gain great practical experience in the area of manufacturing, adding to his excellent theoretical knowledge.

Herr Schlüsser has a thorough University education in general electro-technology and light-technology, and thanks to his continuous interest in problems in his field he was able to contribute to many areas where relevant challenges arose in our company.

Herr Schlüsser leaves our firm of his own free will. We regret this especially as with him we also lose a dependable and always forthcoming colleague whose performance was always highly satisfactory.

We wish him great success in his future work.

G. Schanzenbach & Co.

[signed] Walter Kaesewitz [signature unclear]

[* Translated from the German]

8: Decision from the Russian Military Court, date stamped 2010*

DECISION
of Supervisory Court No. 17
Settlement of Vlasikha, Odintsovskiy Rayon   14 September 2009
Moskovskaya Oblast

Presidium of District Military Court 3

comprising Colonel of Justice S.G. Sokerin, President;
Presidium Members: Colonels of Justice A.I. Massin and B.A. Kozhevnikov;
Secretary: N.A. Agafonova

with the participation of Colonel of Justice A.V. Antyufeyev, Acting Military Prosecutor of the Strategic Missile Forces,

has heard the criminal matter in regard to the finding made by Major General V.N. Samusev, Military Prosecutor of the Strategic Missile Forces, in regard to the sentence imposed by the Military Tribunal of the Garrison of the Soviet Sector of Berlin on 5 April 1948, by way of which

Zinaida Ivanovna* SCHLÜSSER (nee Kungurtseva), year of birth: 1900, place of birth: Irkutsk, Russian, a German national, citizen of Berlin, non-Party member, arrested in regard to the matter on 7 October 1947

was convicted:

– pursuant to Item s of Paragraph 1 of Article 2 of the Control Council Act No. 10 of 20 December 1945 'regarding the punishment of persons guilty of war crimes, crimes against peace and crimes against humanity', in conjunction with the sanction of Item v of Paragraph 3 of Article 2 of the said Act she was sentenced to punishment of 20 years' imprisonment in correctional labour camps

– pursuant to Part 1 of Article 58-6 of the Criminal Code of the Russian Soviet Federal Socialist Republic, to imprisonment in rehabilitative labour camps for a term of 25 years.

For the aggregate of the crimes committed, pursuant to Part 1 of Article 58-6 of the Criminal Code of the Russian Soviet Federal Socialist Republic,

---

* This appears to be an error. Her patronymic elsewhere is 'Demianovna'.

Z.I. Schlüsser was sentenced to a total penalty of imprisonment in correctional labour camps for a term of 25 years, without confiscation of property, as the convict had none.

The verdict was not taken on appeal to an appellate court, and no objection was lodged.

In the finding of Major General V.N. Samusev, Military Prosecutor of the Strategic Missile Forces, the question is raised of leaving the said sentence unchanged and declaring the convict, Z.I. Schlüsser, not eligible for rehabilitation.

Having heard the address of Judge B.A. Kozhevnikov and the opinion of Colonel of Justice A.V. Antyufeyev, Acting Military Prosecutor of the Strategic Missile Forces, who supported the finding, the Presidium

has **ESTABLISHED** the following:

Schlüsser was found guilty of a crime against humanity in the form of hostile acts against the civilian population, persecution of persons on political and racial grounds as well as espionage, the crimes being committed under the following circumstances.

In 1920, Schlüsser commenced employment as a medical nurse at the White Guard Field Hospital of Wrangel's Army, after the rout of which she emigrated initially to Turkey and then to France, where she resided until 1942.

In 1942, Schlüsser became a citizen of Germany and, having travelled to the city of Frankfurt am Main, commenced employment as a guardian for the administrators of German camps housing Soviet citizens forcibly taken away to perform hard labour in Germany. Until 1945, Schlüsser gathered information on the state of mind of Soviet citizens in the said camps, on their relationships to the camp administrators and details regarding persons wishing to join the ranks of General Vlasov's Army. Schlüsser was passing on the information to the Gestapo for reward.

In July 1947, having illegally crossed the inter-Zone border, Schlüsser arrived in Berlin, where she established contact with an American CIC intelligence agent by the name of 'Joerg', by whom she was recruited as a secret agent collecting espionage information detrimental to the interests of the Soviet Union.

In his finding, the Prosecutor is of the view that the court gave a correct juridical assessment of the facts and circumstances of the case. Schlüsser was correctly convicted, her guilt is confirmed by the available evidence, the authenticity of which raises no doubts. On the basis of the aforegoing, Schlüsser is not eligible for rehabilitation.

Having examined the materials of the case and discussed the reasons given in the finding and in the submission of Colonel of Justice A.V. Antyufeyev, Acting Military Prosecutor of the Strategic Missile Forces, the Presidium of the District Military Court holds that the finding is valid and should be upheld.

As is evident from the materials of this criminal matter, in the course of the preliminary investigation and at the court hearing, Schlüsser did not deny the factual circumstances of what she had done and, although her admission of guilt was partial, she did confirm the fact that she had worked for the Gestapo as an agent-informant under the agent number 13 in German camps for Soviet citizens and that she had passed on to the Gestapo for reward information pertaining to persons interned in those camps. These events, according to Schlüsser's testimony, numbered no fewer than 10.

Schlüsser also confirmed that she had collaborated with the American intelligence agent 'Joerg' and had been assigned the agency pseudonym 'Aida' and had been passing on intelligence information to him. Furthermore, as an interpreter, she participated in the recruitment of no less than 7 agents from among the Soviet citizens and service personnel and in the obtainment of intelligence information from them. Nor did Schlüsser deny the fact of her illegal presence in the Soviet Occupation Zone where she had been detained.

Furthermore, the convict's guilt was confirmed by the testimonies of the witnesses N.A. Korepanov and S.I. Negoda regarding the detainment of Schlüsser in the Soviet Zone of Berlin as well as by the confiscation from her, upon her being searched, of documents confirming her collaboration with

American intelligence services.

Thus Schlüsser was validly prosecuted and convicted pursuant to Item s of Paragraph 1 of Article 2 of the Control Council Act No. 10 of 20 December 1945 'regarding the punishment of persons guilty of war crimes, crimes against peace and crimes against humanity' for crimes against humanity in the form of hostile acts against the civilian population, persecution of persons on political and racial grounds as well as for espionage pursuant to Part 1 of Article 58-6 of the Criminal Code of the Russian Soviet Federal Socialist Republic.

The sentence imposed on Schlüsser is just, in regard to its type and severity, and the convict is not eligible for rehabilitation.

On the basis of the aforegoing, pursuant to Articles 407 and 408 of the Russian Federation Code of Criminal Procedure and Articles 4, 8 and 9 of the Russian Federation Rehabilitation of Victims of Political Repression Act of 18 October 1991, the Presidium hereby delivers the following

DECISION:

The finding of the Military Prosecutor of the Strategic Missile Forces is upheld.

The sentence imposed by the Military Tribunal of the Garrison of the Soviet Sector of Berlin of 5 April 1948 on Zinaida Ivanovna Schlüsser shall be left unchanged.

Zinaida Ivanovna Schlüsser is declared ineligible for rehabilitation in regard to the present matter.

An appeal against this decision may be lodged with the Military Judicial Assembly of the Supreme Court of the Russian Federation.

Valid with the appropriate signature.

This is a true copy of the original:

Signatory: Colonel of Justice B.A. Kozhevnikov, Presidium Member

[Issuer's stamp: District Military Court 3]

[* Translated from the Russian]

Select Bibliography

Andrew, C. & V. Mitrokhin, *The Mitrokhin Archive: The KGB in Europe and the West* (London: Penguin, 1999).

Appelbaum, A. *Gulag: A History* (London: Penguin Books, 2003).

Behrman, G. *The Most Noble Adventure: The Marshall Plan* (New York: Simon and Schuster, 2007).

Blagovo, N.V. *A School on Vasilievsky Island: A Historical Chronicle, 1856–1918* [in Russian] (St Petersburg: Nauka, 2005).

Caute, D. *The Fellow Travellers* (London: Quartet Books, 1977).

Churchill, W.S. *Great Contemporaries* (London: Thornton Butterworth, 1938).

Elliot, D. *New Worlds: Russian Art and Society 1900–1937* (London: Thames & Hudson, 1986).

Fest, J.C. *Not I: Memoir of a German Childhood* (New Delhi: Atlantic, 2012).

Figes, O. *Natasha's Dance: A Cultural History of Russia* (London: Penguin, 2003).

—— *A People's Tragedy: The Russian Revolution 1891–1924* (London: Jonathan Cape, 1996).

—— *The Whisperers: Private Life in Stalin's Russia* (London: Penguin, 2007).

Funder, A. *Stasiland* (Melbourne: Text Publishing Company, 2003).

Grass, G. *Peeling the Onion: A Memoir* (Orlando: Harcourt Inc., 2006).

Haupt, W. *Heeresgruppe Nord 1941–1945* [Army Group North; in German] (Bad Nauheim: Podzun, 1966).

Heiden, K. *The Führer*, translated by R. Manheim (New York: Carroll & Graf, 1944).

Heiss, R. *Lebensmitteltechnologie und Verpackung* [Food technology and packaging; in German] (Frauenhofer Institut, Munich, 1984).

Hitler, A. *My Struggle* (London: Hurst & Blackett Ltd, 1936).

Kershaw, I. *Hitler* (London: Penguin Books, 2009).

Kunitz, S. & M. Hayward, editors and translators, *Poems of Akhmatova* (Boston: Houghton Mifflin, 1967).

Kummer, L. & Kummer, E. *Das Land Ohne Sonntag* [Country Without Sunday; in German] (Vienna & Leipzig: F. Salis, c. 1934).

Leinonen, R. & E. Voigt, *Deutsche in St Petersburg* [Germans in St Petersburg; in German] (Luneburg: Institute of North German Culture, 1998).

Pipes, R. *Communism: A History* (New York: Random House, 2001).

—— *Russian Revolution: A Concise History* (London: Harvill Press, 1995).

Porter, C. *Alexandra Kollontai: A Biography* (London: Virago, 1980).

Reed, J. *Ten Days that Shook the World* (Harmondsworth: Penguin Books Ltd, 1966).

Schlögel, K. *Das Russische Berlin* [Russian Berlin; in German] (Munich: Siedler Verlag, 1998).

Roberts, R. *Schroders: Merchants and Bankers* (London: Macmillan, 1992).

Service, R. *Lenin: A Biography* (London: Macmillan, 2000).

—— *Spies and Commissars* (London: Macmillan, 2011).

Shirer, W. *A Native's Return: A Memoir* (Boston: Little, Brown & Co., 1990).

—— *Twentieth Century Journey* (Boston: Little, Brown & Co., 1976).

Solzhenitsyn, A. *The Gulag Archipelago* (New York: Harper & Row, 1973).

Sudoplatov, P. *Special Tasks: The KGB in Europe and the West* (London: Little Brown & Co., 1994).

Swan, H. *Home on the Neva: The Life of an English Family in Tsarist Russia and during and after the Revolution* (London: Victor Gollancz, 1968).

Tolstoy, N. *Victims of Yalta: The Secret Betrayal of the Allies, 1944–1947* (New York: Pegasus Books, 1977).

Valiev, M.T. *The Schlüssers: A Family History of Germans in St Petersburg – a Biographical Perspective*, Vol. 8 [in Russian] (St Petersburg: Kunstkammer, 2014).

Index

For headwords in **bold**, see plate section(s) indicated for illustration.

Academy of Arts (St Petersburg) 17, 63

Adenauer, Konrad 233

Aderkas, Frau 216, 264

Akhmatova, Anna 46, 65–6, 93; memorial statue (St Petersburg) 65, 66, 264

Allendorf (Germany; plate section 2): generally x, 180, 188; Paul and Natalie's family in 180–96, 199, 207, 257, 260 (see also American Occupation Forces)

America (plate section 2): Paul and Natalie's family as potential migrants 74, 211–12, 213–14, 217–18, 236, 242; Natalie's eventual visit 87; Schlüsser descendants in 212–13

American Occupation Forces: in Allendorf, post-World War II 192, 193–4; in Frankfurt, post-World War II x, 9, 10, 193, 199, 200, 201, 203, 204, 206, 209, 221, 239; as 'liberators' to Paul and Natalie 193, 200; Paul's work for 9, 10, 215, 216–18, 223, 231, 243, 260

Argentina (plate section 2), Paul and Natalie's family as potential migrants

Arnot, Monsieur 105

Artsutanov, Yuri 171

Aryan roots (plate section 2), for Paul and Natalie's family 169, 170, 242, 272

Australia (plate section 2): Paul and Natalie's family as potential migrants 236–7, 240, 241, 242, 253, 257–9; making ready 241–2, 243, 244, 245; arrival/ settlement 54, 74, 244, 264

Baker, Josephine 103

Belarus (White Russia), and Kamenzev family 41, 90; and Schlüsser family 73

Berlin: archives in 175; Russian diaspora to 63, 78, 87, 96, 98, 104, 128, 174; Paul and Natalie in 7, 81, 82, 83, 87, 91, 92, 93, 94–8, 99, 106, 107–10, 111–12, 113, 123, 141, 212, 231; wider Schlüsser family in 49, 50, 63, 79, 82, 94–5, 98, 132, 148, 153, 170, 174, 175, 176, 196, 231, 232, 250, 267, 272; Soviet Embassy in 97–8, 109, 112; Zinaida in 259, 260–1, 262, 263, 264, 275, 276–7

Binchenkov, Sergei Afrikanovich 85, 270

Blagovo, N.V. 19, 21

Bolshevik Party: origins 64; rise and rule 22, 28, 29, 30, 32–3, 34, 35, 36, 38, 43–4, 51, 52, 63, 64, 84–5, 109 (see also Cheka; Communism; KGB; League of Struggle; Lenin; Red Army; Stalin)

Bonn (Germany), Zinaida in 210, 260

Bourquine family 222, 226

Brecht, Bertolt 92, 109

Brest-Litovsk Treaty 26, 35, 91

Britain, Paul and Natalie's family as potential migrants 54, 55, 210

Brodsky, Joseph 66

Bruni family 17, 21, 77

Bruni, Anna (plate section 2) 102, 103

Bruni, Fyodor 17, 63

Bruni, Konstantin (Kostya) (plate sections 1&2) 16, 20, 62–3, 98, 102, 103, 160–1

Bruni, Michael Nikolayevich 85, 270

Bryullov, Karl 17

Bukharin, Nicolai 44, 77

Bulgakov, Mikhail 20, 65, 76

Bund Deutscher Mädchen see Hitler Youth organisations

Bunin, Ivan 93

Butzbach (Germany; pre-migration camp), Paul and Natalie's family in 245–9, 251, 257, 258

Canada, Paul and Natalie's family as potential migrants 215

CARE packages, for Paul and Natalie's family 227–8

Carter, (US) President Jimmy 84

Catherine the Great 49; memorial statue (St Petersburg) 45

Charité Hospital (Berlin), Natalie's work at see Robert Koch Medical Institute

Cheka (Soviet secret police) 52, 88

Chekhov, Anton 100

Chopin, Frederic 90

Christo and Jeanne Claude 202

Churchill, Winston 74, 123, 129, 210, 231

CIA/CIC (American secret services) 11; and Zinaida 262, 276–7, 278

Clayton, William S. 207

Civil War, Russian (1918–22): generally ix, 36, 41, 61, 77, 212; combatants 21, 39, 55; dramatic representation 76 (see also Red Army; White Army)

Civil War, Spanish (1936–39), and Hitler 156

Communism/ Communist regime: in Russia 35, 36, 37, 44, 64, 65, 69, 76, 77, 79, 80–1, 83, 85, 91, 113, 118, 119, 122, 229; elsewhere/ internationally 79, 118–19, 122, 132, 144, 258, 259 (see also Bolshevik Party; KGB; Lenin; *Nomenklatura*; Stalin)

Crimea: historically 41; Schlüsser family travel to 14, 34, 47

(J.W.) Croll (company, Lübeck, Germany) 267, 268

Custine, Marquis de 35

Czerny, Professor Adalbert 108

Dahler-Schlüsser, Sophia see Schlüsser, Sophia

Damm family 180, 182–3, 185, 199, 207

Damm, Herr (plate section 2) 180, 181, 183–4, 186, 188, 190–1, 192, 194

Damm, Frau (plate section 2) 189, 190, 192

Damm, Friedrich 180–1

Damm, Heinrich (Heini) 180, 191, 194

Damm, Kathie 188, 194–5

Damm, Margarete (Gretel) (plate section 2) 180, 187–8

de-Nazification process, post-World War II (plate section 2): generally 209, 210; for Paul and Natalie 209–10

Denikin, General 41, 55

den Ouden, Robert (plate section 2) 135, 161

Diaghilev, Sergei 98, 137

Diderot, Denis 49

Diesterweg, Adolph 19

Diesterweg School (primary school, Frankfurt) (plate section 2) 19, 220

Displaced Persons Processing Centre, Hanau (Germany), Natalie's work at 215, 216, 243

displaced persons (DPs), Paul and Natalie's family as 246

Dornbusch police station (Frankfurt), and Paul 12, 187, 200

Dostoevsky, Fyodor 29, 62, 117

Dupond, Anna (plate section 1) 40, 105, 242

Dupond, Louise (Natalie's grandmother) 39, 103, 105, 156

Dzerzhinsky, Felix 67, 68, 142

Dzhennera Institute (Leningrad), Natalie as researcher at 75

Eisenhower, General 201

Elizabeth (Lilibeth; nanny to Paul and Natalie's children) 141, 145, 146

Erhardt, Ludwig 233

Fallerslebenstrasse (Frankfurt) (plate section 2), Paul and Natalie's family in 9–10, 187, 203, 204–5, 231, 251

(I.G.) Farben (company, Frankfurt) 201, 202

Fest, Joachim 133, 140, 146, 173

Figes, Orlando 23, 250

Finland, Schlüsser family *dacha* in 14, 47

Food Technology Institute (Munich) 152, 168, 169

France: rural, Paul and Natalie on honeymoon in 104–5; urban see Paris

Franco, General 156

Frankfurt: historically 92, 222; Paul and Natalie's apartment/ family in 8, 9–11, 12–13, 19, 40, 54, 55, 90, 127, 131, 149, 151–2, 154, 156, 157, 158, 165, 167, 170, 172, 175, 176–8, 186, 187, 190, 196, 199–201, 203, 204–10, 214, 215–19, 220–1, 224, 225–31, 236–41, 243, 245, 257, 260, 264; Vladimir Schlüsser in 165; Zinaida in 40, 165, 171, 172, 210, 257, 260, 262, 276 (see also American Occupation

Forces; Dornbusch; *Fallersleben-strasse*; Ginnheim; Schanzenbach & Co.; University of Frankfurt)

Frankfurt General Cemetery, Paul's burial in 251–2, 265

Frankfurt Russian Immigrants Committee, and Paul 213, 215, 218–19, 228–9, 230, 243, 252

Fröbel, Friedrich 19

FSB (Russian secret service) see KGB

Funder, Anna 263

von Füner, Dr 97

von Füner, Alex 239

Garin, Erast 76

Gehlen, Reinhardt 11

German residency status, for Paul and Natalie: as temporary visa-holders 91; as illegal immigrants 144–5; as non-citizens with limited visas 151, 187, 196, 210; as would-be legal migrants 210–15, 236–7, 241, 242

German War Graves Commission 160, 170, 255

Gestapo (Nazi secret police): and Paul 12, 200, 210, 273; and Zinaida 172, 257, 262, 276, 277

Ginnheim (Frankfurt suburb), Paul and Natalie's family in 149, 151–2, 220, 224; Orthodox churches in 228–9

Gins, Professor H.A. 95, 108

Göbbels, Joseph 111, 173

Gogol, Nicolai 76, 85

Göring, Hermann 156, 168

Gorky, Maxim 37–8

Grimm family 21

Hackenthal, H. 108

Halifax, Lord 152

Harris, 'Bomber' 176

Heiden, Konrad xi

Heiss family 116

Heiss, Dietlinde (plate section 1) 115, 116, 141

Heiss, Rudolf (plate section 1) 115–17, 141, 152, 168–9, 259

Helmer, Alice (née Sevier) 53, 55

Hindenburg, (German) President Paul 132, 140

Hitler, Adolf (plate section 2): as leader and policy-maker ix, 69, 91, 92, 111, 123, 127, 129–30, 131, 132–3, 140–1, 146, 147, 148, 149–50, 151–2, 153, 155, 156, 159, 162, 163, 166, 167, 168, 169, 170, 171, 172, 173, 176, 180, 186, 188, 190, 191, 220, 221, 222, 226, 231; on Russians 93, 127, 130, 210; death 195–6; Natalie's wariness of 93, 129, 130, 140, 141, 163, 192–3; Paul's high hopes of 93, 111, 123, 129, 130–1, 132, 140, 142, 155, 156, 161, 164; Paul's increasing disenchantment with 12, 148, 149, 153, 156, 162, 163, 167, 170 (see also Hitler Youth movements; Gestapo; *Mein Kampf*; Nazi Party; Nuremberg rally)

Hitler Youth organisations (*Bund Deutscher Mädchen* and *Jungvolk*) x, 127, 140, 146–7, 149–50

Hoheneck Prison (former East Germany), and Zinaida 263–4

Holzhausenschule (primary school, Frankfurt) 162

Huvalet, Monsieur 28, 102, 103

intelligentsia: Kamenzev family as 'working' 39, 42, 44, 100; others as 'leisured' 44, 100

International Refugee Organisation, and Paul and Natalie's family 74, 236, 259

Intourist (Soviet travel agency, Moscow), Paul and Natalie's contact with 142, 143–4, 242, 271

Irkutsk (Siberia): historically 41; and Kungurzev family 40

Ivanov, Pavel Feodorovich (plate section 2) 86, 96, 212, 239, 245

Izvestia (News; Russian newspaper) 36

John family (plate section 2) 96, 97

John, Mr 28, 96

John, Lydia Feodorovna (plate section 2) 86, 96, 212

Kamenzev family 39, 41, 44, 73, 83, 90–1, 96, 97, 100, 123, 148, 196, 240; papers/ significant objects of 41, 43, 63, 89, 97 (see also St Petersburg)

Kamenzev, Michael (Misha) (plate section 1) 39, 42, 63, 75–6, 84, 96, 118, 120–1, 122, 123, 133, 134, 148, 162, 241, 253, 270

Kamenzev, Nicolai (plate section 1) 43

Kamenzev, Sergei 39, 42, 85, 121

Kamenzev, Vasily Ephimovich (plate section 1) 39, 40, 41, 42, 84, 85, 96, 98, 120, 121, 123, 270

Kamenzeva, Evgenia Trofimovna (née Rakitsky) (plate sections 1&2) 39, 40, 41, 44, 84, 85, 91, 96, 103–4, 114, 120, 121–2

Kamenzeva, Natalie Vasilievna see Schlüsser, Natalie

Kamenzeva, Natasha (Natalie) 63, 76, 83–4, 118, 162, 253, 254

Kamenzeva, Svetlana 41, 45

Kantstrasse (Berlin), Paul and Natalie in 95

Karl May *Gymnasium* (St Petersburg) (plate section 1): history of 18, 19, 20, 21, 25; Museum of 21; Paul as student 18, 19, 20, 21, 22, 23, 24–5; other alumni 20–2, 25, 29, 30, 34, 77, 99, 112

Karlsruhe (Germany): Paul and Natalie's family in 112, 113–14, 115, 116, 120, 122, 123, 127, 133, 139, 141–8, 152, 216, 253; Michael's visit to 120–1, 122, 148, 253

Karlsruhe Institute of Technology (plate section 2): Paul as student and tutor at 6, 112, 116, 117, 129, 133, 139–40, 141, 151, 168; other alumni 6, 112, 116, 168

Katyn Massacres 173

Kerensky, (Russian) Prime Minister 28

Kershaw, Ian 130

KGB (Russian secret police; previously NKVD and OGPU, later FSB) 66–8, 88, 93, 121, 134, 142–3, 144, 240, 253, 260, 263, 264, 265; and Zinaida 260, 263

Kneipp, Sebastian 158

Kolchak, General 40–1

Koltai, Alexandra 85

König, Adolph 62

König, Albine (plate section 1) 62, 77, 78–9, 82, 89

Kopfstädt, Fräulein 221

Korean War, impacts on Paul and Natalie's family 258–9

Korselt, Herr and Frau 177, 179, 207

Kosmos (science magazine) 241

Kramer family 226

Kresty Prison (Leningrad/ St Petersburg) 66, 68, 264–5

Kronstadt (Russia): and political refugees 63; revolt of 36

Kummer, Ludwig and Elfriede 81

Kungurzev family (plate sections 1&2) 40, 99

Kungurzeva, Zinaida Demianovna see Schlüsser, Zinaida Demianovna

Kutepov, Mr 112

Lanziger, Hubert 129–30

League of Nations: formation 92; undertakings 86–7, 92

League of Struggle for the Emancipation of the Working Class (St Petersburg) 64

Lenin, Vladimir Ilych (formerly Ulyanov): as leader and policy-maker ix, 22, 26, 28, 32, 33, 35, 36, 38, 39, 52, 61, 64, 67, 69, 77, 80, 85, 91, 109, 123, 142; death and memorialisation 37, 64, 65, 134, 249 (see also Bolshevik Party; Cheka; KGB; New Economic Policy)

Leningrad: name change 62, 160; siege of 73, 160, 163–5, 171, 172, 240, 253 (see also Petrograd, St Petersburg)

Leningrad Institute of Engineering (later Lenin Electrical Engineering Institute): Paul as student 31, 39, 75, 112; other alumni 39, 75, 112

Lilibeth (nanny to Natalie and Paul's children) see Elizabeth

Liselotte (wet-nurse to Eugene) 145, 260

Lloyds of London (insurers), and Schlüsser & Co. 47, 49, 153

Locarno Pact (1925) 92

London (plate section 2): Russian diaspora to 53, 55; Paul's dealings 154, 159, 215; Schlüsser & Co. dealings 47, 50, 51–2, 152–3; Schlüsser family in 50, 99, 152–3 (see also Sevier family)

Lubyanka Prison (Moscow) 67, 142

Lunacharsky, Anatole 76, 83

Lutheran Church, and Schlüsser family 50

Lvov, Prince Georgy 26, 27, 28

Madagascar, Paul and Natalie's family as potential migrants 215

Magnus family 251, 252

Makarov family 21, 128, 174

Makarov, Alexander Alexandrovich (Paul's great-uncle) 30

Makarov, Alexander (Paul's cousin) (plate section 1) 95–6, 112, 128, 149, 174, 231–2

Makarova, Mrs (senior) (plate sections 1&2)
Makarova, Mrs (plate sections 1&2) 97, 128, 231
Makarova, Kira (plate section 2) 127, 131, 149, 231
Makarova, Marina (plate section 2) 97, 127–8, 129, 153, 173–5, 231, 232
Mangott, Herr and Frau 222, 247
Mangott, Ursula 222, 226, 246–7
Manteufel, Mr 21
Marshall Plan (post-World War II) 233, 234
Marx, Karl 28, 85
May, Karl Ivanovich 19, 25
Mayakovsky, Vladimir 113
Mayer, Louis B. 110
Mechikov Bacteriological Institute (Odessa), Natalie as researcher 75, 83
Medvedev, Dimitri 36
Mein Kampf (Hitler's book) 93, 127, 130, 133, 140, 152
Melbourne International Arts Festival (2013) 65
Memorial (organisation) 67, 88
Meyerhold, Vsevolod 76, 113
Michael, Grand Duke 26–7
Mikhalkov, Nikita ix, 123
Modigliani, Amedeo 65
Molloy, Peter 263
Morgenthau Plan (post-World War II) 10–11, 13, 203–4, 221
Morocco, Paul and Natalie's family as potential migrants 215
Moscow, historically 29, 35–6, 37, 42, 65, 67, 118, 134, 142, 265
Moscow Show Trials 134
(Albrecht) Müller (company, St Petersburg) 267
Musterschule (secondary school, Frankfurt) 19, 220

Nabokov, Vladimir 93
Nansen, Friedjoef 212
Nansen passports, Paul's attempt to obtain 212
National Alliance of Russian Solidarists (Frankfurt) 240 (see also *Posev*)
Nazi Party (also National Socialist Party): rise and rule of 10, 11, 12, 25, 69, 111, 116, 129, 132–3, 140–1, 146, 147, 148, 149–50, 156, 159–60, 162, 169, 173, 174, 178–9, 191, 193–4, 200, 210, 232, 242 (see also Gestapo; Hitler; Hitler Youth movements; de-Nazification process)
Die Neue Zeitung (newspaper) 210, 234
New Economic Policy (Lenin's) 36–7, 86–7, 250
'New Man' (Bolshevik) 38, 111
Nicholas II, Tsar 17, 22, 25, 26, 27, 35, 48 (see also Tsar's Army)
Nietzsche, Friedrich 127
Nivki (Russia), Vladimir Schlüsser at 166, 167–8, 255–6
NKVD see KGB
Nomenklatura (Soviet) 80–1
Nuremberg rally (1935) 169

Nuremberg trials (post-World War II) 210

Opfermann, Theresa Vasilievna see Schlüsser, Theresa Vasilievna

Orekhovo (Russia): historically 42; and Kamenzev family 42

Orthodox Church (Russian): historically 22, 23, 35, 166; and Paul and Natalie's family 85–6, 117, 148, 149, 215, 222, 228–9, 245, 252, 270; and wider Schlüsser family 22–3, 50, 167 (see also St Andrew's; St Isaac's)

Orwell, George 98

Ostrovsky, Alexander 76

Paasch, Fräulein Elfriede 96, 120, 141

Paris (plate section 2): Russian diaspora to 41, 63, 74, 78, 87, 98, 99, 100, 101, 103, 104, 106; Paul and Natalie on honeymoon in 99–101, 102–3, 104, 106, 137; wider Schlüsser family in xi, 41, 47, 74, 79, 98, 99, 100, 101, 102, 104, 105, 106, 114, 117, 132, 133, 135–8, 139, 148, 156, 159–61, 170, 171, 196, 242, 250, 256–7, 260; Soviet Embassy in 100–1; Zinaida in 41, 74, 99, 104, 135–6, 256–7, 260, 276

Paris International Exhibition (1927): Beatrice at 137; Paul and Natalie at 102, 137

Paris World Fair (1937) (plate section 2), Natalie at

Pasternak, Boris 55

Pasteur, Louis 75

Patton, General 193

Paul I, Tsar 49

Paulus, General von 167, 168

Pavlov, Ivan 36

Pencost, Mr 217, 228

Pestalozzi, Johann Heinrich 19–20

Peter the Great 14, 48, 49

Petrograd, name changes 26, 62 (see also Leningrad, St Petersburg)

Pipes, Richard 37, 48, 80

Piroth, Peter 220, 221, 222, 226, 241

Poland, Natalie's family connection 41, 91, 123

Posev (Russian language weekly newspaper) 229, 240, 252

Pravda (Truth; Russian newspaper) 36

Preobrazhensky, Evgeni 44

Provisional Government (Russian, post-Tsarist) 26, 27, 28

Pushkin, Alexander 90, 148, 242

Putin, Vladimir 36, 264

Red Army (Bolshevik): 29, 36, 39, 41; and Paul 188

Red Cross 259, 261, 264

Red Terror (Lenin's) 32, 33, 52

Reed, John 51

Repin, Ilya 63

Reval (later Tallinn), Schlüsser family/ Schlüsser & Co. in 49, 51

Rieman, Erika 263

Robert Koch Medical Institute (at Charité Hospital, Berlin) (plate section 1), Natalie's work at 7, 75, 83, 95, 96, 107–8, 112, 141, 216

Roosevelt, (US) President Franklin 10,

74, 231
Royat, Monsieur and Madame 105
Rudolstadt (former East Germany), Theresa Vasilievna Schlüsser in 175, 176
Russian Liberation Army 172, 257, 262, 276
Russian Military Courts/ Tribunal, and Zinaida 210, 260, 275–8
Russian/ Soviet citizenship status, for Paul and Natalie: on special purpose exit visas 82, 83, 97–8, 112, 117, 132, 143; as would-be legal emigrants 143–4; as illegal emigrants/ defectors 143, 144, 161, 196, 271; as potential involuntary repatriates 210, 261
Russian nationalism, Paul's vision 130, 131, 142

Saalburg (Germany), Roman fort at 238
Sablino (Russia; plate section 1): Schlüsser *dacha* at 34, 56, 57–8, 59–60, 61, 62–3, 89, 91, 160, 164, 249–50, 269; township see Ulyanovka; train station 34, 56, 57, 58, 60, 61, 269
Sachsenhausen Concentration Camp (Germany) 203, 260; Museum at 259–60; Zinaida as prisoner 260–1, 263
Samoilov, Lev (cousin-in-law of author) 58, 66, 67, 255
St Andrew's Orthodox Cathedral (Vasilievski Island) 14, 15, 16, 35, 50
St Isaac's Orthodox Cathedral (St Petersburg) 17–18

St Petersburg (also Petrograd, Leningrad): generally and historically 14, 26, 27, 29, 30, 32–3, 35, 55, 64, 65, 73, 160, 163–5, 171, 172, 240, 253; name changes 26, 62; Kamenzev family in xi, 63, 75, 84, 96, 97, 101, 114, 117, 120–1, 122, 123, 133, 134, 143, 148, 161–2, 163, 186, 196, 240, 242, 253–4, 255; Natalie in 44, 74, 75, 79, 95, 101, 113, 212, 270; Paul in 14, 15, 16–17, 26, 29, 31, 32, 33–4, 36, 37, 38, 44, 62, 74, 75, 78, 79, 95, 96, 101, 112, 113, 212, 270; wider Schlüsser family in 14–17, 18, 26, 27–8, 29, 34, 36, 37, 44, 45, 46, 55, 81, 88, 96, 98, 101, 160, 163–5, 264, 267 (see also Vasilievski Island)
St Petersburg Cemetery, and Schlüsser family 50
St Petersburg Public Library 45–6
St Petersburg Stock Exchange (Vasilievski Island) (plate section 1), and Schlüsser family 48–9
St Petersburg (Petrograd) University 19, 30, 99
Sardier, Monsieur 105
Schanzenbach & Co. (company, Frankfurt), Paul's R&D work at 12, 13, 108, 151, 152, 153, 155, 181, 187, 188, 210, 215, 216, 261, 274
Schliemann, Heinrich 47, 153
Schlisselburg fortress prison (Russia), Paul in 32
Schloegel, Karl 93, 265
Schlüsser family significant objects/ papers (plate sections 1&2) xiii, 12, 15, 18, 20, 21, 22, 23, 29, 34,

47, 50–1, 56, 58, 62–3, 75, 86, 88, 89–90, 99, 105, 108, 113, 114, 122–3, 129, 135, 142, 143–4, 146–7, 157, 158, 163, 169–70, 175, 190, 192, 194, 207, 209, 241–2, 252, 266, 267–78

Schlüsser Trading Company/ Schlusser & Co. (Vasilievski Island) (plate section 1) 27–8, 36, 37, 46, 47, 48–9, 50–2, 53, 77, 81, 96, 102, 152, 153, 159; and 'lost fortune' 47, 51–2, 96, 101, 102, 153, 159, 175–6

Schlüsser, Alexander (Justus's son; plate section 2) 50, 152–3

Schlüsser, Alexander (Paul's brother) 14, 15

Schlüsser, Andrei (Paul's brother) 15

Schlüsser, Antonia (plate section 1) 34, 61, 62, 249–50, 269; and will 22, 34, 57–8, 61, 242, 249–50, 269

Schlüsser, Artur Arturovich (plate section 1): and Sablino *dacha* 22, 34, 269; education 21–2, 34; incarcerations and execution 66, 67, 68, 88, 96, 264–5

Schlüsser, Beatrice (plate sections 1&2): as child/ young woman 98, 99, 100, 101, 104, 105, 135, 137; as wife/ mother 101, 135, 161; and family research project 25, 29, 101, 102, 104, 135, 136–7, 159, 160; career 99, 137; education 100

Schlüsser, Carl (Justus's son) 50

Schlüsser, Dagmara Arturovna (plate section 1): and Sablino *dacha* 22, 34, 269; education 22, 34

Schlüsser, Dorothea Elisabeth (née Bode) (plate section 1) 267, 268

Schlüsser, Eveline see Schroder, Eveline

Schlüsser (later Schlusser), Eugene (Evgeni) (plate sections 1&2): as child/young man xiii, 5, 7, 8, 9, 79, 90, 96, 115, 127, 128, 145, 156, 157, 165, 176–8, 179, 180, 181, 182, 183, 186–7, 188, 189–91, 193, 195, 199–201, 203, 204, 206–7, 208, 210, 211, 213, 215–16, 217, 218–19, 220–1, 222, 223–4, 225–6, 227, 228, 233–4, 236–7, 238, 239, 242, 244, 245, 246, 247–8, 249, 251–2, 258; as family researcher ix-x, xi, 4–5, 6, 7, 8, 11–13, 18–19, 23, 34, 45–7, 53–5, 56–8, 59, 60–1, 63, 64, 65, 66–8, 73, 75, 80, 86–7, 88, 89, 93, 99, 101–2, 105, 114, 115–16, 127–9, 131, 135, 142–3, 146, 153, 157–8, 160–1, 162, 167–9, 170, 171, 173–6, 194, 201–2, 203–4, 209, 210, 217, 229, 242, 243, 250–1, 255–6, 259–60, 261–6; as husband/father 7, 53, 65, 79–80; appearance 7, 226; career 4, 7, 53, 118–19; citizenship 211; education 7, 19, 220–1, 237, 247–8; health 4, 7, 24, 227, 228, 238, 239, 246; language skills xi-xii, 145, 222–3, 237, 247–8; reflections on migrant experience 243–4; significant objects 241, 242, 244, 247; survival instinct 246

Schlüsser, Fyodor (Paul's grandfather) 50

Schlüsser, Fyodor (Frederick; Paul's father): as businessman 16, 64, 65; as husband/ father 15–16, 94; death 16; education 20; religion/ spirituality 17, 22–3

Schlüsser, Fyodor (Paul's brother) 14, 15

Schlüsser, Friedrich (Justus's son) 50

Schlüsser, Heinrich (Justus's son) 50

Schlüsser, Justus Friedrich (plate section 1): as businessman 47, 48, 49, 51, 169–70; as 'enemy of the people' 51; as 'honorary hereditary citizen' 51; as husband/ father 47, 267, 268; death 49–50; oil portrait 47, 50–1, 242

Schlüsser, Ludowicka 34

Schlüsser, Margaret (plate section 1)

Schlüsser, Nadya (Nadezhda) (plate sections 1&2): as co-heir 153; as daughter/ sister 99, 106, 135, 153; death 47; significant objects 47

Schlüsser (later Schlusser), Natalie (Natalya Vasilievna; née Kamenzeva) (plate sections 1&2): as child/ young woman 5, 40, 41–2, 43–4, 73, 123, 240; as daughter/ sister xi, 39, 63, 75–6, 83, 84, 85, 86, 90, 95, 96, 97, 100, 114, 117, 120, 121–2, 123, 133, 134, 148, 161–2, 163, 164, 171, 186, 196, 240, 241, 242, 253, 254; as mother x, xiii, 4, 7, 8, 9, 11, 108, 112, 113, 114, 115, 117, 120, 121, 131, 133, 141, 148, 149, 156, 165, 176–8, 180, 181, 182, 186, 189–90, 193, 196, 203, 206–7, 214, 215–16, 220, 225–6, 227, 228, 236, 239, 241, 242, 244, 251, 252–3, 257–8, 264, 266; as sweetheart/wife x, 5, 9, 39, 70, 73, 74, 76, 78, 83, 84, 85–6, 87, 94, 95, 96, 97, 100–1, 102–3, 104–5, 106, 107, 112, 113, 114, 122, 131, 141, 142, 177, 178, 186, 187, 188, 196, 212, 215, 228, 229, 241, 243, 248–9, 251, 252, 258, 260, 264, 266, 270; in old age 3–4, 5, 6, 69–70, 74, 156, 194–5; appearance 3, 6, 39, 103, 141, 228; career 3, 7, 44, 75, 83, 89, 95, 97, 99, 100, 107–8, 112, 114, 141, 175, 210, 215, 216, 236, 242, 243; character 6–7, 20, 40, 41, 75, 94, 97, 100, 116, 133, 141, 189, 254; death 128; education 5, 22, 39, 44, 74, 95, 99; health 8, 161, 163, 214–15, 263, 264; language skills 5, 6, 39, 40, 95, 103, 189; leisure interests 76–7, 90, 97, 102–3, 104, 105, 109, 110, 113, 122; portrait 63; religion 85–6, 229, 270; resilience ix, 6, 7–8, 20, 44, 65, 74, 93–4, 116, 181, 196, 206–7, 216, 240–1, 251, 254; secrets and lies 4–5, 6, 8, 9, 13, 54, 73–4, 75, 86–7, 96, 99, 161–2, 210, 212, 213, 215, 253, 257, 259, 260, 262–3, 264, 265; significant objects 43, 63, 70, 75, 86, 87, 89, 90, 105, 108, 122, 123, 163, 192, 194, 241, 242, 252, 266

Schlüsser, Nicolai (plate sections 1&2): as co-heir 34, 57, 61, 153, 159, 269; as husband/ father 29, 98, 99, 100, 102, 137, 159, 160; as (step) son/ brother 28, 99, 100, 102, 105, 153, 170; career 27–8, 98, 159; education 20; health 24, 29, 160, 161; military experiences 25–6, 27, 28–9

Schlüsser, Oberstfeldmeister (of Parchim) (plate section 2) 169–70, 175, 255, 272

Schlüsser (later Schlüsser-Sabline), Oleg (plate sections 1&2): as child/ young man 98, 99, 100, 104, 105, 137; and family research project 45,

46, 51, 170, 212; career 99, 170; education 100, 170; health 24; significant objects 51, 170

Schlüsser, Olga (sister of Raymond; later Sternat) (plate section 2) 15, 94, 153, 174

Schlüsser, Olga (née Malinovskaya – Nicolai's wife) (plate sections 1&2): as wife/ mother 29, 99, 100, 104, 105, 135, 136, 137, 138, 159–60, 161, 170; career 98–9, 100, 136, 137, 138; education 29

Schlüsser (later Schlusser), Paul (Pavel Fyodorovich, Pavlusha) (plate sections 1&2): as child/young man 14, 15, 16–17, 20, 55, 221; as co-heir 34, 56, 57, 61, 62, 63, 153–4, 159, 215, 269; as 'enemy of the people' 31, 32, 33, 132, 214; as family photographer x-xi, 104–5, 107–8, 117, 120, 158, 248, 260; as father xiii, 7, 10, 96–7, 114, 115, 117, 127, 128, 133, 139, 141, 143, 144, 145, 148–9, 155, 156, 158, 162, 163, 167, 176–7, 178, 179–80, 181, 199, 200, 204–5, 207, 208, 211, 214, 217, 218, 220, 221, 222–4, 225, 226, 228, 231, 237, 238, 239, 240, 241, 244, 245, 246, 247, 248, 249, 260, 266; as (step)son/brother xi, 36, 37, 63, 79, 88, 94–5, 96, 97, 100, 102, 114, 117, 133, 135, 140, 153, 161, 163, 164, 170–1, 172, 174, 175, 196, 250; as sweetheart/ husband x, 5, 8–9, 10, 13, 39, 73, 74, 76, 78, 83, 85–6, 87, 94, 95, 96, 97, 100–1, 102–3, 104–5, 106, 107, 109, 112, 113–14, 122, 131, 141, 142, 143, 156, 178, 187, 196, 200, 212, 228, 241, 258, 260, 264, 266, 270; as (possibly) US secret service agent 53, 55, 131, 217–18; appearance 34–5, 40; career 9, 10, 12, 13, 16, 75, 81, 89, 99, 108–9, 111–12, 115, 117, 139, 140, 151, 152, 155, 158, 161, 181, 187, 188, 196, 210, 215, 216–18, 223, 236, 243, 273, 274; character 8, 14, 40, 75, 78, 94, 96–7, 223; death/ burials 5, 249, 251–2, 258, 265; education 6, 16, 18, 19, 20, 21, 22, 23, 24–5, 31, 39, 55, 62, 74, 81, 98, 99, 112, 116, 117, 139–40, 143, 168, 221; health 8–9, 10, 13, 20, 24, 32, 33–5, 37, 131, 158, 161, 214, 215, 229, 243, 248–9, 253, 259, 262, 264; language skills 95, 218, 222, 230; leisure interests 76–7, 97, 102–3, 104, 105, 109, 110, 113, 122, 238; military call-up averted 188; religion/ spirituality 17, 18, 22, 23, 62, 85–6, 148, 149, 214, 215, 222, 223, 228–9, 245, 252, 270; resilience ix, 7–8, 65, 74, 123, 143, 144–5, 148, 151, 156, 161, 196, 200, 210–12, 213–15, 251, 265; secrets and lies 8, 9, 12, 13, 54, 73–4, 86–7, 88, 96, 139–40, 144, 149, 153, 175, 212, 213, 214, 215, 218, 222, 237, 242–3, 257, 259, 260, 261, 262, 265; significant objects 18, 20, 21, 22, 23, 29, 34, 47, 56, 58, 62–3, 86, 89, 90, 105, 113, 122, 135, 142, 143–4, 158, 169–70, 241, 242; suspected affair 260

Schlusser, Paul (William's son) 109

Schlüsser, Raymond (Raimund) (plate section 2) 15, 94, 153, 174

Schlüsser, Sophia (née Dahler), as wife/ mother xiii, 14–15, 16; death 14–15; religion/ spirituality 17

Schlüsser (later Schlusser), Svetlana (plate sections 1&2): as child/young woman x, 6, 9, 12, 113, 114, 115, 117, 120, 122, 123, 127, 139, 144, 145, 146–7, 148–9, 155, 156, 158, 162, 180, 181, 185, 190, 193, 194, 206, 220, 230, 236, 237, 239, 248, 249, 251, 252, 258, 260; career 4, 6, 9, 230, 243; citizenship 117, 211; death 146; education 146–7, 156, 158, 162, 185, 220, 230, 237; health 6, 114–15; language skills 145, 148, 230, 243; leisure interests 239; religion 117, 148, 149; significant objects 114, 146–7, 190, 242

Schlüsser (later Schlusser), Tatjana (Tanya) (plate sections 1&2): as child/ young woman 9, 115, 145, 156, 162–3, 171, 180, 181, 185, 195, 207, 211, 215–16, 220, 224, 236, 237, 248, 249, 251; as adult 249, 264; career 4; citizenship 211; education 162–3, 185, 220, 237; health 4; language skills 145; significant objects 241–2

Schlüsser, Theresa Vasilievna (plate sections 1&2): background 15; as co-heir 154; as mother/ stepmother 15, 16, 20, 28, 46, 94, 95, 160, 174, 175–6; death 176

Schlüsser, Vasily (Paul's great-uncle) 61

Schlüsser, Vladimir (Volodya) (plate sections 1&2): as co-heir 153, 159; as husband 41, 99, 135, 159, 160, 165; as (step)son/ brother 28, 99, 102, 106, 135, 136, 153, 159, 160, 165, 255; character 99, 136; career 159, 160; death/ burial 167, 170–1, 210, 225, 256; education 20, 27, 99; death 91; language skills 160, 165, 166, 168; military experiences x, 25, 27, 28–9, 140, 160, 161, 163–8, 171, 225; military secrets and lies about 170–1, 255–6; religion 167

Schlüsser, Wilhelm (Justus's son) 50

Schlüsser (later Schlusser), William (Vasily, Wilhelm, Bill) (Paul's son) (plate sections 1&2): as child/young man x, 5, 9, 25, 109, 115, 116, 133, 135, 145, 147, 149, 156, 157, 167, 180, 181, 182, 185, 191, 205, 208, 219, 220, 223, 227, 233, 236, 237, 239, 241, 243, 248, 249, 251, 258; and family research project xi, 47, 63, 101, 105, 109, 116, 157–8, 168, 259; as husband/father 4, 249; career 4, 116, 122–3, 241; character 94; citizenship 211; education 19, 25, 156, 185, 191, 220, 237, 241, 243; health 7, 227, 249; language skills 145; leisure interests 238, 239; significant objects 241, 242

Schlüsser, Zinaida Demianovna (Zina, née Kungurzeva) (plate sections 1&2): as child/ young woman 40; as daughter/ sister 99; as reputed spy (post-World War II) 11, 172, 259, 261–2, 275–8; as wife/ widow 99, 104, 106, 135–6, 160, 165, 170–1, 210, 255, 256, 259; career 11, 40, 55, 104, 257, 276; character 104, 135, 260; citizenship 256, 276; language skills 172, 257; political activism 11, 104, 257, 259, 262

Schopenhauer, Arthur 127

scout groups (Germany, post-World War II), American-funded 239

Schroder, Eveline (née Schlüsser) 50

Schroder, John Henry 50, 152–3

Schroder, (Sir) Henry 50

(J. Henry) Schroder & Co. (bank, London) (plate section 2): and Paul 154, 215; and Schlüsser family 50, 152–3, 154

Segelins, A. 86

Sevier family 53, 77, 154

Sevier, Alice see Helmer, Alice

Sevier, Frederick (Fedya, Fred) 15, 16, 53–4, 153, 154, 175, 210, 217

Sevier, Richard 54

Sevier, Robert 53, 99, 152, 153, 154

Shapoval, Olga 162, 163, 240, 254

Shaw, George Bernard 98

Shirer, William xi, 107, 130

Shoopinsky, Mr and Mrs (plate section 2) 213, 228

Shuisky, Vladimir Vladimirovich (plate section 1) 5–6, 8, 76, 253

Siemens-Schuckert (company, Berlin), Paul as intern at 81, 89, 108–9, 111–12

Slepnova, Tatyana Nicolaivna 59–61, 164

Smolensk (Russia), and Kamenzev family 41, 42, 44, 73, 84, 91, 123

Solovetski Islands (penal colony, Arctic Circle) 88

Soloviev, Vladimir 62

Solzhenitsyn, Alexander 31, 43, 240

soviet, original scope/ function 22

Soviet Union (magazine) 79

Sprenger, Jakob 178

Stalin, Joseph: as leader and policy-maker ix, 17, 33, 36, 37, 38, 41, 48, 57, 60, 65, 66, 69, 74, 76, 77, 80–1, 88, 91–2, 98, 101, 104, 110, 111, 112–13, 118, 122, 123, 134, 142, 144, 155, 156, 165, 166, 167, 172, 173, 182, 229, 231, 234–5, 240, 250, 264; death 263 (see also Cheka; Communism; KGB; 'New Man')

Stalingrad, battle of 166, 167, 168, 169, 173

Stasi (East German secret police), and Zinaida 263

Sternat, Herr 174

Sternat, Olga see Schlüsser, Olga

Stolypin, (Russian) Prime Minister 30

Stravinsky, Igor 98, 137

Sveshnikova, Valentina Nicolaivna 244

Swann, Dr Herbert 55

Switzerland: Natalie's family connection 39–40, 105, 123, 156, 242; Paul and Natalie on honeymoon in 104, 105

Tallinn see Reval

Tashalgu, Professor 75

Tolstoy, Countess Alexandra (Lev Tolstoy's cousin) 62

Tolstoy, Alexandra (Lev Tolstoy's daughter) 211

Tolstoy, Alexei 93

Tolstoy, Lev 62, 104, 118, 211

Tolstoy Foundation (New York) 211, 240

Trotsk (region, Russia) 56, 57, 91, 269

Trotsky, Leon ix, 29, 36, 41, 77, 91,

112–13, 122, 142

Truman, (US) President Harry 207, 234, 258

Tsar's (Imperial) Army: and Kamenzev family 42; and Schlüsser family 25–6, 27, 160

Tsvetaeva, Marina 93

Tukhachevsky, Mikhail ix, 36

Tver (later Kalinin), and Kamenzev family 40, 41, 73

Ulyanov, Vladimir Ilych see Lenin, Vladimir Ilych

Ulyanovka (formerly Sablino township) 57, 58, 60, 61, 62, 164

United Nations Health Organisation 216

University of Frankfurt 201–2

Uspensky, Lev 21

Vasilievski Island (St Petersburg): Schlüsser & Co. on 27–8, 36, 46, 48–9, 50–1; Schlüsser family on 14, 18, 27, 29, 34, 44, 46; Paul on 14, 29, 44 (see also Karl May *Gymnasium*; St Andrew's Cathedral; St Petersburg Stock Exchange)

Veitel, Fraulein 162–3

Venezuela, Paul and Natalie's family as potential migrants 215

Versailles Treaty (post-World War I) 91, 92, 132, 133

Vlasov, General 172, 257, 262, 276

Voildo, Ekaterina Kor 106

Voildo, Michael Evgenovich 106

Voltaire 49

Waggeg family 12, 177, 226

Waggeg, Herr 12, 176, 177

Walter, Ellery 69

Wannsee agreement 173

Webb, Beatrice and Sidney 98

Weber family 206, 226

Weber, Christa 206, 221–2, 226, 245

Weber, Marek 109

Weigel, Professor 151

Weill, Kurt 109

White Army (anti-Bolshevik): and Schlüsser family 28–9, 41; and Zinaida 40–1, 55, 99, 276; and others 55

Wildflecken (Germany; pre-migration camp), Paul and Natalie's family in 259

Witte, Sergei 48

Wolff, Herr 49, 267–8

Worishofen, Bad (Germany) (plate section 2), Paul and Natalie's family in 156–8

World War I: and Kamenzev family 43; and Schlüsser family 25–6, 27, 43

World War II: and Kamenzev family 43, 152, 162, 163; and Paul and Natalie's family 152, 153, 154, 155, 156–7, 158, 161, 162, 163, 164, 167, 169–70, 171–2, 173, 176–96; and wider Schlüsser family 152, 159–60, 161, 163–8, 174, 175–6

Wrangel, General 41, 276

Yalta Conference (1945) 74, 210, 231

Yeltsin, Boris 67
Yesenin, Sergei 77
Yezhov, Nicolai 134
Yudenich, General 29

Zamyatin, Evgeni 113
Ziehenschule (secondary school, Frankfurt) 162, 220

About the Author

Eugene Schlusser has written film documentaries on diverse subjects but this is the first time he has written about his family. He draws on his Russian and German heritage, the memories of his three older siblings and photos and documents to explore 'why the secrecy in the family?'. He was born in 1939 in Frankfurt, Germany. His family came to Australia in 1950. But why? He has been a filmmaker, drama teacher and occasional actor. He has two sons and three grandsons. He lives in Melbourne.

www.ingramcontent.com/pod-product-compliance
Lightning Source LLC
Chambersburg PA
CBHW030850170426
43193CB00009BA/557